One More Horizon

The Inspiring Story of One Man's Solo Journey
Around the World on a Mountain Bike

Scott Zamek

A photo companion of this journey is available at

scottzamek.com

We shall not cease from exploration
And the end of all our exploring
Will be to arrive where we started
And know the place for the first time.

—T. S. Eliot

CONTENTS

To those who helped along the way.

Foreword

BY ALL RIGHTS, I should be dead—many times over. This is the twenty-fifth anniversary of my journey around the world on a mountain bike, and the tenth anniversary of the first publication of *One More Horizon*. The world has changed since I hopped on that GT Timberline all those many years ago, and for many Americans the door has slammed shut on the type of solo travel I experienced in certain out-of-the-way places. Yet the fact that I am not dead is a testimony to one unchanging human factor, and that is that ordinary people around the world retain a generosity of spirit not always reflected in the behavior of their governments. For it was they—the average citizens—who came to my aid time and time again, most probably saving my life on more occasions than I care to remember.

At the same time, travel has become easier and more modern in certain countries. Twenty-five years ago, it was not possible to move freely throughout China; I traveled with forged permission papers that made me cringe whenever I presented them at a military checkpoint or border crossing. Today, the country is awash with Western journalists and American companies—even an airport in Kashgar, a city that was once a remote Taklamikan border town accessible only to those who traveled by camel or mountain bike. The southern coast of Spain, the Costa Del Sol, was once a quaint collection of inns and cafés frequented by backpackers, but now boasts a series of high rises and modern restaurants catering to a much different traveler.

Yet other areas of the world have not been so kind to the would-be tourist. Syria, for example, would be impossible to travel across today, especially by mountain bike. Although, those who have read the first edition of *One More Horizon* might argue that it was impossible twenty-five years ago as well, since I ended up in a Syrian prison.

Readers of the first edition have not been shy over the years. One of the most requested items has been to include maps and photographs in the second edition. Alas, the publishing costs to do so would have been prohibitive; the best I can do is refer you to my website, scottzamek.com, where readers can follow along by visiting the photo journal page. It is always a risk to include a web address in a printed book however, so I apologize in advance to those who pick up this book ten years in the future and find the website no longer exists.

Another pervasive request from readers, one which surprises me a bit, is to start the "action" sooner. Of course, when writing a travelogue, if the story starts in America, then . . . the story starts in America. Not much is going to happen on the safe streets of the Western world. Take solace in the fact that those who continue past twenty pages or so claim they cannot put the book down, so be patient.

Which brings me to the ultimate question. By leagues, the most common query I get is, "Why?" Why explore? Why adventure? Why put your life at risk?

These are difficult questions to answer, because the people who do these things do not know why. To them, it is as natural as walking or talking, as necessary as breathing, eating and sleeping. In Gibraltar, I met a traveler who had been on the road for twenty years. When he told me he was about to get married, and his fiancée in England had insisted he remain home, I asked him why, then, he found himself in Gibraltar. "Because I wanted to see one more horizon before I settled down," he told me.

Robert Louis Stevenson answered the question a bit differently when he wrote, "I travel not to go anywhere, but to go. I travel for travel's sake. The great affair is to move; to feel the needs and hitches of our life more nearly; to come down off this feather-bed of civilization, and find the globe granite underfoot and strewn with cutting flints."

But for those who have no desire for adventure, almost any explanation represents a vague philosophy. Readers want neat beginnings to things, and neat ends. They want unanswerable questions tied up with ribbon and bow in a comprehensible package, then presented so they can clutch the idea and understand. They want the inception of an adventure, the motivation, distilled down to where domestic life ended and travel began. They want to know what spark initiated the fire, so they can hold it in their hands and make it a part of themselves.

They want to know, "Why?"

My beginning, my addiction with adventure, began when I was twenty-one. I hoisted a tattered pack, put out my thumb, and made my way for an entire year around the dusty roads of America. The year lasted what seemed like five lifetimes, and I experienced a freedom I had never before known. I learned to push my body and mind to their ultimate limits, and each time the limit was reached, my boundaries became wider—limits farther away. And I reveled in my newfound abilities: a mountain top that was before unreachable, a forest that was inaccessible, miles that were then unattainable.

In the achievement of certain goals, life became at once simpler. In walking that last mile beyond all strength, trivialities faded. The basics became important, they became luxuries, and it was during those times I found myself most fulfilled. I learned that the trifling day-to-day expectancies of American life obscured life's basic rewards.

When I returned home after twelve months of travel, everything seemed to have changed. People's goals and aspirations appeared constricted, dreams were a thing for children or nighttime, and no one cared what was over the next mountain top. The topics of discussion concerned the immediate environment—the town, the school, the surrounding ten miles—that was the entire world. I had returned home to my own people, my own community, but they were no longer mine. I had become a citizen of my experiences; while surrounded by those with less, I would forever find myself on the outside looking in, even in my own home town.

It was then people began greeting me with a blank, vacant stare, empty, devoid of any thread of commonality—like a floating object with no frame of reference. The look was often accompanied by a squint of the eyes, wrinkled nose, and stretched lips, as if to suggest I were some circus novelty to be viewed safely from afar.

It was then I knew I would leave again.

Seven years after returning from the American adventure, having been congratulated by family and friends for "getting it out of my system," the travel seed began to bloom anew, but a seed that blooms also must grow. All my other adventures had been on a small scale, the North American continent. This time I wanted to see the world, and my experience hitchhiking in the States told me I wanted to travel in a manner that would help me meet the people, incorporate myself into the culture, as well as add a little spice and challenge to my journey.

Secretly, I made a list entailing different modes of travel. I told no one, fearing my friends and coworkers might think me crazy. The list included canoeing, walking, bicycling, hitchhiking, motorcycling, and driving—among others. I began reading everything I could get my hands on regarding these subjects and, as the research intensified, the list slowly narrowed. Hitchhiking was eliminated since I wanted a new experience after my American adventure. With more reading, others were rejected for various reasons until, remaining on the list was left one word—*bicycle*

1
Preparations

THE MAN on the phone sounded like Marlon Brando in *The Godfather*, but not quite as endearing. He was a public relations executive for one of the major mountain bike companies, and I was attempting to find a sponsor.

"Bicycle around the world, eh?" he said, his voice raspy in my ear. "Are you a professional cyclist?"

"Not exactly."

"Do you train a lot?"

"Ah—no." The fact was, I hadn't cycled since high school, and I had only recently quit smoking. I decided to keep those details to myself.

"Have you done anything like this before?" the man asked.

"Well, I . . ."

"Never mind," he interrupted." Call us when you get to Africa."

Perhaps finding a bicycle was not the best way to start. I decided to call a camping supply company instead.

"Call us when you get to Africa," they said.

A magazine.

"Call us when . . ."

It was obvious I would have to buy the gear myself. I sought out a private bicycle designer who advertised as "specializing in expeditions." The man lived in a small house on the outskirts of Akron, Ohio, where I had been working and saving money for a year in preparation for the trip. He was tall and wiry, with a backwoodsman's beard and eyes peering through coke-bottle glasses. His living room was a mass of spare parts and bicycle frames, with odd cables and worn tires dangling from the ceiling. I told him of my plans to ride a bicycle around the world.

"Hell, yeah! I'll help ya. What an expedition." He wrung his hands in excitement.

"Just think of the publicity. Why, we'd be written up in every magazine in the country." He wandered around the shop, muttering more to himself than to me.

"My business would prosper. Never done anything this big before. Did a trip across New Zealand once . . ." He went on as I stood by, unnoticed.

"Wait a minute." I felt compelled to interrupt. "I just want to know a price range."

"Hell, we can build ya' a bicycle from scratch! All the best parts. Best frame. I can even getchya' the best bearin's to throw in yer bottom bracket."

"How much?"

The man rooted for a pad and pencil and began tabulating. While he was scribbling, I thought about asking him what a bottom bracket was, then thought better of it.

"Twenty-five hundred for the bike," he pronounced. "Then there's spare parts and supplies." He scratched his head in thought. "We'd have to mail caches ahead to different cities. I would say another five thousand for that."

"All I have is seven thousand dollars," I sheepishly admitted.

"For the bike?"

"For the entire trip."

He looked at me, an expression of horror crossing his face. His enthusiasm deflated like a leaky balloon.

"This is impossible," he said after overcoming his shock. "It can't be done."

I explained my intention of camping out most nights, leaving food as my main expense.

"Call me when you get to Africa," he said—and showed me to the door.

I PUT MY SEARCH for a bicycle aside and began planning my route. Research encompassed all my spare time. My room became a collection of maps, travel guides, and library books. As I discovered places I wanted to visit, I marked that place with a pin on my world map. I became obsessed. By the time I was done, there were 358 colored pins stuck in the map, ranging from Tierra del Fuego to Vladivostok, from Addis Ababa to Tashkent.

My mind wandered to all the exotic places I'd read about and desired to see. The vast expanses of Asia called with a single, undeniable voice. What treasures and tales awaited in Kipling's India or Stanley's Dark Continent? China seemed so distant that it could not be reached by imagination. Although the art and culture of the world intrigued me, I would need to avoid major cities to have access to camping and stay below my five-dollar daily budget. But wilderness intrigued me as well. My reading brought me to ancient cities and fabled gardens, to holy rivers and sacred lakes, to wide rivers and wider mountains.

I began writing the countries that drew my attention. I wrote travel bureaus, tour companies, health departments—anyone that could give me information on the journey. The replies trickled in slowly, and many were discouraging.

Extreme Adventure Tours
122 E. Sir Edmund Hillary Blvd.
London, England
January 12

Dear Sir,

Regarding your request for travel information of Africa, Asia, and the former Soviet countries. We are sorry to inform you that Extreme Tours cannot help you with an itinerary of that kind. Our office does not organize individual travel in Asia and points east. We do not advise traveling to some of the areas you suggested. Thank you for your interest in Extreme Tours.

—Tour Director, Extreme Adventure Tours

Ohio Department of Health
14 Oak Street
Canton, Ohio
February 14

Mr. Zamek,

The following vaccinations and medications are recommended: oral polio vaccine, typhus series, rabies series, tetanus, hepatitis, diphtheria; Chloroquin and Fansidar for malaria. These are available through the Ohio Department of Health.

—G. William Zack, M.D.

Any spare time between work and route planning was spent buying gear. My tent was one of the lightest models available; at just over two pounds, it stood like a cocoon when fully extended. My sleeping bag, lined with Mylar to prevent loss of body heat, was rated to twenty degrees below zero. Other miscellaneous gear came together: ground mat, camp stove, mess kit. The last major item remained a bicycle.

I visited my third bike shop in as many days and described my plans to the two men behind the counter.

"It's impossible," one of them said after I explained what I needed. "Where would you get spare parts? Food? How would you carry it all?"

"You would need to pull a wagon behind you," said the second man. "It's the only way."

Shop after shop brought the same reply, until I found myself at a bike dealer located near Cuyahoga Falls, Ohio. The salesman had toured Europe by bicycle and served as the perfect advisor.

"Nonsense," he said when I mentioned the wagon idea. "All you need are some good panniers and a few tools and spare parts."

He showed me the equipment he had used in Europe, then he recommended several brands of bicycle. There were traditional ten-speed road bikes, light and sleek for racing. There were dozens of mountain bike models, each equipped with enough gears to tackle any terrain. There were hybrids, a combination road/mountain bike. There were collapsible fold-up models for easy transport.

How and which one to select? I knew nothing about bicycle touring.

"I would go with a road bike for the paved roads of Europe," the salesman said. "But you may need a mountain bike in Asia."

I deferred to the expertise of the salesman, and he obliged. He knew my financial situation, and I sensed that he did not care about making a high-priced sale or securing a commission. It seemed he was caught up in the spirit of adventure, and he suggested gear based on moderate price, as well as the unique requirements of the trip.

The bike chosen was a GT Timberline, a mountain bike, with a bronze-colored frame and twenty-one gears for the rough roads of the Third World. Two sets of panniers, front and back, with a handlebar bag for maps would carry my supplies. A guaranteed-for-life Blackburn rack supported the entire rig.

Spare parts and tools completed this stage of my preparations. My spare tires were made of bulletproof Kevlar which could be rolled up like paper to be stowed in the corner of a pannier. I bought two extra inner tubes and enough tire patches to see me through Europe. The salesman threw in some extra spokes and cables, free of charge, then equipped me with the tools necessary to make basic repairs. The entire setup ran less than $600, and I felt grateful for the salesman's help when I left the shop. My last major hurdle was behind me.

A few loose ends still remained. I applied for my passport at the post office, then I went to the health department to be immunized. Through a cut-rate travel agent, I bought a one-way ticket to Oslo on Scandinavian Airlines. At $250 it was the cheapest ticket available over the Atlantic, but it would be an easy matter to cycle south into Europe, spending only a few days in Scandinavia. Realizing a crash course in mechanics was in order, I bought a used bicycle for twenty dollars which, with the help of a roadside repair manual, I completely dismantled and put back together, piece by piece. Eventually, I learned what a bottom bracket was.

My confidence was growing daily, although the letters that continued to trickle in were not encouraging.

China National Tourist Office
60 East 42nd Street
New York, NY
March 23

Dear Mr. Zamek,

Hotel and transportation arrangements must be confirmed before a visa will be issued.
Visa applications must be submitted in duplicate with a valid passport and two photos.
Travel to areas of China not open to tourism is prohibited. Bicycle travel outside of open
cities is prohibited. Importation of the following articles is prohibited: arms, ammunition,
radio transmitters, manuscripts, printed matter, films, photographs, gramophone
records, loaded recording tapes, video tapes, any matter detrimental to Chinese political,
economic, cultural, and moral interests.

—China National Tourist Office

I removed the pins from the countries that refused me entry, and my route began to take shape. When I intersected all the remaining dots on my map, the resulting path looked more like a coiled snake than a straight line. It began in Scandinavia, curled westward through Europe, then north into England, Ireland and Wales. The course veered south through France and Spain, east through Africa and continued around the Adriatic Sea following the coast of Italy and the Balkan peninsula. I would then cycle east through Greece and Turkey. None of the countries bordering Turkey agreed to issue me a visa, so I would continue east by any possible route that became available. It was a tentative plan, subject to change due to weather, political volatility around the world, and luck.

With the route set, the time had come. I quit my job, then sat down to write letters to friends and family. My unvarying sign-off was, "with luck, I'll see you again in two years."

2

Europe

north of Vejle, Denmark

THE CARDBOARD BOX containing the pieces of my bicycle came rolling down the long luggage belt at Fornebue Airport. Like Dr. Frankenstein, I was expected to rebuild the thing. Perhaps sometime in the future, my bike, like Frankenstein's monster, would require repairs beyond my ability. I opened the box and placed the pieces about the hard floor of the luggage room. Norwegians gathered in curiosity, forming a circle around me as they pointed at bicycle parts and discussed what they thought to be my mission.

"National Geographic . . ."

"Crazy cycle stunt . . ."

"Typical rich tourist . . ."

A few of the spectators offered misguided advice while I assembled the bike. Pedals threaded on easily, the way they had in the beginning. Handlebars turned to the proper position, and panniers snapped securely against the rear rack. All was as I had practiced at home.

Cycling away from Fornebue airport, I thought of the journey from Ohio to New York, where the airplane had awaited to fly me over the Atlantic. At first, it seemed as if my bike grew heavier as the east coast drew nearer. I was beset by constant knee and ankle pains, a grim reminder of a previous sedentary lifestyle. My muscles grudgingly ached into action each morning like an old car being jump-started after a long spell in the garage.

Time, and the constant undulation of the Appalachian roadways, slowly strengthened my legs. Once Pennsylvania was left behind, I gradually began to feel more comfortable atop my bronze-colored bicycle. I covered greater distances each day, and found it easier to camp, my new gear becoming more familiar with each stop. By the time I reached the Blue Mountains, I had worked out many of the kinks that haunted me my first weeks on the road. The trip from Ohio to the coast, five hundred uneventful miles, had taken me more than two weeks.

FOLLOWING MY PLAN, I cycled south through Norway toward Europe. My stay in Scandinavia would be brief, spending a single day in both Norway and Sweden before taking a ferry to the northern tip of Denmark. I stopped in the village of Ellos, the first across the Swedish border, cradled in rock above an inlet of pellucid water set against a turquoise sky. A hilltop café serving breakfast overlooked the fjord referred to on my map as Koljofjorden. Small white fishing shacks seemed strewn about like dice on a green carpet of grass, which stretched down to meet a fleet of idle fishing boats floating along the banks. In the distance, framed in azure, black-feathered sea birds flew, their orange beaks angled toward the North Sea.

The ferry to Denmark floated me through Koljofjorden, emerging in the Kattegat Strait and on to Fredrickshaven at the northeastern tip of Jutland. From the coast, I cycled toward Germany, four hundred kilometers south along the length of the peninsula. I rode past sandy shoreline scattered with driftwood, and solitary trees which stood black and warped against the seaside air. A gray ocean whispered its waves forward, over tidal flats and onto the shore, in an effort to reach the thin, one-lane road. With my approach, cormorants bobbing with the wind-blown waves fluttered for the sky.

I pumped south over flat countryside, a refreshing respite from the mountainous roads of American Appalachia. Denmark's intricate series of well-kept bicycle paths allowed me to traverse three-quarters of the country, north to south, without having to face a strenuous incline, a potholed road, or a traffic-ridden highway. The trails took me through, one day a wooded lane; the next, a stand of antique windmills stretching over an endless expanse of green.

A forested section along the path attracted me to a picnic area. An old man sat at the lone table, pen in hand, scrawling deliberate notes on a yellow pad. I sat and broke out a can of sardines, the only food available at the small country store I had visited to the north. In an act of good will, the Dane offered a package of crackers. I thanked him, but it became clear we did not share a common language. No matter, the old man rose from his bench, remaining hunched over like a half circle, then motioned for me to follow. He led me to a stone cross, shoulder high, with no markings or signs save five bouquets of flowers planted at the base.

"Kalmonk," he said, pointing a thin finger at the cross. "Do you know?"

I admitted that I had never heard the name.

"Nineteen . . . four . . . four . . ." the Dane continued in an effort to conjure up what little English he knew. "Denmark's man . . . writer . . . Germans kill." The old man uttered a word or two, paused to gather the next translation in his mind, then continued with another set of words.

"Kalmonk write . . . Germans no like . . . Germans kill."

It seemed as if my companion wanted to be more specific but was being patient to be sure I understood.

"He . . ." The old man pointed to the grave and stood as if in prayer.

"Great man?" I asked.

"Yes." He raised his head toward me.

"President?" I guessed.

My companion motioned up to the sky, "Higher."

"Holy man?"

He tilted his hand in the air as if to say "sort of." But as we walked back to the Dane's car he said, "Kalmonk in Underground?" forming his statement as a question to be sure I understood.

"Yes," I assured him I knew what he meant.

"Me in Underground?"

"You knew him?" I asked.

"Yes," he said, saddened.

"You were his friend?"

"Yes." He gazed at the ground in memory.

"Denmark has lost a great man."

"Yes, great man," he said, then he reached into the front seat of his car and brought out a box of apple juice, which he offered to me.

"Where in England are you from?"

"U.S.A.—Ohio."

"How far today?" He motioned toward the bicycle.

"A hundred kilometers."

The old man rolled his eyes, as if that were a great distance, then he climbed into his car and drove away.

MAY 19th

moors near Lubeck, Germany

GERMAN BREAD served as my breakfast, thick and doughy, baked to a bronze crust and auburn through to the center. The loaf of bread I bought before camping on the banks of the river Elbe weighed a good three pounds, and was dense enough to stand up to a tightened bungee cord for days on end without exhibiting the slightest indentation. Since entering Germany, the local bread served both as my breakfast in the morning, and my pillow at night, giving my overused shoes a much-needed hiatus.

I broke camp and gave my legs that first, tight stretch over the pedals. I had been cycling fifty to eighty kilometers per day, but Germany marked the peak of a gradual rise in fitness which began when I was reduced to walking up my first Appalachian hill. By midafternoon, I had accomplished the 200 kilometers to Lubeck. I wanted to see the border—or what was left of the border between East and West, and cycled eastward, beyond the city to where the wall once stood. Gray cinder blocks remained half-buried where the wall had been dismantled to its base. Everything else was gone, except a graffitied guard tower blackened by fire, as if someone had tried to erase the concrete testimony to the past then decided to leave it black as a lesson to the present. An open field stretched from each side of the former border. There, an old man paced the eastern side of the cinder-block line, as if some mental, impenetrable barrier still existed in the German psyche.

I was looking for a place to stay that would conform to my five-dollar daily budget, a place where a shower would mean more than a sliver of soap and one liter of water poured from a cycling bottle. "The youth hostel," I was told at every turn, "but you will have to go through the moors."

Just before nightfall, a dirt road brought me through a swampy area with no suitable ground for camping other than the thin path itself. On my map, the trail continued through the moors to emerge on the other side. In reality, the path came to an end at the youth hostel, where an expansive green lawn opened up from the tangled swamp. Ivy crawling up the worn black walls of the stone building brought to mind a medieval castle.

Through the heavy front doors, a caretaker stood behind an oak counter.

"Name?" he asked me when I walked inside and leaned the bicycle against the front desk.

I gave him my name.

"Number of people in party?"

"I'm alone."

He wrote "lonely" in the space. "Occupation?"

Taking note of his last entry, I said "wanderer," which elicited a smirk. Under sex he put the word "man," then he looked at the form and read through the entries. "Lonely wandering man." He paused in thought. "Touring by bicycle are you? We'll give you a room to yourself so you can build up your strength."

The caretaker, who introduced himself as Bart, led me to a large room with four bunks, which he said were "for you and your bicycle." I brought in the bike and unpacked, then I went out on the sprawling front porch to review my maps. From inside the dining hall came the melodious sound of a singing choir. I thought about the incongruity of it all—a youth hostel and a choir in the middle of the moors—while I planned my route to Holland.

An hour passed before I was interrupted by one of the other guests—a robust, bearded German—who walked out onto the porch, beer in hand. He tipped his bottle in greeting.

"Are you guys singing in there?" I asked him.

"Ja," he said, his voice gruff." We from Bavaria—we drink beer un sink!"

"Sing?"

"Ja—drink un sink."

"That sounds like fun," I had to admit.

"Come, drink beer un sink with us!"

We went into the wide dining hall where several tables were linked end to end in a long row. The Bavarian seated himself at the far head of the tables. Next to him was a tall barrel filled with beer and ice. I was given a chair in the center, among twenty of the other guests. The Bavarian reached into the barrel, grabbed an Einbecker beer and slid it down the table. It came to a slow stop in front of me.

"Do you know any American folk songs?" a woman across the table asked me. Bart was seated at the head of the table opposite the Bavarian. I gathered from his expression that he had already explained my nationality.

"Folk songs? Well, none that I could sing. The truth is, I can't sing."

"Where are you from in America?" the girl next to me asked.

"Well, I was born near Detroit. It's a city in Michigan."

Against all odds, they flipped through their songbooks and came upon a song called "Oh, Detroit."

"Surely you know this—being from Detroit," one said. I had never heard of the song, but they sang it in my honor anyway, and afterward came a soon to be familiar sound. Down slid another Einbecker; the first was only half gone.

"Ha! You must drink," insisted the Bavarian." You must drink faster to keep up with us!"

"I'm drinking," I said." I'm drinking already."

"You say you were born in Detroit," said Bart." Did you live somewhere else after that?"

"My most recent home was in Ohio," I admitted, but soon regretted my answer. After a moment's pause, the group found a seldom sung song in a dusty song book entitled, "On the Banks of the Ohio."

"You must know this song," said one, "being from Ohio."

I shamefully admitted my ignorance, as murmurs of suspicion wavered down the table. But they sang with gusto, and after the song, down slid another Einbecker. The Bavarian glared across the table with approval as he saw my previous beer had been drained.

The evening began to fade into a pleasant haze of Einbeckers, conversation, and song. The moors were locked safely outside, and bike repairs and nighttime campsites were worries for another day. There were no dangers here, only the lyrical sound of song, laughter around the table, and a quiet room to myself in which to study my maps and reflect upon a journey put at bay for one serene night.

SIGNS OF CIVILIZATION crept back into the landscape with my westward advance. The moors disappeared, giving way to scattered stands of trees tilting over the gray coated road, an occasional car rolling by to shudder some leaves from dead branches. Canals appeared across the Dutch border, paralleling the road beyond a thick shoulder of sunlit grass flecked with dandelions. Undulating countryside across the chocolate water held brick cottages with pointy roofs, and black windmills the shape of silos, their sails slowly cranking in time with the breeze. Some bridges made of metal, with white metal railings, swung out parallel to the channel to let boats pass; some arched over the water like a frown, solid, unmoving. I watched the boats glide soundlessly down the canals, the scenery broken only by an occasional cow sedately working her lower jaw back and forth in tedium.

By nightfall, the canal roads brought me to the small Dutch village of Geithoorn, and it seemed as if I had cycled into a tiny replica of Venice. Appearing like the subject of a Rembrandt landscape, the town was built upon a network of canals crisscrossed by humped bridges made of brick, and carved white stone stained green with lime. Along the main canal stretched a line of cafés, with tables facing the small boats that plied up and down the waterways of Geithoorn. Guitar music wafted from the cafés and wavered over the water, setting a rhythm for the boatmen only to fade in the wake of their dripping oars. The setting seemed uniquely European.

I sat at a canal-side table while the day grew long. The sun's glow on the eddies dimmed and the boatmen deserted the darkening canal. I left when the rivermen left, and wandered through the labyrinth of Rembrandt bridges, past the darkening canals and along the shaded cobblestone lanes leading westward. As I slowly, reluctantly, turned the pedals out and away from Geithoorn, the guitar music faded, leaving me with the feeling I had found a prize seated in the center of Europe like a proudly displayed gem.

In the tradition of Geithoorn's embodiment of art, the byways and canal paths of Holland brought me past scenery which implanted itself in my mind as flashes of portraits and pastels. My route followed the coast, over the offshore islands north of the Zeeland peninsula and along the massive dikes built up on sand dunes between the islands. Rather than the thin road alongside, I learned to cycle on top of the dikes where the view held my attention with the lure of an endless seascape. Below on either side was nothing but ocean, and ahead stretched only a thin line of mounded earth crooking left, then right before disappearing over the horizon into the distant sea.

Each village I came across was numbingly attractive. Delft was a city preserved in its seventeenth-century state, with church spires and minarets and bell towers rising above the brick cottages of small-town Europe. While sipping espresso in the central square, I was surrounded by the architecture of two ancient cathedrals. Geode Ree, regardless of the fact the town was very tiny, supported a sprawling cathedral, a windmill built in the eighteenth century, and a maze of cobblestone streets squeezed between the walls of antique houses.

Such visions along the road from Geode Ree to Bruges made the eighty kilometers feel like ten. I cycled past windmills, archaic bridges, many of the dikes which make Holland unique, alongside canals and through narrow town streets. The only thing to distract from the landscape was a lingering thought of the imminent French border.

I had spoken to other travelers, but no one seemed to know what was required to enter the country. Some said a visa was required. Others said it was not. Some people told me of bureaucratic logjams, one-hour border searches, and time-consuming paperwork.

When I approached the border, I didn't know what to expect. It was the first time since landing in Norway that I'd even seen a border post. I cycled up to the guard booth ready for a long battle with bureaucracy.

The guard gave my passport a cursory glance. "American? Okay," he said, and he waved me on with the twitch of a finger without looking up. My confidence in the traveler's grapevine had dwindled greatly.

The northern coast of France was industrialized, with factories spewing white smoke into the sea air. Skirting Dunkirk, I cycled into Calais and boarded a ferry which took me over the English Channel to Dover. The white cliffs, seeming to shore up the earth of a continent, stood in contrast to blue-gray waves below and a meadow of green grass above. Dover castle dominated the horizon beyond the wharf.

I exchanged money in Dover then began searching for a bike shop capable of repairing my rear rim which had become damaged on the cobblestone lanes of small-town Europe. Country roads brought me to Sandwich, where I found a shop at the end of the main street. There was no one at the counter, so I wheeled my bike into the back where the mechanic was preoccupied with a bottom bracket repair. I explained my problem, and realized how refreshing it was to be able to express myself without the hand gestures and broken English of recent weeks.

"Right," he said after analyzing the rim. "Gotta get the free wheel off."

"I know," I said. "I don't have the tools."

He hoisted the bike up on a hook and chain apparatus then began the operation.

"I always wanted to know," he said while he worked, "why do Americans call biscuits, cookies?"

"Well, because biscuits are something else completely in America."

"What are they?"

"They're, well . . . they're, ah . . . like round baked bread shaped like a muffin."

"You Americans. You always make things so complicated." I was suddenly nostalgic for the days of hand gestures and language dictionaries. I was still thinking about biscuits when the mechanic finally lifted the wheel off the frame. He produced the precious freewheel removal tool, a tool conspicuously absent from my tool kit, and inserted it into place. To this he attached a wrench then, with opposing pressure from a chain, he tried cranking off the freewheel. A few grunts and as many minutes later produced no results.

"Can't get it off." He stood up with hands on hips. "You sure it comes off this way?"

"Well, yeah. I mean, I've never actually taken it off. Don't they all come off that way?"

"Well . . ." he said, almost to himself as he stood staring at the bike wheel. "As far as I know they all come off that way." He continued to stare at the bike as if in deep thought. "Better get the boss." He went into the recesses of the store and returned with a slim man in his late forties.

The new man looked at my panniers. "Touring huh? We're always glad to help someone touring. Let's see what we've got." After analyzing the project for a minute or two, he repeated the same procedure his employee had tried.

"Where you headed?" he asked with familiar grunts while he struggled with the wheel. I told him about the trip past and the trip yet to be in what had become an almost encyclopedic litany, memorized and repeated at every city, village, and turn of the road.

The boss stopped and put his wrench down. "That's quite a trip," he said and reached into a tool box pulling out a two-foot-long wrench. "This should do it."

He placed the wrench in position. "Here, take that side and crank down." He produced a chain when I'd taken my position.

"You know, I once cycled across the Sahara." The wrench was in place and I held it down as the chain was adjusted.

"The Sahara?"

He relieved me on the wrench.

"Three of us went. A quarter of the way the road disappeared— just disappeared. There was nothing but sand and wind and sky."

"Whatd'ya do?"

"What did I do? I turned back. The others, they kept on for a while but eventually came back to meet me."

He was momentarily distracted by our lack of success. "No, this isn't working. Hold on, let me make a phone call." He looked up the freewheel brand in a catalogue then called a fellow shop owner who told us to do exactly what we had just tried. "You sure it turns counter-clockwise?" the owner asked just before hanging up the phone, then he went in back and returned with a long, hollow pipe.

"You remember my story," he said, emerging from the back room, pointing the pipe in my direction. "When you cross North Africa, turn back if it gets too bad, or turn north—toward the sea." He slid the hollow pipe over the handle of the wrench. "Grab the pipe and crank down," he told me. "But if it puts up too much of a fight, ease up. You could strip the threads."

The pipe was attached to the wrench, which was in turn attached to the freewheel removal tool, which was itself attached to the freewheel. I pushed down on the pipe with all my weight . . . then came a long click. Then *click, click*.

"Stop!" the junior mechanic shouted. "You're stripping it!"

I was tired of waiting and expended one last effort. The freewheel gave a metal-tearing screech then dropped to the ground in defeat.

"I've never seen one that tight," said the red-haired mechanic. "How many miles you got on that thing anyway?"

"I'm not sure. I came through a few states in America. Then there was a little of Scandinavia . . . Denmark and Germany, Holland . . ."

"No wonder," the boss said while he set about repairing the spokes and rim.

Two hours after I walked into the shop, the repair was done. The owner gave me twenty spare spokes, two extra inner tubes and a spare tire. He showed me how to true my wheels properly and gave me some traveling advice before sending me on my way—no charge. Just a wave and the satisfaction that he'd helped another cyclist.

JUNE 6

London

WHILE I CYCLED through the sunlit countryside toward Canterbury, I took the opportunity to think about what the mechanics in Sandwich had told me about my bike. Many of the sprocket teeth were broken and would have to be replaced before Africa. My cables were frayed and all the bearings needed new lubricant. Depending on the availability of parts, I was hoping to make the repairs myself rather than pay a professional mechanic.

In addition to the repairs, I wanted to formulate some changes for the remaining journey. My original plan was to see Scotland, Ireland, and Wales, but the advantage of traveling alone was I could go wherever I pleased. I was well over my five-dollar daily budget, which worried me. At the rate I was spending, my money supply would be gone in a year. The weather also plagued me. Although it was June, fifty degrees and sporadic rain remained the norm. For those reasons, I decided to turn south, return to France, then make for Spain and warm weather with all possible speed. I was eager, as well, to see some of the countries outside Europe.

First, I was due in London to collect some money wired from my bank account in the States. I spent the night in Chatham before setting out, but as the miles toward England's largest city ground by, I began to realize that cycling into the capital would not be an easy task. The only routes on my rudimentary map were highways, and the traffic north of Chatham was steadily increasing. I asked several pedestrians about a less-traveled way north, but soon discovered that no one in the suburbs had any experience entering London on anything less than a motor-way.

Ten miles south of the city, I came upon a cyclist at the side of the road. He was an elderly man, perhaps in his sixties, sporting cycling shorts and a massive set of calves. I slowed and asked him if he knew a good route into town.

"Sure," he said. "That's where I'm headed. You can cycle along with me."

He rode an old-fashioned bicycle, but a well-kept antique, and with it he set an impossible pace for my overweight and fat-tired mountain bike.

"You see this bike?" he called while we rode. "It's a fifty-four classic. Built it myself—that's my hobby, rebuildin' bicycles. These pedals I found in a junkyard. Originals, they are. The whole bike has original parts. All I added was the gears."

"You must cycle a lot. Is this your normal pace?" Wallowing in false pride, I was trying to disguise my labored breathing.

"No, I'm goin' slow 'cause you're loaded down. I go a hundred and twenty miles in a ride sometimes. I just get on and keep goin' and can't stop. My wife hates it—thinks I'm daft, she does." He paused for a second. A bead of sweat dripped along his bald head. "We got some good hills comin' up." He'd given his warning and picked up the pace into the hills. I was forced to get out of the saddle to keep up, and eventually the frame of the old man grew smaller and smaller into the distance of the rolling hills until I was on the road alone once again.

Fifteen miles later, I came upon the English cyclist standing in front of a local brewery alongside his 1954 classic. "C'mon, I'll buy ya' a pint," he shouted and waved me inside the small wooden inn.

He threw down his pint fast, as if it were a glass of water, and he talked about himself, his bicycle touring club, his restored bicycles. He discussed cycling as if it were theology, and never asked about my trip—a refreshing break from all the inescapable questions. To him, I was merely a member of his religion: omniscient in the realm of the bicycle, a comrade in sport not to be asked questions, but to be joined in discussion. Just as a church member would not ask "Who is Christ?" or "Is there a God?" so the old man would never ask where I was headed. That was not the point. The point was to be cycling regardless of the destination. The point was to be part of the brotherhood. The cyclist finished his pint. "Straight down the road is London," he said, and stood, then left without ceremony. I saw the shrinking frame of the English cyclist for the second time in the day. I was once again on my own.

There were a few tasks to accomplish in England's capital. I sought out the American Express office where I collected the $1,000 required to last me across Africa, then I went to the headquarters of *Euro-Biker Magazine* to inquire about a scenic route through France. In the wide main lobby, I was greeted by a receptionist sitting in the hole of a doughnut-shaped desk.

"May I help you?" she asked, with a sideways look of suspicion.

I explained my trip to the secretary and that I was seeking information about the route. Surely someone at the magazine would know the bicycle-friendly areas of France.

"One moment please," she said through her nose. "Someone will be out."

"Can't I go in?"

"I *said* someone will be out."

I waited in the austere lobby, standing. After a curiously long delay, someone came out. He came through a steel door and greeted me with his back to it, guarding the passageway to the office with suspicion. This was not what I had envisioned, but I explained my needs despite the lack of hospitality.

"Where's your bike?" the magazine representative asked when I had finished the explanation. His tone indicated that he didn't believe my story.

"It's there." I pointed to the bike which was leaning against the lobby window.

"You're going across France on a GT Timberline!" he sneered. "Better you than me!"

So much for camaraderie. I walked out without another word spoken.

My last stop was the London library, where I read about

Denmark's war history. I found no reference to Kalmonk, my apparent misunderstanding of the spoken word, but the name Kaj Munk was listed.

"On January 4, 1944, the murder of Denmark's great priest, poet, and dramatist, Kaj Munk, horrified the free world. His body was found in a ditch on Horbybund Hill, near Silkeborg, in Jutland. His face had been battered savagely and he had been killed by five pistol shots, fired at close range."

Kaj Munk was an outspoken opponent of German occupation, and his influence irritated the Germans. His assassination was carried out by the Peter Group, a roaming Nazi death squad. The poet's funeral was conducted in a small church but, despite German threats, thousands attended, content to stand outside and mourn.

When I cycled out of London, I was reminded of the stone cross that marked the site where the priest had been murdered. I remembered the old man, the five bouquets of flowers, the apple juice box.

JUNE 11

south of Le Mans, France

ONCE OUTSIDE London's city limits it was an easy ride south to Portsmouth, where the ferry carried me back over the English Channel to Le Havre, France. In the middle of a long line of cars snaking its way from the ferry to customs stood my rather conspicuous GT Timberline. While the procession passed the French officers, I was singled out of the line to show my passport. A senior official asked me about my destination. "Spain," I told him, in the offhand manner of one who's been asked the same question a thousand times.

"On that?"

"Oui."

A younger officer wandered over. "Move on, you must move on."

I grabbed for my passport, but the older man wasn't finished with me, and he wasn't about to give my passport back until his curiosity was assuaged.

"How far do you go in a day?" he persisted, with a twinge of mockery.

"It varies," I said, as I tentatively reached for my passport. I

20

hoped that he would let me get out of there if I gave him the shortest answers possible.

The younger officer came back over. "Move on!"

"I'm trying."

"Where's your tent. Do you have a tent?" the senior man asked.

"Move on!" said the younger.

"I need my passport!" I shouted, exasperated. The two officers began arguing with each other, in the midst of which I was handed my passport, almost subconsciously by the older man.

"American tourist!" came a voice from behind before I made my escape. One hour in France, and I already felt as if I were ready for the scenic hills of the south.

JUNE 21

Pau, France

THE COUNTRYSIDE south of Noir was covered with grapevines, which made finding campsites exceedingly difficult. Directly to my west lay Bordeaux, so I assumed the grapes in the area were destined for a wine of the same name. Three days to the south stood the great Pyrenees—my first significant mountain range.

The landscape became more grand in the Mediterranean south. Sprawling chateaus dominated the skyline of each vineyard. Mercedes and red convertibles replaced the matchbox-like Trabants of the north. Campers and bulky mobile homes appeared on the scene and these, along with the sports cars, almost exclusively owned the roadways. North of the Dordogne River, I had no worries in staking my claim to a thin stretch along the side of the road. Cars would swerve into the opposite lane to give me space, leaving me with an entire lane to myself. If there was oncoming traffic, drivers would wait, lingering behind me until the way was clear to pass.

Different customs held true in the south, among the young vacationers dominating the roads and the reckless mobile home drivers, half of whom, I suspected, were not from France. For the first time since entering the country, I suffered a few near collisions and was subjected to the once familiar cat-calls which were prevalent in some of the other areas of Europe and America. Northern France had spoiled me with its memorable courtesy.

I made my way through the traffic of Perigord and into Gascogne, where the population thinned and I glided past trestles supporting brown and green vines burgeoning with purple fruit. The chalets of the terraced countryside became the squat, whitewashed houses of Pau, and the climate graduated to almost tropical with temperatures well into the nineties.

Pau was a preparation stop, since the Pyrenees mountain range began its rise thirty kilometers to the south. I gave the bike a complete overhaul. I replaced cables, oiled parts, put on new brake pads and adjusted some nuts and bolts that had worked loose. After cleaning and lubricating the bearings in the bottom bracket, I bought food supplies sufficient for a week in anticipation of some mountain camping. At a used-book store, I bought two books written in English, *For Whom the Bell Tolls* and *Papillon*.

Beyond Pau, I felt France was almost gone. The last of the grapevines melted behind me. The whitewashed houses, endless vineyards of Burgundy, and fear of being run over by a mobile home were all in the past. I felt as if beyond the Pyrenees, as if beyond some unannounced border, Europe would be left behind. I hoped that my time in Europe had prepared me for the countries to come. With the mountains nearing, I hoped the memory of the English cyclist on his refurbished bicycle would help me over the border and into Spain.

Those thoughts overtook me when the dark apparition to the south slowly revealed itself as a long, high, mountainous barrier—the Pyrenees. I thought of the lands, mysterious to me, which were yet to come. My daydreaming brought me excitement, hope, and anxiety. While traversing the deserts of north Africa, would I think of apple juice boxes and stone crosses in a Danish town where no tourists go, or would I instead be hearing the echoing voice of the man from the magazine, "better you than me"?

3

A Spanish Summer

SWITCHBACKS ran up and out of sight, becoming lost in the foothills of the Pyrenees. The thirty-kilometer ascent, represented on my map as the least traveled road from France to Spain, would be my longest to date.

The road tilted upward. My legs strained against the pedals as my lungs rebelled in memory of relentlessly flat Europe. I began pumping the pedals to a slow cadence, exerting a paced and consistent effort which reduced the mountainous climb to a measured rhythm. The exertion became enjoyable, interrupted only when I dismounted to explore some paths that wandered off from the main road. A river joined my progress below a sloping shoulder, and I stopped to eat lunch with my feet dangling over a cliff face.

My ascent continued when night slowly fell, and I caught sight of the grassy banks of a stream far below. I climbed down the slope carrying my bike and glanced around at the night's campsite. I stood atop a knoll, surrounded on three sides by a clear stream which flowed slow and straight over tossed rocks, except for a small curl in its course that passed around my encampment. The stream was shallow, showing its pebbled mocha bottom, with a transparent green reflected by the setting sun.

On the opposite shore, a steep, sandy bank rose into a blue mountain filled with stubby ocher trees, their trunks interspersed with the same green moss that made up the floor of my campsite. On the near shore, a few feet from the green peninsula that held my tent, a foaming waterfall tumbled two stories down. The river's rushing hiss over lichen-coated rocks brought a sense of comfort with the darkness. The cascading water, plunging into the slackened stream at dusk, lulled me to sleep with pacifying rhythms when night closed in.

I bathed under the waterfall with the rising sun's reflection, the thought of a winding mountain climb ahead, and a restful night behind. I packed slowly, surrounded by the beauty of the river and the falls, then carried my bike back up the side of the mountain to continue the ascent. I thought my legs might give, never having attempted such a climb, but instead they felt stronger with the rising altitude. It seemed my lungs could fail, but instead the cadence of the climb elicited a new harmony in my body.

When I achieved the summit and passed into Spain, the novelty of cycling in the mountains became apparent. If, during the climb, the curling road gave way so slowly as to imprint every crack and crevasse on my thoughts, then the descent stole those details away, blurring them into a patchwork of sights, cacophony of sounds, and mesh of colors.

I was on my second descent by midday, having climbed two passes over 2,000 meters high. The mountains continued their rise to the south like an undulating sine wave. When night approached, I set camp in a long, gradually descending ravine that paralleled the road, as if nature had engineered its construction for the benefit of cyclists in need of a campsite at sunset. An isolated chalet stood around a bend in the valley, like a fortress of ancient gloom and rustic elegance. Warped mountain shadows rose with the lowering sun.

While I organized my gear around the tent, a gathering storm closed in over the surrounding landscape. A dark, misty cloud slowly crept up the valley along which the road climbed. Like a vaporous claw, it reached its way up the road with thin fingers that curled around every tree and rock, each dale and hill. By the time camp was set, the cloud engulfed the mountains to the south and pressed into the valley as if a blanket were being draped over the land. In places within the mist, sparks flew from the ground like exploding fireworks, a form of lightning I had never seen. Rolling thunder marched up the valley as the sky went black. Rain followed in a seething rush.

I huddled inside my fragile tent, the mounting storm battering thin synthetic walls. Aluminum poles bowed as the tent flap whipped with the wind in a constant nervous vibration. Lightning turned the black sky white. Thunder arrived in a long, low rumble.

I crawled out and secured the tent by attaching extra ropes to the rainfly, but even with this precaution the tent shook and threatened to collapse. I sat inside, terrified by the sight of lightning strikes through dark tree branches. One instant revealed falling branches and a violent, white sky—the next, darkness and rushing wind. Viewed from the safety of a secure house the storm would have been terrifying. From inside a tent, it was like being carpet bombed.

I could hear sharp cracks like the snapping of a whip in the wind. Dozens of tree branches fell. Peering beyond the tent flap, I saw branches scattered along the grass. Shaken leaves and tree limbs littered the ground with the constant drone of a rising wind. I looked up in fear of being crushed by a branch or a tree. Suddenly, a large chunk of hail the size of a baseball fell in front of my tent.

Two more landed, then a machine gun fire of hail pelted the ground. My tent buckled after a few strikes. I took the tenting between my forearms and stretched it over my head. If one were to hit me squarely above the shoulders, I would surely be knocked out. The battering hail rained against my arms. Those that struck above my head sprang against the tenting, hit me with reduced impact, and bounced away.

The hail thickened and I was battered into a crouch. My arms numbed. I could no longer keep the thin synthetic above me. The machine gun fire slowed to a steady *crack crack* then plop—plop—plop. This was my chance to run for cover.

Abandoning everything, I ran toward the chalet around the bend in the valley. I ran, surrounded by trees and jagged hills. Hail fell with intermittent thuds and splashes on the rain-drenched grass. The chalet took form through rain, nestled in the cliffs beyond two grassy hills. A mother and daughter watched the spectacle from a covered porch, and I hurried underneath, orphaned and drenched by the storm. Through mime and my rudimentary French, I explained that I had been caught in my tent during the storm and had left all my gear to the mercy of the rain. The woman assured me I could stay until the storm was over. I was led inside and given a towel before the woman turned up the fire under a teapot.

Calm, safe, I had time to take in my surroundings. The room was large and welcoming, the size of a restaurant kitchen, yet the wooden tables, hanging oak cupboards, and well-used cookery made it seem small and comforting. A high window inset in stone faced the Pyrenees. Outside, through blackness, hail rattled the window glass as wind and rain battered the walls of the safe, well-lighted kitchen. The chalet was a fortress made of large stone bricks, a haven both mentally and physically.

When the hail stopped, I made my way in the driving rain to recover my gear. My former camp was gone, and a rivulet flowed over the grass where my tent once stood. My bike laid submerged in muddy water, and the tent, poles warped and damaged, wavered a hundred yards downstream, everything inside drenched. It took me over half an hour to drag it all, waterlogged, back to the chalet. When the task was finally complete, the mother insisted I hang the gear out to dry underneath the porch.

The rain slowly abated. The mother and daughter went inside to clean up the mud I had tracked in earlier, while I tended to the gear dangling about the porch. The sight of my damaged tent and the comfort of the hillside chalet made me ponder the perceptions brought on by a safe, domestic lifestyle. Spending the majority of my nights in a tent gave me a newfound respect for the true dangers of weather.

"Uh campeh," came a voice from behind, shaking me from my thoughts. The mother appeared in the doorway, pointing into the blackness beyond the porch. "Uh campeh," she repeated, then motioned for me to follow. I was led to the side of the chalet, where a large camper was parked next to a decayed stone wall. The woman opened the side door and began methodically preparing the camper for my occupation. "Uh campeh," she repeated for the third time, while turning down the sheets of a small cot in the corner, then she left, closing the door behind.

JULY
south of Madrid

THE MAP I acquired from the Spanish tourist board showed a large green crescent extending the length of the country, north to south. The green represented forest, bypassing all major cities. This was the route I followed through Spain, a route of green mountain trees, rocky valleys cut by clear, spring-fed rivers, and row after row of Spain's most pristine mountain ranges.

By the time I reached central Spain, June was almost at an end, the temperatures were sweltering, and I found my mountain legs. Ascents became enjoyable, even exhilarating, and the beauty of the Spanish mountain ranges seemed unrivaled. Each night was filled with some of the best camping Europe had to offer, and each night I stopped cycling before the sun set, sought out a comfortable campsite, and built a raging fire to keep the darkness at bay. Some nights I camped in abandoned villages of adobe brick, wild chickens scuttling around the deserted streets in testimony to a living community long since move away.

When June passed into July, I was quickly approaching the southern coast of Spain, Costa del Sol. Following my present line, the coast would be reached at Malaga, a city of which I knew nothing. From Malaga, the road followed the coast westward to Gibraltar and my final stop in Europe. The Dark Continent was less than a month away.

My last day in the Spanish highlands entailed a climb to 2,000 meters—an altitude I reached while the morning sun was rising over the distant blue mountains—followed by a 20-kilometer freefall descent into Malaga. Central Spain had shown me a civilization almost third worldly, which made modern Malaga a lesson in culture shock. I hadn't spoken English since leaving France, but the first person I questioned in Malaga, to my surprise, was from England. In fact, it seemed half the people in Malaga were English, and the Spanish residents were all bilingual, making life in southern Spain much simpler for me, albeit less exotic.

Lacking the price of the expensive hotels of this coastal resort, I decided to sleep on the beach amidst the never-ending rows of lounge chairs rented during the day by sunburned English tourists. Before dawn, I was awakened by a beachcomber wielding a metal detector.

"Sorry to wake you," he said when he saw my head rise up from between two chairs.

"I thought you were the police."

"Naw, they don't care as long as it's one person. Now, a large group, they'd break up." The man sported long, scraggly hair, easy-flowing clothes, a dark tan and flopping sandals, like someone who had spent his life forever near an ocean shore.

"You ever find anything good?" I asked, while contemplating the option of beach-bumming as a full-time profession.

"Sure, once I found a diamond ring. Mostly coins and bottle caps though."

"Say, as long as I'm up, you know a good place for breakfast?" I was still bleary eyed from having been awakened so early, but my stomach wouldn't let me rest with the anticipation of Malaga's Western-style restaurants.

"Andy Capp's," the beachcomber said as he moved away. Then, from over his shoulder he called, "Just ask anyone, everyone knows it." He swung his detector into the darkness back and forth, back and forth. In the distance, a periodic beep would give away his location.

The sun came up to turn the Mediterranean blue, while the beachside shops opened their doors one by one. Waking on the beach in the glow of the rising sun made me feel like a free and careless gypsy, who need only eat and sleep to be content.

I went to the boardwalk where I bought a *Herald Tribune* at a shop touting international newspapers. At Andy Capp's I ordered eggs, hash browns and toast. After living on the scraps of camp-stove cooking for so long, it seemed to me I was immersed in culinary treasures served up by the greatest chefs in Europe.

The owner was reading the morning newspaper in the booth next to mine. Due to the early hour, we were the only two in the restaurant. I savored my breakfast and the news from America while the dining room filled, until the overflow of customers brought two young Englishmen to my large booth.

"Name's Malcolm, this is Dave," said the brown-haired half of the pair. Dave had red hair and a bald pate, giving him a clown-like appearance.

"We noticed the bleedin' bicycle," Dave said, his northern accent contrasting sharply with Malcolm's proper, Lawrence Olivier English. "Where might ya' be goin'?"

"Headed to Gibraltar, then Africa."

"Here's the deal," Malcolm explained. "We were wondering if you might like to join us."

"Join you?"

"Yeah, we're cycling too. Along the Costa del Sol. We don't go fast but if you want to join us you can tag along."

The following morning we left for Torremolinos and cycled into the heart of Spain's splendor. It seemed the extent of Mediterranean colors was unlimited, or limited only by one's own ability to perceive beauty. At times, it seemed I was staring at a postcard of stucco-white houses with blue shutters, each village set upon pastures of emerald grass adjoining the cerulean sea. At times, I felt the front wheel of my bicycle was rolling over into a land of hallucinations, while my rear wheel maintained a tenuous anchor in reality.

Having traveled alone for four months, riding with partners was almost as unique to me as the scenery. Malcolm was new to cycle touring so he most often brought up the rear. I became used to riding with Malcolm, partly to rediscover the art of company and conversation, and partly to bask in the grace of the Mediterranean. Dave, unlike Malcolm or me, either took in the scenery at high speeds, or preferred to gaze while motionless. He would usually race far ahead, and we would later come upon him while he was finishing a second pint of beer at some roadside café. Malcolm and I were then obliged, after catching up on bicycle, to catch up in pints as well.

We arrived in Torremolinos to find Dave, true to form, waiting for us at a pub at the edge of town. Malcolm's Spanish wife had recommended a hotel, the Hotel Italia, and the place turned out to be a vision from a travel brochure. We were given a room overlooking the central plaza which held a high-spewing fountain and sprawling garden. The familiar blue shutters on white walls encircled the plaza, contrasting with the brilliant red and yellow flower garden. Floating mist from the fountain added a surrealistic, dreamlike effect to the entire scene.

We unpacked our gear then went downstairs to the café, where small round tables supported umbrellas tipped at artistic angles toward the sun. We ordered prawns and *bocadillos*, leaning back in our chairs to watch the evening bustle of the streets. I felt at ease, my feet propped up on the next table, a cup of espresso in my hand. Here were all the necessities needed for life and living: carefree company, an easy chair, bags packed with a tent and food. "And I thanked god I was free to wander, free to hope, and free to love," came to mind the words of a distant poet.

Voices broke me from my thoughts when the owner of the café approached our table and addressed Malcolm in Spanish. The two held a lengthy conversation before Malcolm turned to us and translated.

"You see that girl over there?" A lone girl sat sobbing at a corner table, head in her hands. "She was here with her boyfriend for two weeks but when it came time to pay and leave, she discovered her boyfriend had crept away in the night. The girl has no money."

"Didn't they have to give their passports before checking in?" I asked.

"That's what's keeping her here. Apparently, the boyfriend stole his back the night he left."

Normally, the affair would have been none of our business, but, since the girl could speak no Spanish and the owner no English, Malcolm had been asked to interpret in an attempt to resolve the situation.

Malcolm agreed and accompanied the owner to the girl's table. Not ten minutes had passed before screaming broke out and the girl's sobs turned into wails. Malcolm sat in the middle of the maelstrom, red-faced, rubbing his palms against his pants.

Dave found the predicament to be so humorous that he was awash in tears of laughter throughout the entire negotiation, and began ribbing his friend during Malcolm's periodic visits to our table. "Got it all sorted out, Mr. Ambassador?"

After an hour of discussion, the owner left in a rage and the girl had adopted Malcolm as her savior. As the evening went on, through those subversive and subtle developments that no one can ever grasp, Malcolm somehow came to be attached to the girl's debt, even responsible for it. And, since Dave and I were acquainted with Malcolm, we had garnered some of the responsibility as well.

"See what you get," Dave said, determined to be of no help.

"We could help her pay," suggested Malcolm.

"No! How much is it?" Dave and I said at the same time.

"About seventy-five dollars."

Seventy-five dollars would last me until Africa. I couldn't justify paying for someone else's relative luxury while I continued on a shoestring budget. "Let's call her embassy," I suggested.

"Call her embassy," Dave said, raising his eyebrows, "of course."

Malcolm called the British Embassy with the girl at his shoulder. He was still pressed into service as liaison even though the girl and those at her embassy obviously spoke a common language. The owner became involved on the phone and finally, through a master stroke of diplomacy, Malcolm had replaced himself with the embassy and was once again sitting at our table enjoying his food. "Bloody humanitarian," was all Dave could say the rest of the evening, always followed by a self-satisfied smirk.

WE CYCLED along the remainder of the Costa del Sol in the usual fashion, with Dave leading the way while Malcolm and I pedaled easily behind to take in the distracting views of this tropical coast.

Fuengirola turned out to be our last stop together. Malcolm and Dave would stay to enjoy the rest of their vacation on the southern shores of Spain, and I would continue west, toward the Straits of Gibraltar and Africa. We spent the evening in Fuengirola's *tapas* cafés, eating prawns and drinking thick red wine. In the morning, I left Fuengirola alone and cycled to Gibraltar, stopping my last night in Spain at a seaside campground.

Crossing into Gibraltar was similar to entering Canada or Mexico from the United States—a cursory glance at the passport, a few obligatory customs questions and a walk through the processing line into a miniature England. I felt as if I had been transported across the English Channel a thousand miles to the north, complete with the high-priced hotels and endless barrage of, "Sorry, we're all full."

I was directed to a tourist office which, I was told, helped travelers and their pocket books match up with comparable accommodations. Camping would have been possible, but only the clandestine style, since camping was prohibited in Gibraltar, and Gibraltar's cramped geography provided very few places to hide a tent. The tourist office itself was no more than an outdoor kiosk with brochures attached around the outside and a tour operator attached by ear to a phone on the inside.

The woman recommended the "only cheap place in town," a place I had already found to have no vacancies. "There's the fire department," she persisted. "Sometimes they let people camp on their lawn."

I had heard that rumor as well, a rumor which was directly contradicted at the fire department, where they didn't seem to know what I was talking about. Her suggestions went on for some time, as option after option was eliminated due to expense, or lack of vacant rooms. Eventually, we ran out of list.

"Well, there's only one hope, but I hesitate to tell you this," the tour guide said.

"Tell me what?"

"It's Miss Segura's Guest House, but . . . well . . . she's a little strange."

"Strange?"

"It's just that we've had complaints . . . no, not complaints. We've been informed by some people who stay there that she's a little crazy, so I don't like to send the average traveler there."

"Why send *me* then?"

"You travel by the bicycle?" pointing to my bike.

"Yes."

"I think you can handle it."

At a price of fifteen dollars per night, I could suffer a little strangeness. She gave me the address and directions. When I cycled away, I heard the clerk call after me, "Don't say I didn't warn you!"

I arrived at the guest house to find an archaic, two-story building, equipped with four sleeping cubicles on the top floor each separated by paper sliding doors. The cubicles were located upstairs from a cavernous main hall which echoed footsteps whenever someone walked through. A winding staircase swept down from the cramped, rented quarters to the wide Elizabethan lobby. Lateral doors adjoining the lobby led to Miss Segura's section of the house. There were no furnishings in the broad lobby, which led out through a small door onto the narrow streets, making the descending walk down the staircase a lonely, self-conscious affair. Patinaed wood, aged lamps, and dim light added a lingering uneasiness to the atmosphere.

But no matter how strange the house itself, nothing could outmatch the infamous Miss Segura. She was a woman of perhaps sixty, with red hair and black-rimmed glasses. She wore a tight dress glittering with beads, her hair piled straight up in a column on her head. Odd hairpins stuck out of her bundled hair, some of them remarkably similar to those cocktail umbrellas placed in daiquiris at overpriced night clubs.

"Now, don't put anything on the bed," she said when she showed me upstairs to my room." I haven't changed the sheets yet." Her voice was coarse and cracked.

"In here are the showers," she said and swung open the door to the shower room. "You come to take a shower in the morning when the water's hot. Here's your room. Now remember, don't put anything on the bed. And take your shoes off if you lie on the bed." I thought at any moment she would offer me a cup of hot chocolate.

At length, she left me. I moved my gear in and slowly unpacked, when the sliding paper door to the next room opened. In the doorway stood a young, skinny Englishman.

"She's a weird old bat, isn't she?" he whispered with a mischievous grin on his face. Behind him stood a woman with light brown skin and thin, Cleopatra eyes.

"I'll say," I replied. There was not much more to add to the statement.

"Makes you feel like . . . well, like . . ."

"Like a relative coming home for a day before returning to boarding school?"

"Unwanted relative," the girl said.

"I think she really cares though," I said." Maybe she's just lonely."

"Maybe," the Englishman said, "but she makes me feel uncomfortable, like I shouldn't touch the furniture or something. Name's John by the way. This is Waridi."

"That means 'flower' in Tanzania," said Waridi." I was born in Tanzania." She spoke perfect English, with an accent similar to John's, which prompted me to ask how long she'd lived in England.

"Oh, all my life. I was only born in Tanzania."

The echo of footsteps could be heard coming up the stairs punctuating the muttering of Miss Segura. "Good—good," a few more steps then, "good, that's good." She arrived at the top of the stairs. "That's good, you've met each other, good, good. It's always good to meet your neighbors." Turning to me, "I've brought your clean sheets. Now, you three chat while I fix the bed." John was in the corner trying to control a sudden fit of laughter, which made him sound like a clucking chicken.

After Miss Segura left, John produced a six-pack of beer and the three of us settled into our rooms and exchanged travel tales. "I'm worried," I told them after we had finished a few beers and joked about lying on the beds with our shoes on. "I've started talking to my bicycle."

"That's normal," said Waridi, "after having traveled alone for so long."

"Maybe you should give it a name," John said and turned toward me.

"I already have. I've started calling it Papillon."

"What does that mean?" Waridi asked.

"Butterfly. It's the title of Henry Cherrier's book about his adventures in South America."

"Well, you've named him," John said. "Now we've got to christen him. You know, break a bottle of beer over the frame or something."

"In here!" Waridi laughed. "Miss Segura would hang us!"

We settled for a small splashing of beer over Papillon's seat and a modest libation, with John stating rather reverently, "I christen thee—Papillon!"

After the naming ceremony, we turned in. I finished Cherrier's book and wondered who was crazier, Miss Segura, or the three of us.

The following morning I wandered around Gibraltar. I had entertained the thought of finding a job for a few months in order to wait out the summer heat of the Sahara, but after a day of inquiry, I realized the bureaucracy made that impossible.

When I went back to Miss Segura's Guest House, I discovered John and Waridi had already checked out. The upper level, quiet, lonely, closed in on me. I packed my gear in silence, contemplating the ferry crossing to Tangier and my last moments in Europe. With Papillon loaded and prepared to go, I checked out of Miss Segura's and pedaled down to the port, ready for Africa.

4
African Sand

Tangier, Morocco

AT THE DOCK, where the ferry to Tangier awaited, a crowd had already gathered. Groups of Arabs waving passports were barging through a tiny gate in an attempt to avoid passport control. Directly through the gate, the ferry waited, whereas customs was through a building to the left. The Arabs, seeing the ferry straight ahead, could not understand the point behind traveling in the opposite direction.

Members of the mob were carrying their gear from Spain back to Morocco. Some clutched live animals, others carried carpets, televisions, stereos. One man was bent beneath the weight of a porcelain sink, and one group flocked around a refrigerator which they were trying to cram through the minuscule gate. Guards at the gate attempted to beat back the crowd in a scene depictive of an ancient flight from Egypt.

Using Papillon as a battering ram, I made my way through the chaos to the gate. Several guards with batons were pushing the crowd back to the customs side of the threshold. A ranking officer stood at perfect ease with the confusion around him, staring straight ahead, ignoring the crowd, but he turned when he heard my American accent.

"Can I put my bike beyond the gate?" I shouted to him over the din.

"Beyond the gate?"

"There's no way I'll get through the mob with this bicycle," I explained. The end of the bulging line spilled out on the other side of

35

the fence, after winding through the customs building. If I left the bike on my side of the gate, there would be no way to retrieve it after going through customs and arriving on the other side.

"Yes, I see what you mean," said the senior officer. "C'mon, bring it through and I'll watch it until you clear customs." The guards parted to let me through. When I passed through the opening, a dozen Arabs slipped by with me and made a frantic dash for the ferry. The guards corralled the runners, bringing them back to the morass.

"Is it like this all the time?" I asked a younger official.

"No," he said. "But that bloke put the refrigerator by the gate. It's blocking most of the people from tryin' to come through customs."

"Right," I said, and elbowed my way through to customs. Inside the building stood a master sergeant barking orders and pushing the Arabs into line. I went up to him and sheepishly handed over my passport, expecting abuse. A smile came over his face.

"Nice ta' see one of our own," he said. "Hogs, nothing but hogs these people are! "He glowered down upon the surrounding mass. The Moroccans looked at me with disdain. One said, in English, "Look how he treats the American while we are treated like dirt."

"They're not civil," said the master sergeant to me, while staring at the man who had made the comment. "Not one of them knows how to act civilized!"

My passport was stamped and I was rushed through the customs process in VIP manner, always greeted by a smile, while the Arabs were harassed, yelled at, and searched. The Moroccans began to regard me with more and more contempt, and I began to wonder what the repercussions would be once aboard the ferry—in their domain.

After being processed, I was deposited on the opposite side of the gate, but a back-logged crowd waited at the gangplank. The group with the refrigerator had managed to get it through the gate and onto the ramp, where it blocked everyone else from boarding. A few guards were arguing with the owners of the fridge, while attempting to move the obstacle from the gangplank. The group that seemed to be responsible, perhaps a dozen in all, were sharing duties arguing with the angry mob, fighting with the guards, and sitting on top of the refrigerator so it could not be moved. In the end, and much to my surprise, the persistence of the Moroccans won out and the frustrated guards helped move the refrigerator to the hold of the ferry where it would be out of the way. The crowd settled down, and the passengers boarded.

Most of the ferry was equipped with wooden, bucket-style chairs crowded together on the main level. Below deck was a relatively deserted area with benches and tables covered with red plastic. I opened up *For Whom the Bell Tolls*, sat at one of the benches, and prepared for a leisurely crossing.

The ferry docked in Tangier well after nightfall. I was destined for Rabat to apply for an Algerian visa, then I planned to cycle east, through the valley created by the Riff Mountains and the Middle Atlas. The route would take me across the northern edge of the Sahara, a daunting prospect in the middle of August.

I disembarked and was met on the quay by the ever-present hordes of hawkers and lurking guides. They descended like vultures over a day-old carcass, and I, new in Morocco, was walking carrion. I had not yet discovered the proper prices, armed myself with key Arabic phrases, or learned to barter with any skill. I planned to pitch my tent at the campground I had read about in another traveler's guidebook. But I attracted so many would-be guides while I analyzed my map that it became impossible to concentrate over the constant din.

"Guide, meestir?"

"Taxi, meestir?"

"Change money, meestir?"

I scrambled atop Papillon and cycled away from the crowd. A few enterprising Moroccans ran after me, and when I needed to stop to check the map, they caught up to me.

"You are looking for a hotel?" one asked in perfect English. "Mookhaiyem," I said in reply, the Arabic word for "campground" which I learned in Gibraltar with the knowledge that even one word of any local language gains at least a little sympathy.

"Ah! Mookhaiyem! It is very good you know this word meestir. Come, I take you to mookhaiyem."

I instantly regretted learning the word.

"I don't need you to take me. I know the way."

"Yes, but you will never find it by yourself." The guide adopted the posture of a schoolmaster. "It is very difficult to find."

"I have this map."

"Still, you will never find it." The guide shrugged his shoulders and crossed his arms as if to indicate I would be a fool not to hire him. "Besides, I know the man who owns the campground."

"So what?" I knew he would get a kickback.

"I will get you a special rate!"

"No thanks."

"*Extra* special rate, meestir!"

"Sorry." I jumped on Papillon and cycled away. Around the next corner was the campground, a straight ride down the road from the quay.

MID-JULY

Rabat, Morocco

SEVERAL DAYS of cycling along the Atlantic coast brought me to Rabat, the center of Moroccan officialdom with a prominent police force roaming the streets along with uniformed military personnel. Even though the history of Morocco's capital could be traced back to the 3rd century B.C., I found it to be contemporary and clean when compared to Tangier. The design of the city left the broad streets open to the air, and although there were many historical sites in Rabat, quite a few of the buildings were modern consulates and embassies.

The medina was far easier to explore than that of Tangier as well. Its streets were broad and linear, crowds were smaller, and the "guidemeestirs" were not as persistent. This tranquility was due to the large number of government officials who held office in the city, and my goal was to acquire a visa from one of those officials. After my cursory exploration of the city, I set out to find the Algerian embassy. I knew the general location of the embassy, and how to say "Algerian Embassy" in Arabic. Armed with that information, I was able to get within a block of my destination, then started interrupting unsuspecting passers-by and saying, "Safarah Algerie?" with my shoulders shrugged and arms waving side to side.

It seemed to me that most people understood what I was asking, but I was unable to find the embassy after a dozen sets of directions. After traveling in circles for well over an hour, I approached a military officer who was buying spices at a street-side stall. Surely he would know where all the embassies were located.

"Salaam Alaykoem," I shouted as I approached, "Safarah . . . "

"Algerie!" the man said, finishing my question.

I looked at him closer. It was the same man I had asked an hour earlier.

He glared at me as if to say, "Yes, you are an imbecile."

I found the embassy just before closing. Inside, I asked one of the officials about an Algerian visa.

"Oh, you don't get that here," he said. "You must go to the Algerian consulate, but they are closed now. You must go tomorrow."

An entire day wasted. In an attempt to salvage some progress from my visit, I asked the official to write down the Arabic for "which way to the Algerian Consulate" with the address, then I returned to my hotel for the night.

Over the course of the following week, I learned there were a few prerequisites to acquiring an Algerian visa. Three passport photos were needed, to accompany three sets of forms made out in triplicate. A letter from the U.S. Embassy was required, exonerating the Algerian government in the event an American traveler found himself shot by Muslim extremists. Things became even more bizarre when, arriving at the U.S. Embassy, I learned that I was expected to write the letter rather than an embassy representative. A secretary then typed the "disclaimer" on government letterhead.

The U.S. diplomat who returned the typed copy advised me "in an official capacity," not to go to Algeria. "They are in civil war," he insisted. "Tanks in the streets."

By the time I collected all the information necessary for an Algerian visa, I had explored the city and was anxious to head east, so I arose with the sun hoping to collect my visa and get an early start out of town. But my hopes were dashed when I arrived at the consulate. Inside, a throng of Arabs was massed around the visa window. I asked one man what was going on.

"No visas today. Civil war."

"In Algeria?"

"Yes, in Algeria."

"When can we get visas?"

"Maybe tomorrow."

"The civil war will be over by tomorrow?" That seemed a dubious hope at best.

"Inshah Allah," replied the man. If Allah wills it.

Disregarding the fatalistic reply, I went to the window and asked about a visa.

"No visas today," the woman behind the window shouted over the crowd.

"Why not?" I shouted back.

"No visa today!" That was the only reply I could get. It seemed I was committed to a long wait in Rabat. When I went back to the consulate the next day, I held little hope of success. But patience is a virtue in the Arab world. By the end of the morning, I was given my visa and was finally able to cycle eastward out of Rabat. Later that afternoon, the Algerian consulate stopped issuing visas indefinitely. If I hadn't secured my permission on that particular day, I would have been forced to wait months. The civil war had begun in earnest.

MID-JULY

Fez, Morocco

BEFORE LEAVING RABAT, I bought a five-liter water jug which I attached to my rear rack. With my water storage capacity up to seven liters, I made a mental plan for the ride across Morocco. I anticipated a conservative ten days of cycling to reach Oujda on the Algerian border, 540 kilometers from Rabat. Towns along the way were no more than 100 kilometers apart. I could afford, at a conservative progression of fifty kilometers per day, to carry a two-day supply of food and some emergency rations without worry. Water would be a different matter. My map showed two stretches of 100 kilometers or more containing no towns at all: between Fez and Taza, and between Taourirt and Oujda. If no villages existed between those points, I would be forced to carry twenty liters of water.

The first day out of Rabat offered some insight into the rest of the journey. The temperature was a sweltering 105 degrees, and my seven liters of water were gone by nightfall. The town of Khemessit saved me from a slow death of thirst, where I refilled my five-liter jug and two one-liter cycling bottles before setting up camp for the night.

The disappearance of the sun made the desert less brutal, almost welcoming, with cool breezes wafting over a flat land of dead vegetation and dry rock. The darkness was translucent, a half moon and stars revealing a dimly lit landscape. The sounds were that of the night: wind moaning through the far away Atlas, a beetle scratching at my tent walls, the whispering hum of my camp stove.

The day revealed thorns, flat tires, and higher temperatures: 110 degrees Fahrenheit. A transient summer sun rose, red in the morning, yellow, then white, turning the desert white with the day's advance. But the sixty kilometers to Fez revealed more than desert heat when a malicious side to Morocco became apparent. Gangs of children roamed the desert scrub beyond the road, and my appearance provided the perfect panacea for their boredom. One teenager fired rocks from a pellet gun, and some groups chased after me brandishing club-sized branches.

It was as if I did not represent anything real within their world. I was not a human being, but a thing, an anomaly, entertainment on a high-tech bicycle. And it was my bicycle, my mode of travel and where I was able to travel—off the beaten track—that made me a novelty.

I reached the outskirts of Fez at noon. Beyond Fez, my map showed 120 kilometers of barren hills. I would have to re-supply before moving on to Taza, another two days' ride. I explored the city and was accosted by the usual crowd of hawkers, hotel touts, and guides selling their services for a few dirhams. One bearded young Arab sprinted beside me as I rode along, breathless but delivering his sales pitch anyway. "Meestir, I think you are needing a guide."

"I don't want a guide." The main duty of "guides" in Morocco was to lure travelers to a friend's jewelry or carpet shop, where the prices rivaled my monthly budget. Local hotel prices were doubled to provide a kickback for any guide able to lead unwary tourists through the doors.

"But meestir, I am very good guide. I speak five languages!"

"Five?"

"Si. Buongiorno Signoré, Signoré buongiorno," he shouted, as if on stage. "That was Italian!" he proudly pronounced.

Although this guide obviously spoke no Italian, it was not unusual to meet a Moroccan who did speak five languages. I had already been asked for dirhams in French, Arabic, English, Spanish and Italian—all by the same beggar.

"Please, meestir," the man kept badgering me. "I am going to medical school. I need the money."

I did need a guide. I needed supplies for the expanse beyond Fez and a few minor bike parts. In the medinas of Fez, it would have taken me days to find the gear. This man spoke perfect English. Why not him?

"All right," I agreed. "I'll pay you ten dirhams."

"Don't worry meestir. My name is Abdul. You won't be sorry."

"First I need a hotel."

"No hotel," said Abdul. "You will stay at my house."

Abdul insisted. He wanted me to meet his friends. "We can sit and smoke hashish," he urged. "I will send my brother Abdullah out for your supplies. He will get a better price by himself than with a tourist."

Abdul took me to his house after a meal of chicken and couscous at a local restaurant. Abdullah was given my list of supplies and sent out to fulfill his duties. I was led down a set of stairs to a room more like a dungeon than a basement. A mattress rested on the concrete floor in one corner, illuminated by a single, bare light bulb dangling from an electrical cord. Abdul and his friend, Sa'id, sat on a blanket in the middle of the room and smoked hashish.

Although Abdul was married, Muslim tradition prevented his wife from being seen by guests. She worked in the kitchen while Abdul retrieved the food himself and placed it on the blanket. We ate with our fingers from community bowls: stuffed peppers, couscous, and some dishes I could not identify. One looked like brown calamari in a curry sauce.

"What's in this brown dish?" I asked.

"I don't know the word for it. Like a snake in the water."

"Eel?"

"Yes, that's right, eel."

The evening wore on and Abdullah returned. The price he charged was about half what I normally paid for food. The bike parts seemed reasonable as well, especially since he succeeded in buying toe clips, an item that I had given up trying to find. I gave him twenty dirhams.

"It is not enough," Abdul protested on behalf of his brother.

"What do you think is fair?" Here we go, I thought.

"You must decide, but you would have paid double the price Abdullah asks from you, plus he spent all day finding these things."

I ended up giving Abdullah fifty dirhams, the equivalent of the price of the items. I couldn't deny the fact that I would have paid twice as much for the items and spent two days finding them. Essentially, I received Abdullah's services for free.

Months later I would realize I had committed a typical traveler's error. I grossly overpaid for services, thus boosting the price for any and all travelers to follow.

The next morning I asked Abdul why tourists were charged so much more than natives. He retreated into the safety of the Koran.

"The Koran states that no one should charge more than a six percent profit, but many people do not follow this rule."

His answer did not seem to hold true in my experience. I asked Abdul if he believed in the Koran's six percent rule.

"I believe," he said.

"Then maybe you can help me understand the rule."

"Yes?"

"Abdullah bought fifty dirhams of supplies for me, right?"

"Right."

"But he made fifty dirhams on the deal. That's a one hundred percent profit, not six percent, isn't it?"

"No, that's not correct," Abdul said, supremely confident. "You see, the real price for you would have been one hundred dirhams. So there was no profit made. Really, you owe Abdullah another six percent."

I left Abdul with a parting gift of a hand-held tape recorder I had carried from Ohio. It was inundated with sand and long since broken, but he and his brother looked at the machine as if it was a bar of gold. I had no doubt they would repair it and make a Moroccan fortune before I cleared the hills of Taza.

LATE JULY

Taza and the road to Oujda, Morocco

BEFORE I ARRIVED in Taza it was nothing more to me than a mental goal beyond 120 kilometers of barren hills, but in Taza I found more than a mental oasis. I found a town that was devoid of tourists and suffered from a refreshing lack of overpopulation, guides, souks, medinas, loud markets, or any of the other nuisances that are the bane of the tired Westerner's existence in Morocco.

These factors made the town a perfect rest stop, a rest I badly needed. I had cycled across two days of sun-cracked hills with temperatures above 110 degrees. I was dangerously dehydrated and the intestinal adjustment that plagues all travelers throughout Africa had descended upon me with a vengeance. Every piece of my gear was clogged with sand, including my food. It was time for a two-day rest.

Taza must have been a tourist attraction at some time in the past, or during certain parts of the year, since the hotel was luxurious enough to accommodate the most elite tourist crowd. The decor looked as if it came out of a nineteenth-century novel, with leather-backed chairs and wooden furnishings polished to a deep mahogany brown. My room was no different. Although small, it was equipped with a leather chair, writing desk, and a bathroom that contained two sights I hadn't seen since southern Spain: a bathtub and Western toilet, complete with toilet paper.

I went downstairs to check in and found the Arab behind the counter to be fluent in English. I mentioned my surprise in finding a tourist hotel here in the desert.

"Oh yes," he told me. "We have many tourists. There is so much to see in Taza. More than you think."

"Then why is the hotel empty?"

"Wrong time of year. Everyone is being at beaches; only you two cyclists come through."

"Two?"

"Yesterday we had one—like you, with the baggages, except he had a bag for carrying on the shoulders and tied it to the back of his bicycle." I looked at the register. Checked out yesterday, one Miguel Megias of Venezuela; occupation: cyclist; destination: Oujda. Only one road ran to Oujda from Taza, but there would be no way to catch the other cyclist. If I stayed in Taza for two days, Miguel would have reached Oujda by the time I checked out of my hotel. I put the matter out of my mind, went to my room, and poured a long-awaited bath.

Over the course of the next two days, I cleaned my gear, washed my sand-riddled clothes, and stocked up on supplies for the three-day crossing to Oujda. After two days of rest, I set out with a tailwind to Guereif and the Moulaya River, across sixty kilometers of sunbaked desert.

I estimated three days to reach Oujda across 240 kilometers of desolation. The foolhardiness of washing my clothes in Taza struck me, since everything I owned was covered with sand within minutes of setting out. It was like blow drying a bathing suit before taking a dip. Even my hair was bleached sandy brown from the constant dust lingering in the air.

Twenty-eight kilometers into my first day out from Taza, I arrived at the small town of Msoun. The searing heat made my skull ache, despite the T-shirt wrapped around my head for protection. One of the outdoor stands lining the road sold chilled lemonade from a plastic cooler like those seen at ice cream parlors in the States. When the shopkeeper noticed me, he rushed over with a sample of his product and I was soon surrounded by an assembly of curious Arabs. The vendor spoke English and translated questions from the crowd while plying me with glass after glass of cool liquid. Normally, I tried to avoid these crowds, but the lemonade planted my feet firmly in their tracks. I stood, straddling Papillon, answering questions and savoring my small, golden oasis in a glass.

"Tell me," I asked the translator after cooling down a bit, "how hot is it today?"

"Very hot today. Fifty-five degrees."

"Fifty-five degrees! That can't be right. That's more than a hundred thirty degrees Fahrenheit." The vendor beckoned and a newspaper was brought. The text was in Arabic, but the number 55 was printed.

"It says fifty-five degrees today," explained the English speaker. The information was hard to believe, but, even if the forecast was close, it explained my pounding headaches of late.

The thirty-six kilometers to Guereif was unbearable. Anything more than ten minutes of cycling was virtually impossible. I was forced to stop at the slightest opportunity for shade and rest. My routine became ten minutes on, ten minutes off. Whenever I stopped, I was swarmed by flies which attacked my eyes and mouth for moisture. My water bottle nipples always supported a globule of flies, each vying for the drop of water left on the end. By the time I reached Guereif, I had gone through ten liters of water and a liter of lemonade.

I filled my water bottles in town then cycled into the desert, the sun, and the sand. A few kilometers east of the village I approached a small wooden bridge. Below, a muddy waterhole was left in an otherwise dried up stream bed. A group of half-naked children wallowed in the hole. Arab women washed pots and clothing in the muddy water. Wetness in this dry land was irresistible, beckoning with the undeniable promise of coolness, of shade, of a few moments respite from the searing sun. Wetness in this dry land was like a five-course meal placed in front of a starving man.

I climbed down and soaked in the pool. The children saw me and flocked to my position. Women pointed and gawked. Papillon, resting high on the dry bank, was mobbed by a swarm of children. Seconds after I dipped my first toe in the muddy water, I was forced to beat a hasty retreat. My five-course meal was left uneaten.

I stopped to fill my water bottles in Taourirt among the usual crowd of curious onlookers, well-wishers, and children seeking to break the endless monotony of their desert lives. One of the men in the audience, for that's what these groups truly were, asked me if I was in a race.

"Why would you say that?" I was curious.

"Because the other man is two days ahead of you." It was Miguel again, the elusive cyclist from Venezuela, and I hadn't gained a single day on him.

I would hear no more stories of the other cyclist; between Taourirt and Oujda was nothing but 100 kilometers of heat-induced pain. I cycled through the soaring temperatures in fits and starts. Two kilometers, find shade. Two kilometers, find shade. There was dry scrub. Desert. A town—fill up on water. Two kilometers, find shade. Two kilometers, find shade. A bridge—hide from the sun.

The day wore on and the Atlas Mountains rose to the south. Dry scrub stretched into sand. Sand rolled into undulating, barren foothills. Foothills rose into opaque, blue mountains, perpetually hazened by the dusty gray air.

Two kilometers, find shade. I filled my water bottles in a small village fifty kilometers from Oujda. "The road is flat to Oujda," a villager informed me. An odd statement, since the road had been flat for weeks.

Two kilometers, find shade. Flies continually attacked my eyes and mouth. The sun attacked my body, took what water it liked from my cracked skin. I cycled the last few kilometers to Oujda in darkness, without water. Dazed and depleted, I checked into the first hotel I came across and collapsed into bed from heat exhaustion.

The next morning I awoke worried that I hadn't bartered a price before checking in. By not agreeing on a price beforehand, a traveler puts himself at the mercy of whatever the proprietor wishes to charge, or at the very least, places himself in a weak bargaining position. My fears, as it turned out, were unfounded. The young man behind the desk was a student—his father owned the hotel—who was afflicted with a wanderlust that made recounting my journey a pleasure rather than a rehearsed litany. He was eager to help me with any services he could provide, free of charge. It was a highly unusual offer in Morocco, a country in which the main source of income seemed to be guide services.

I stayed several days in Oujda, gathering information about Algeria, buying supplies, resting and rehabilitating. Ali, the student-clerk, tried to fix my sand-riddled radio. Ultimately we found it to be, as Ali put it, "beyond repair." Supplies were easy to find in Oujda, a thriving border oasis with an ample medina. With limitless access to food and water, my body slowly rejuvenated until I felt recharged and rested.

There was only one remaining item that vexed me. During my search for supplies in the medina, I had been unable to find a map of Algeria. Throughout the entire city of Oujda there was not one Algerian map to be sold. Ali even sent his friends out to scour the town, but they returned without success.

"You will have to go on with no map," Ali said and shrugged. "You will be traveling blind."

EARLY AUGUST
Sidi Bel Abbes, Algeria
WITHOUT A MAP, I was left with no recourse but to hope fortune favored the foolish and blindly head east. I knew the distance to the

Tunisian border was roughly 1,500 kilometers. As for towns, distance between water stops, availability of food or type of terrain, I was in the dark. All these questions had to be answered before I could possibly venture forth into the desert. Even though my water-carrying capacity was still seven liters, it would not be enough if I were to run into a two-day stretch with no stops. In the town of Tlemcen, fifty kilometers east of the border, I upgraded that carrying capacity to nine liters with the addition of a two-liter water jug. It would still be less than a day's supply.

In Tlemcen, I again asked about maps and about the terrain that lay to the east.

"No maps," one man told me, "and as for terrain, this time of year—desert." He laid his hand flat as if to depict an endless, level expanse of baked earth.

Indeed, my first 100 kilometers in Algeria had been a lesson in dust—brown dust. The roads were the same brown as the scenery which surrounded them. The vegetation was brown. The mud buildings were brown. There were few color variations; an occasional eucalyptus tree showed itself in welcome contrast to the surrounding monotony. In large red letters, a hand-painted sign on the wall read "Bush Assassin," a lingering reference, no doubt, to the Gulf War.

One hundred twenty kilometers into Algeria, on the outskirts of a town named Sidi Bel Abbes, I came upon a building clad in the familiar color of dun. The structure was flat and square with a blue sign that said "Gendarmes," the Algerian police. Since maps in Algeria seemed to be government secrets, I thought the police might be of some help in obtaining one, or at least have a dependable knowledge of the immediate area. I cycled toward the gendarme station, but a few worries came to mind. Was what I was doing legal? Did I have the proper forms and permission to be cycling across Algeria?

I approached the building and opened the door. Inside the sparse station were three officers suffering from the same boredom that afflicted all those I met in certain, underdeveloped parts of our planet. They were enthusiastic about my journey, and displayed an almost comical concern about my well-being which made them instantly likable. The three took the responsibility upon themselves to see me safely on my way, while exhibiting a sense of camaraderie that seemed uncharacteristic for a government official in any country. I filled up my water jugs at their outdoor well then asked the three about maps.

"No maps," I was told.

"Can't we draw him a map?" one of the junior guards suggested.

The ranking officer produced pen and paper. Much to my dismay, the three immediately began arguing over details.

"You will go to Mascara first," the leader said while sitting at his desk, hunched over the blank paper soon to be a map. "It is eighty-five kilometers east." He drew a line and two dots on the page. One dot, Sidi Bel Abbes, the town we were in, and the other, Mascara. On the line between the two he wrote "85 km." Upon this fact they all agreed, Mascara was indeed eighty-five kilometers away.

"Then you will go to El Chlef," the captain said and drew another circle on the map, east of Mascara. "It is one hundred and fifty kilometers from Mascara."

"No it's not," said one of the junior officers.

"No, the captain's right, it's one hundred and fifty kilometers away," the third man insisted.

"I tell you it's farther away."

"I should know," repeated the supporter of the captain. "I am from there. It's a hundred and fifty kilometers from Mascara."

The captain settled it by writing "150 km" in the space between Mascara and El Chlef. This went on for another half hour until I was presented with a map that I looked upon with some suspicion. The final version looked like a fallen totem pole.

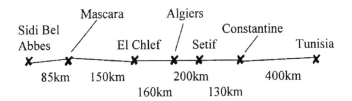

AUGUST
El Chlef, Algeria

I LEFT THE GUARDS with my thanks and headed east. Mascara came, and went. The captain was right about the distance. I checked into a hotel in El Chlef, after more than 200 kilometers of desert cycling, anticipating a refreshing change of pace from desert camps and camp-stove cooking. Still wearing my cycling shorts, I went down to the restaurant for a much-needed meal. The place was full of Algerians, some leisurely eating, others shouting harsh Arabic at one another. Through some small miracle there was a bar with alcohol being served, despite my preconception that alcohol was forbidden in Algeria.

Bellying up to the bar, I asked for water. I was badly dehydrated, so I planned to drain my two-liter water jug as many times as was physically possible. Arabs mingled around the bar, arms the size of watermelons, looking as if they had come off an oil rig somewhere south of Texas.

My water jug wasn't half drained before a round-bellied Arab leaned toward me and began screaming. He was pointing at my cycling shorts which, I had to admit, were inappropriate in Algeria, a Muslim country in which arms and legs were required to be covered in public. But what could I do? With temperatures continuing at a sweltering 120 degrees, it would have been impossible to cycle in long pants. And my cycling shorts were the only thing I possessed that was lined with the protective padding necessary for a full day in the saddle.

The man continued to scream at me in Arabic. He was blatantly drunk. I heard the words "George Bush" repeated several times. I readied myself for a hasty retreat back to my room, but several of the others at the bar stood up and intervened. A shouting match ensued. The original Arab began to look sheepish and apologetic. Eventually, one of the bigger men turned to me and said, "Come, sit down," waving his hand toward an empty stool.

I sat down, more out of fear than gratitude. The man bought me a drink. By this time everyone who had been sitting at the bar was gathered around, mumbling in hushed Arabic.

"That man is stupid," the Arab seated next to me announced to the crowd. Then, turning to me, his tone became more subdued. I felt his intentions were sincere and friendly. "He hates you because you are American . . . for what your government does. I told him you are not George Bush. You are not the American government. You are a traveler come to Algeria to meet the Algerian people, person to person." He stopped to take a gulp of his drink then turned and said a few words in Arabic to the intent crowd surrounding us.

"That man disgraces Algeria," the Arab said, turning back to his beer. "You came to meet Algerians and he shows you only anger and stupidity. If he went to America, would he want to be seen as the Algerian government? Would he want Americans to hold him responsible for how our government acts?"

As the conversation continued, I actually began to enjoy myself. We were given another round, on the house, and the crowd started to ask questions about America, about my trip, and about hospitality.

"We are Muslims," one member of the crowd said as a precursor to a question." As Muslims we are taught to treat travelers like our own family. Would you treat a traveler the same in America?"

"I would now," I said.

The night escaped into a few more beers, many more questions, and an atmosphere of sincerity that is unique to travel. All the questions were genuine, with no hidden meaning or attempts at evasion. In return, I gave answers as honestly as I knew how, and tried to give them an understanding of American culture and ideals. At one point, the drunken tyrant who terrorized me when I first sat down at the bar came over and apologized. "I am drunk," he said, "and you probably did not know to keep your legs covered."

Hours after I first entered the bar, overcome by fatigue, I negotiated my way through the crowd's good-night wishes and returned to my room. It was late, and the night air of Algeria's August was moderate, contrasting the white-hot sun of midday. A slow-moving fan dangled from the ceiling of my room, a luxury only dreamed of in my desert camps.

I laid my head on the dingy pillow and recapped the last four days in my mind. I had come almost 400 kilometers through Algeria, each of the six nights camping in the desert. I had learned to judge the temperature by the liters of water I consumed throughout the day. My carrying capacity was nine liters, but every day had been a ten-liter day, and I would have gone through twice that if it had been available.

My thoughts while cycling always turned toward the concept of shade. Two kilometers of cycling would result in ten minutes of grace in the shade. Being exposed to the sun became my curse. Whereas most tourists spent their vacations worshiping the sun, my only thought was to hide from it, like a rat scurrying from a hovering vulture.

I hugged my pillow before falling asleep. There would be precious few pillows in the thousand kilometers of sand between El Chlef and Tunisia; precious few ceiling fans or bars, and precious few moments to reflect on the comfort of companionship within the cool shelter of a safe hotel.

MID-AUGUST

the road to Blida, Algeria

I LEFT EL CHLEF later than I would have liked. The combination of dehydration, alcohol the previous night, and knowledge of the hard cycling to come kept me in town until noon. I began my eastward effort in the heat of the day, while the residents of El Chlef were retreating into the protective shadows of the buildings— hurrying away from the heat, the sun. On my way out of town, I bought a tunic of the sort the Arabs wore in the desert. The clerk included a lesson in tunic-wrapping in the sales price.

Two kilometers out of El Chlef, I wilted under a eucalyptus tree, my body seared by the heat. It occurred to me what a petty stash was my nine liters of water. I could have gone through nine liters in half a day if not for restraint. My palate was perpetually dry. My tongue perpetually swollen and sticky. My mind was constantly bent toward the consumption of water.

The day persisted in much the same manner. Two kilometers of mind-wrenching heat and dust, then ten minutes in any small bit of shade that made itself available. At times I found myself curled underneath a meager and scrubby little bush like a snake squirming on its belly.

By the end of my first day out of El Chlef I had gone through a gluttonous ten liters of water and traveled a pitiful thirty kilometers. My goal was to make the distance between El Chlef and Algiers in two days, which meant covering eighty kilometers each day providing the map drawn by the gendarmes was correct. At sunset, instead of setting camp, I sat by the side of the dusty road and cooked a stew on my camp stove. I was hoping the cooler night air would clear my mind and result in some solution to my pitiful mileage.

The sky grew darker, and a full moon rose which lit the sky a dusky orange. Suddenly I was struck with an idea. Why not cycle by moonlight? The moon was surely bright enough, at least to allow moderate progress, and the temperature was perfect for cycling, almost too cold just before sunrise. I never dropped off to sleep until well after midnight anyway, when the night air became comfortable enough to allow me some physical peace. When I put the idea into practice, I found cycling was feasible if I kept my eyes fixed on the patch of road directly in front of my tire.

Eventually, the night air became bearable. The dim light made it seem as if I was speeding into an endless void. In reality, my progress was miserable, but I was certainly making better time than during the heat of the day. I began to enjoy cycling for the first time in a long while, with the refreshing night air flowing past and the radiance of the cool orange moon lighting my way.

Around midnight, some bright white lights came into view on the roadside up ahead. They seemed strange in the blackness of the surrounding desert, somehow threatening, as if the moon's power had been invoked to warn people away from this one spot in all the vast and empty darkness.

A police checkpoint became visible beneath the lamps. There had been fighting in the area between Muslim extremists and government forces, but since the road led to the capital of Algiers, I assumed the roadblock was intended to deter revolutionaries rather than innocent tourists, albeit unconventional tourism in my case. I cycled up to the roadblock and gave the guard my passport.

"American?" he asked as he slowly scrutinized the pages.

"Yes, American."

"Why do you travel at night?"

"It's too hot during the day, and I am looking for a place with a hotel." I didn't want to tell him I camped in the desert. He would surely have forbidden me from doing so.

The guard opened a ledger signed by all those who passed the checkpoint. "Sign the book please. You will find a hotel in Blida."

The columns printed in the register required name, nationality, occupation, destination, coming from, time of entry, and religion. I filled in all the relevant information, writing "Zoroastrian" under the religion column, then looked at the previous entries. Most were in Arabic, some in French, but I noticed one in English written on the previous day's listings: Miguel Megias, Venezuela; occupation: cyclist. It was the same cyclist I had heard about in Morocco who was a scant day ahead of me when I arrived in Taza. Eight hundred kilometers later Miguel Megias of Venezuela was still exactly one day ahead of me. I looked at the time of entry: 10:30 p.m. Miguel was doing the same thing I was. He was cycling at night.

The fact that I was once again on the heels of the Venezuelan cyclist gave me a new-found energy. I passed through the gate and continued through the morning hours with a redoubled effort. At around two o'clock, I set camp, exhausted. My new plan was to sleep until six or seven in the morning, cycle until the heat became too unbearable, usually around eleven, then take a midday siesta. When the sun retreated far enough toward the horizon, I would resume cycling and continue through the night until I reached Algiers.

In the morning, the white light of the sun shocked my eyes in harsh contrast to the cool orange glow of the midnight moon. Even at seven o'clock the heat was so overbearing it awakened me in a pool of sweat inside my oven-like tent. I was on the road by ten after seven, but I had not been able to find water the previous night. My bottles were dry by nine o'clock and I found myself spent beneath the shade of a eucalyptus tree. The only town on my rudimentary map was Algiers, seventy kilometers away, an impossible distance without water. The guard at the checkpoint had mentioned a town called Blida, but I had no idea in which direction or how far the town lay. There was nothing in sight but heat and dust and brown, dead scrub. I slumped against a twisted trunk, too stricken with thirst to cycle on, a prevailing sense of gloom and defeatism overcoming me. "At least I have the protection of my tree," I told myself. I became so apathetic I could have allowed myself to lie there until time and decomposition melted me into the base of my shady haven.

I AWOKE some hours later. Had I passed out, or fallen asleep? My tongue felt like a swollen wooden branch. There was no feeling when I licked my lips, like wood grating against dry bark. I did not know how long I had been out, yet the sun was still high and the thick air was like a suffocating prison. Finding water was now a priority. Slowly and with effort, I forced myself onto Papillon, made mental preparations to leave the protective shade, and moved myself east by cranking the sandy pedals.

Ten minutes later my rear tire went flat. Delirious with thirst, I looked around. There was nothing to be seen but the same white-hot sand, the same sun overhead, and a new-found despair spurred from an insane desire for water. I climbed off Papillon and sat on the burning sand. I lingered for the timeless period of delirium, unable to comprehend any clear course of action.

I kept babbling the word "patch" as if saying the word would patch my tire, or give me strength to do it myself. I was defeated both mentally and physically, yet in the back of my mind I kept alive the word, "patch." I held on to it, wrapped it up in a mental package and relegated the idea to some corner of my mind, a corner with one function, to persevere. I rolled over to look at the sun, the poison of my existence in Africa. I looked up to see what I thought at first was a hallucination. Around the sun circled a ring of vultures, this time not imaginary.

One of the large birds landed next to me, and that was enough. I opened my panniers and searched for the patch kit. I pulled my camp stove out of the bag and threw it at the squatting vulture. Behind me, the clank of the stove brought the sound of flapping wings. The bird shifted and fidgeted back into place with a sideways eye fixed in my direction.

In my delirium, I patched the tire. While I worked on the repair, I talked to the black-eyed vulture as if he were my neighbor over the backyard hedge. When the tire was patched and the tube swollen with air, I straddled the bicycle and it obliged. I slowly moved away from the godforsaken site, away from what must have been a disappointed bird.

But there was still the more deadly vulture, that hovering scavenger, the sun. This vulture had a single white-hot eye and it did not merely stare and squawk, but suffocated, surrounded, bore down with a relentlessness to outlast any determination. I pedaled on, stopping often to rest, all the while muttering thanks to some unknown deity for the fortune of a flat and sandless road.

The miles ground by, and I was reduced to a walk. I wasn't sure if I was leading the way, or if some other force was guiding me to Blida, a town which I prayed was nearby. I rounded a bend obscured by dunes and saw a reflection denied from the sun, like the white parts of a negative photograph. As I advanced, the reflection became defined. Three Arabs in white, desert dress walked on the road. The vision was made unclear to my mind by my swollen eyelids and a pervasive wavering in the desert air. With my approach, it became obvious one of the Algerians was carrying a jug like the one strapped to my rear rack. I had found what I sought. I had found water.

MID-AUGUST

west of Algiers

THE DESERT ARABS watched me with curiosity as I sucked on their water jug like a desperate camel. I used some of the water to pat on my burning face then poured a precious dab into a cupped hand and soaked each of my swollen eyes. I filled one of my cycling bottles using the last of their supply. I felt guilty but I still didn't know how far away Blida lay, or if the town existed at all. Even though the day was in decline, I could still have ended up in the same desperate shape I was in before stumbling across these Arabs.

"We have more water at our house," one of the Algerians said suddenly." If you come with us we can give you more."

I was at once grateful, but also shocked at myself. I hadn't thought to ask if there were any towns nearby, how far it was to Blida or, most importantly, if the three could replenish their own water supply. The sun had made me a danger to myself. I would have cycled off with less than a liter of water.

"We live in Blida," one said, snapping me back to my senses. "It is just up the road."

I followed the three home. They lived in a mud hut on the western edge of town. There were two other huts surrounding a compound of swept dirt. A well stood at the far end of the clearing. Although there were no other houses in sight, I was assured they did in fact live on the outskirts of a small desert village.

The Arabs gave me enough water to fill my jugs to their nine-liter capacity, then, in a gesture which seemed to deny the fact we were far from any tourist resorts, asked me if I wanted to see their museum.

"Museum?" I asked, wondering if I had heard them right." You have a museum in this town?"

"Yes, we have a museum," one said.

"For tourists!" another said, grinning.

After all their generosity, I felt obligated to accept the offer and investigate the tourist museum of Blida. I was led to a mud structure similar to the house, yet smaller. When the door was opened, the light of the setting sun highlighted clouds of billowing dust agitated by the long sedentary door, just as the same light scheme revealed a bizarre scene through the murky air. It was a scene characterized by the glint of white canine teeth, and a view through the haze of what looked like two-dozen Bengal tigers standing artificially erect on either side of the room.

"This is our museum," I was told, an outstretched arm ushering me forward. We entered a stark room containing twelve stuffed trophies mounted in threatening poses. Other than two or three of the trophies, I could not identify any of the animals frozen before me. Most of them were canines, similar to hyenas or large jackals, whereas some were rodents the size of a castle gargoyle.

"Us shoot," the third Arab who had stayed silent for most of the afternoon said.

They claimed they had shot all the animals in the mountains, which I took to mean the Moyen Atlas in the shadows of which I had been cycling since Rabat. None of them knew the English names for the animals and I was surprised not to have encountered any of them in the desert. But I began to suspect foul play. Who knows to what lengths a poor Algerian farmer living on the outskirts of a tiny desert village would go to open a tourist museum in his own backyard? I was then prompted to ask about the popularity of the obscure museum, wondering if the door was kept so dusty merely for effect.

"How many tourist have you had here anyway?"

"Oh, you are the very first!" one said.

"But our friends come to see—when we shoot another animal!" interjected another.

The sun had just slipped below the Atlas when I mounted Papillon and readied myself to leave. The three curators warned me of the dangers of camping in the desert "with all the wild animals," and told me Algiers was fifty kilometers to the north-east. Fifty kilometers with the sun setting was more than my dehydrated body could bear, even by moonlight, so I cycled ten kilometers into the desert and set camp for the night.

MID-AUGUST

Algiers

MY CAMPING TECHNIQUE had changed dramatically since the friendly hills of America and the relatively safe fields of Western Europe. I learned to keep everything packed in my two panniers which were left open and upright inside the tent. Any supplies needed during the night could easily be obtained from the open bags. That left me with the ability to pack and leave at a moment's notice. Keeping my gear packed and close also reduced the possibility of theft. My bicycle was the only thing left outside the tent, the frame securely chained to a tent loop. Any thief attempting to steal Papillon in the night would find a tent dragging along behind him, with me inside.

On occasion, I used a second style of camping which I dubbed "the slash and burn method." The technique entailed laying the bicycle on the ground fully loaded, rolling out my sleeping bag and sleeping in the open with my head on one of the panniers. I could then quickly pack the sleeping bag in the morning, climb aboard the bike, and set out within minutes of awakening. It was the slash-and-burn technique I used in the desert outside Blida. As a result, I reached Algiers before the light of the sun began to scorch the desert sand its afternoon shade of white.

There were duties to perform in Algeria's capital. I needed to plan the onward route and budget my finances to last until the next money transfer. Since the trouble in the Adriatic region was escalating, I would no longer be able to cycle the length of Italy then south through what was once Yugoslavia. Instead, I would cross Sicily and the boot of Italy, then take a ferry across the Adriatic directly to Greece. My next American Express office was likely to be Athens, and I was left with barely enough money to make the distance. Before leaving the city, I also needed to find a map. The item had become a necessity of late since, although the map drawn by the gendarmes was amazingly accurate at first, the farther I traveled from Mascara, the more useless the map became. The inaccuracy was a direct cause of having run out of water in the desert near Blida.

The medinas in Algiers were small and cramped compared to those in Morocco, but to compensate for their size, they seemed to cram twice as many dark doorways and shady deals into half the space. In the threshold of one doorway, I finally bought a map of Algeria from a nervous Arab who treated the document as if it were a pound of hashish. The price he insisted upon reinforced my notion that maps were indeed State secrets in Algeria. The price also precluded any hope of making it to Athens with my remaining money supply. To add to my frustrations, after selling me the map, the Arab unfolded the document on the ground and began describing the symbols as if he were explaining a complex calculus equation to a child. "These are roads," was a typical comment, while the Arab pointed to a road.

LATE AUGUST
near Bordj-bou-arreridj, Algeria

SEVEN HUNDRED KILOMETERS of desert cycling separated Algiers from the Tunisian border, and to my chagrin, it was back to the same grind from the first kilometer. The daytime temperature continued to be sweltering, and the tunic I bought at the border became indispensable for protection from the sun. The full moon, my companion, had disappeared, so I was forced back to the painful day-time cycling routine. Two kilometers—find shade. Two kilometers—find shade. Afternoons were spent underneath the most minute patch of desert scrub, withered, feeling as if I were being slow-baked in an oven.

The days were gray. The white haze of dust blanketed the air as if the land had been submerged in milky-white absinthe. The road was tan dirt, and the desert was tan, like smooth clay fresh from the kiln. A dense vapor hovered in the air above hot earth, like a clinging fog, thick, palpable, with substance. There was no salvation, no refuge, where I didn't feel as if I were swimming at the bottom of some great ocean of heat, sun, and sweat-dried earth. The air breathed a viscous life of its own.

I set camp early, underneath a small cement bridge barely wide enough to accommodate my tent. I made it a short day due to the pervasive dehydration which, this last week, had slowed my pace to that of a child. All my jugs were full to the brim with water, so, once camp was set, I leaned back, began sipping tea from my tin cup and guzzling from my five-liter water jug. I was in my own private quarters—the bridge forming a tunnel around me—hidden from the sun that was now lowering on the horizon to relieve the desert of its triple-digit temperament. The BBC kept me company on my shortwave radio, and I began to relax with the retreating temperature.

The following morning I cycled toward a small town that my map showed to be five kilometers southeast. I had finished most of my water the night before with the knowledge that I would be able to refill my bottles at the town labeled only in Arabic on my map.

Five kilometers later, there was no town within sight. The landscape once again changed from the dry brush which surrounded my nighttime camp under the bridge, to the ever-familiar desert rock and searing sun. By noon my water was gone. With nothing but wavering air on the horizon, I pushed east. There would be no stopping every two kilometers underneath some bit of shade. There would be no avoiding the midafternoon sun. I was forced to cycle on in the familiar pursuit of water.

It didn't matter. There was no shade anyway. This was a barren land. No water. No trees. No towns or people. No sign of civilization. I pushed east through the gray landscape. The relentless sun again sculpted my tongue and lips into the familiar swell and crack of the desert. My head tingled with the heat like a thousand tiny pins needling at my skull. A chill overtook me despite the heat. Blood pumped through my temples bringing a dull pain.

With effort, a village came into view. The locals, somehow realizing my condition, rushed out jugs of water which showered upon me like gold coins. I had been subjected to this clairvoyant treatment twice before; both times I had run out of water and both times I was beyond desperation. I assumed that the people could see my physical condition or, noticing my bicycle and realizing the distance to the nearest town, understood I could not possibly have carried enough water.

The boredom of the desert played a role as well; the arrival of a foreigner on a bicycle was the equivalent, in some of these villages, to the circus coming to town.

I drank the water the villagers gave me. I drank it, poured it over my head, and felt it between my fingers as if it were rare saffron. The usual crowd gathered around, and the usual questions were asked. There were no fluent English speakers in the village, so communication took place in mime, my few words of Arabic, and their few words of English. I was told I was on the outskirts of the major city of Setif, a day and a half out of Constantine. That meant I was six days from the Tunisian border. One of the Arabs indicated that another cyclist had recently been through the town, and like me he drank much water. Could it have been Miguel? With my limited vocabulary, it was difficult to know if I was getting the message right. When I asked if anyone remembered where the other cyclist kept his bags, one of the villagers recalled that he carried only one bag, which he attached to his rear rack.

It was surely the Venezuelan.

Before I left town, I soaked my turban in water and filled my bottles. On the way through Setif I drank every drop of the nine liters of water in my bottles then filled them again before cycling into the desert. The sun was slowly setting when I made camp at the foot of a sand dune ten kilometers east of Setif. I was stocked with a full supply of well water from Setif. I laid back in the sand by my tent and tuned in to the AM radio band, while the sun widened into a dying half-orb encompassing all the sand dunes on the horizon. When the first English song I'd heard in months came over the airwaves, I climbed to the top of my sand dune and listened to the sound of the whispering wind and the words, "Hey where did we go, days when the rains came . . ."

LATE AUGUST
Tunisia

SIX MORE DAYS in Algeria went much like the others—dodging the sun, scavenging for water and staying one step ahead of dehydration. A few kilometers short of the Tunisian border, I came upon an ascent that wreaked havoc on my bicycle. Halfway up, my bottom bracket froze. My pedals had been grinding for weeks, but I was unable to get the collar off and check the bearings. My procrastination resulted in welding the pedals fast, so that they could no longer turn. I was left with no choice. Lacking the proper tools, I would have to walk. Pushing Papillon to the summit of the hill, I then glided down to Tunisia.

Upon reaching the border, my troubles worsened. Three customs officials descended upon me with Third-World vigor and began dissecting my gear. They started with my tent. One official tore it open then handed it to the next, who then searched through the folds with his nimble fingers. By the time the assembly line of gear reached the third man, obviously the boss, he was left with nothing to do but feel the seams, stand rigid in an imperious pose, and utter a few English comments in my direction.

"Tent?"

"Yes, tent."

"Expensive."

"Not really."

"Not for you Americans."

My sleeping bag went down the assembly line next, then my ground mat, camp stove, mess kit. When they came upon my tent poles, the third man asked, "Camping?" My mental response was, "What do you think you've been tearing apart for the past half hour you moron, fishing gear?" My vocal response was, "Yes, sir."

My camera came next. When it reached the ranking official he said, "Open." When I explained to him my film would be ruined if I opened the camera, he said, "Open!" I opened the camera.

The real problem came when they found my talcum powder. I bought it in Gibraltar to apply over a new patch. This prevented the patch from sticking to the inside of the tire. I also bought some vitamins in Gibraltar which were packaged in a plastic tube with a green label. When the vitamins ran out, I put the talcum powder into the vitamin tube. When the green label fell off the vitamin tube, my talcum powder was in a clear, plastic tube. When the third man, the boss, saw my talcum powder in the plastic tube, he shouted, "Cocaine!"

Two guards were summoned to stand behind me as I tried to explain the function of talcum powder. After some more in depth analysis (sprinkling, dabbing, tube-tapping) a senior customs official was brought to the scene, who gingerly tapped a half gram of the powder onto the table. Methodically, he pinched a little of the dust between his thumb and forefinger, then rubbed the fingers slowly together, while bringing the pinch up to his mouth and then his nose. Finally, he proudly proclaimed, "Cocaine!"

"It's not." I protested in my own defense. "It's talcum powder."

"Cocaine!" said the official.

I suddenly realized the seriousness of the situation that had developed. This was not an American legal system with laboratory analysis and fair trials. This was Tunisia, where the opinion of the highest official rules. If the customs people decided I was carrying cocaine, then I was carrying cocaine, and I would pay the penalty regardless of the facts. As a last resort, I decided to show them how the powder was used to patch a tire.

They allowed me to go through the five-minute procedure which culminated in dusting the patch with talcum powder. I did one patch without the powder to demonstrate how the patch tore off by sticking to the inside of the tire. As a result of my demonstration, a yet higher-ranking official was summoned, who quickly tasted the powder, the only one to do so thus far, then went into a tirade in Arabic. The reprimand was directed at the other, lesser officials, and I interpreted it to mean something like, "You idiots! Don't you know talcum powder when you see it!"

The senior official left in a rage, leaving me at the mercy of the original, inept guards. They had, to this point, only examined half my gear. When they resumed their search, they came upon a tinfoil bag of leaf chewing tobacco, also from Gibraltar. The label had long since fallen off. The third man opened the bag and peered inside, then, wide-eyed, exclaimed, "Marijuana!"

FIVE HOURS after arriving at the border, I finally escaped Tunisian customs. I explained the tobacco pouch by piecing together the cornflake-sized remnants of the label which were buried in five inches of sand at the bottom of my pack. With a bit of coercion, I managed to borrow a hammer from the immigration people and free up my pedals by beating on the bottom bracket until metal fragments began to fly through the air like sparks. I hoped to reach Tunis, where I could find the tools necessary for proper repairs.

I limped toward Tabarka with my pedals turning like a grist mill, metal against metal. But repairs were a lesser priority than my more immediate concerns, which happened to be food. I had run out of Algerian dinars long before crossing the border, with the hope that my supplies would carry me to Tunisia. They had, but there were no facilities for changing money at the border. I needed to find a bank or tourist area before I could eat. Only half a loaf of stale, rock-hard bread remained of my supplies, which I had been rationing for some time.

The combination of cycling eight hours a day and rationing food sent me into bizarre daydreams as I cycled. I imagined I was at the Thanksgiving table looking at turkey dripping with gravy, glistening cranberries, fluffy-white mashed potatoes, and dense, steaming stuffing straight from the turkey's belly. I dreamt about foods I rarely ate in America, about Kentucky Fried Chicken, Big Macs, eggs fried in bacon grease and sausages laden with glistening fat.

I arrived in Tabarka in the midst of such a dream, while jealously hoarding my half loaf of stale bread. Tabarka lies on the southern shores of the Mediterranean, which led me to believe there would be enough tourism in the town to allow me to change money. I went to the shore which was lined by low, white houses much like those shoe-box dwellings I'd seen in southern France and Spain. I stood at the shore leaning against Papillon, watching the waves of the blue Mediterranean lap away my hunger and listening to the sea-wind tell me to forget my repairs.

Suddenly, a voice called in English from behind me. I turned to see a tall, muscular Arab, dressed only in shorts, leaning against the open door of his seaside bungalow.

"Do you speak English?" the Arab shouted to me again. He was the first adult Arab I had ever seen without a shirt. With his deep tan and careless mannerisms, he seemed more like a vacationing American than a Muslim in Tabarka, Tunisia.

"I speak English very well," I said as I wheeled Papillon over to the doorway.

"Ah, you are English," the Arab said and extended a lanky arm in my direction. "I could not tell with your black skin."

"American," I corrected him as I shook his hand. I hadn't looked in a mirror in months, but, judging from my arms and legs, I had no doubt my face was as dark as any Arab's.

"My name is Achmed," the easy-going Arab said as he flapped

over to Papillon in his sandals. "Cycling?"

"Cycling," I answered, followed by a description of my trip. Achmed spoke perfect English, complete with Western gestures and American slang. This made me feel, while talking with him, as if I had been transported back to America—the perfect panacea for a traveler who hadn't heard proper English in months. I complimented Achmed on that point.

"Oh, well," he mused, "I have been in America many times. Actually, I am the coach for the Algerian Olympic Volleyball Team." He knelt down to look more closely at Papillon, then stood up and, in turning back toward me, leaned his hand on the rear rack. "I know all the American players," he continued, then began naming the members of the U.S. team. "I am only here in Tabarka on vacation with my family."

While Achmed talked, he moved his hand in the air with the confidence of a man who is an Algerian state treasure, a celebrity given special privileges. We discussed the state of Algerian sports, and Achmed leaned yet farther on the rear rack, until his hand came upon my stale loaf of bread. Suddenly he stood erect, then tentatively tried to squeeze the unsqueezable, rock-hard loaf.

"Is this what you are eating?" Achmed asked.

I explained my predicament, and that I hadn't as yet been able to exchange money for Tunisian dinars.

"This will not do," Achmed said, almost to himself, then he called through the darkness beyond the open door of his house. In an instant, his wife emerged from the doorway with a slice of watermelon, handed it to me, then just as quickly returned into the bungalow.

I was in no position to argue. I ravaged the watermelon as fast as I had gluttonized the golden, life-giving water in Setif. As I ate, visions of Kentucky Fried Chicken came to my mind, and visions of eggs dripping with bacon grease, and sausages soaking in glistening fat. No sooner had I finished the watermelon than Achmed's wife came out with a thick, fresh slice of baked bread and a long finger of white cheese laden with light green olive oil. Another slice of watermelon followed, then a square hunk of mutton, more cheese, more bread. Achmed stood with hands on hips, regaling in the effects of his Muslim hospitality.

"Eat," Achmed urged and laughed. "We will get you to Tunis after all." Again his wife appeared with more bread, more watermelon. Achmed's sense of pride made me hesitant to tell him I had eaten enough. In fact, I was stuffed to the point that the memory of sausages glistening with fat elicited an entirely new reaction. Achmed's wife emerged yet again, arms laden with meat, white cheese dripping with oil, thick doughy bread and watermelon. I resorted to storing the supplies in my panniers and satisfied myself with sucking on watermelon rinds in the hope that the longer I milked an individual slice, the less likely Achmed's wife would be to emerge from the dark recess of Achmed's inexhaustible larder.

Finally, when my belly was extended as tight as an inflated inner tube; when my panniers were stuffed with smuggled supplies that would easily last me to Tunis, only then did Achmed's wife relent. As I prepared to leave, Achmed insisted I take even more food with me. Here was an example of hospitality that made me feel that Africa had taken me on a roller-coaster ride, revealing the peaks of human kindness, and the valleys of bureaucracies and border guards.

I made it to the center of Tabarka having barely escaped Achmed's generosity. A tourist hotel, the Hotel du France, exchanged one of my three remaining $50 travelers checks for Tunisian dinars. The exchange left me with so much local currency that I decided to stay a night in the hotel and recover from the past weeks of desert cycling. After all, it was only a two-day ride to Tunis and I was on the Mediterranean, in a small, quiet town equipped with good food, water, and tourist amenities. What better place for rest and recovery? My only reservation was that I was carrying around twenty days' worth of Tunisian dinars for a short two-day ride to Tunis, where I would take a ferry to Sicily. Once in Sicily, my dinars would be worthless. I hoped to exchange the Tunisian currency for Italian lira, either before leaving Tunisia, or once in Sicily.

After securing Papillon safely in my room, I went out to explore the town and soon found myself sipping coffee at a small seaside café. Watching the white waves of the Mediterranean rise from the clear blue water, I reflected on the hardships of the desert. From the severe beauty surrounding my café table, the hot and sere Sahara seemed two lifetimes distant.

While my thoughts wandered beyond the desert toward Europe,

Scandinavia, and my inept beginning in America, the café began to fill, and the overflow guided a young Arab to the extra chair at my table. It soon became clear we spoke no common language, nor did either of us, I think, want to talk, with the relaxing waves of the sea so easily distracting. I looked over at the Arab sharing my table and, although he was properly dressed for a Muslim, with legs and arms covered, he somehow looked like a vacationer as he relaxed and leaned back in his chair. I stared at the turquoise water of the Mediterranean thrusting like gull's wings at the clear white sand of the beach. It was good to be relaxing, beyond the searing heat of the Sahara.

The Arab sitting across the table turned from his thoughts and tipped his glass in my direction. Not a word was spoken, yet I knew what was on his mind. I knew he was melting into the sea air as I was. I knew he was watching the grains of beach sand fade one by one to start their journey back into the eternity of the ocean. I knew, with the sun setting in a golden display of ecstasy, that words were not necessary.

The sun held onto its life as if it enjoyed living as much as we enjoyed watching it die. With its last flicker, the sinking orb sent a beam of orange across the water. From the bent edge of the curving ocean all the way up to our seaside table, a thin sliver of light served as Taps to the glory of the day. We watched the clouds turn fire red, to purple, to obscurity, then went our separate ways—I to the Hotel du France, and he to a place I envisioned was peaceful and silent and without the normal strife of Tunisian life.

AS THE ROAD bent north into Tunis, I thought of my silent Arab companion and the tasks ahead of me. Once in Tunis, I cycled down to the wharf with the thought of arranging a ticket to Sicily. At the landing, I was greeted by a mob of Arabs much like at the port in Gibraltar. The ticket office was hidden behind a beehive of swarming, impatient tourists.

Then, I spotted it. Against a tall white wall, secluded from the crowd, leaned a lone bicycle guarded by a black-skinned man with stark white hair. I approached and could see the thinness of the man's cheeks and the peeling of his weathered skin, which hung down in papery sheets from his dark face. His clothes were the color of the desert; they were drab, tattered and torn. His hair stood straight up and bleached on his head.

Sitting on the rear rack of his common ten-speed bike rested one pack, a backpack. I wheeled Papillon over to the man when his sunken eyes lifted. They seemed dull and thin from the insufferable desert sun. I came up next to the man and I offered him my hand.

"Miguel Megias of Venezuela, I presume?" I said, and privately hoped I did not look as disheveled as the man who had constantly stayed one step ahead of me across the top of Africa.

5
Italy

SOMEONE SLAPPED ME hard on the back while a customs official was examining my passport. A musty cloud of dust rose from my tattered shirt to linger in the air. I turned to see a man with a long gray pony tail and an American flag printed on his T-shirt.

"What the hell you doin' man?" he said, laughing." Dude, they'll never let ya' back into the States lookin' like that!"

"Do I look that bad?"

"Put it this way, you look like that guy in Treasure Island who was trapped on the island."

It's true I hadn't seen a mirror in a month, or taken a bath in weeks.

"You mean Ben Gunn?"

"That's the guy."

"How did you know I was American anyway?"

"I saw your passport. Ben Archer," and he offered his hand. "Whatch'ya doin', some sorta' crazy cycle stunt?"

During the time we spent going through the boarding procedure, I told Ben of my trip. I told him about Miguel, the elusive cyclist who was now aboard ship. I told him about buying the ferry ticket just when the ticket office was about to close, and persuading the clerk to let me board the ferry on such short notice. The sights of Tunis did not matter. After trailing days behind Miguel throughout three countries and having finally caught up to him, I simply could not be satisfied with a short five-minute encounter.

Ben stared at me blankly while I finished the story. He began to say something then stopped. "Don't take offense," he said finally, "but I can't figure out if you're brave or just crazy."

We found Miguel in the small bar area below deck. He was trying to find a place to eat, but none of the shops would accept his Tunisian currency and the bartender looked upon our dinars with disdain. "This money is worthless outside of Tunisia," he insisted.

"Then what do we do with all these dinars?" I asked, frustrated.

"To the sea!" he said, and made a motion to throw the money overboard. Miguel and I hadn't eaten in some time, but we now had no way to buy food until the ferry docked and we could cycle to a Sicilian bank. We were reduced to sitting in the bar restaurant, drinking water, where I learned a bit more about this cyclist who had led me through three countries.

Miguel was fifty-five years old, although apart from his sun-scorched skin he could have passed for thirty. His silver hair, streaked white by the sun, matched his thin, silver-rimmed glasses. Born in Venezuela, Miguel taught electrical engineering at a university in Spain. His recent divorce had given Miguel the freedom to undertake the bicycle journey he had long dreamed about, across the top of Africa then on to Italy and Greece. We decided to cycle together across Sicily to Messina, where Miguel planned to catch a train to Brindisi. The professor's command of five languages, including Italian, meant I could put aside my mime act until we parted.

Forty-five minutes into the crossing, we had planned our route across Sicily. Ben, realizing we were temporarily without funds, brought three coffees to our table. "I've arranged a cabin for myself," he said and sat down. "I thought you guys might want a coffee before I go." And then he added in a low voice, "I can't stand sleeping in those plastic chairs."

We drank our coffees. Ben went on to his cabin while Miguel and I leaned back in our plastic chairs, our minds swimming from a full day of activity. To us, the plastic chair was a luxury. We faded into sleep in tune with the humming engine of the ferry, and the thought we were skimming along at a pace ten times that of our bicycles.

LATE AUGUST
Strada 113 to Palermo, Sicily

BY THE TIME we docked in Trapani, Miguel and I were thinking only of food. We thanked Ben, who gave us his card "If you ever need any help," then we sprinted to the nearest bank. A multinational riot awaited us at the door, with Italians, Arabs, French, Germans, Americans—and one Venezuelan, Miguel—all pressing toward a tiny slot in the middle of a single, two-foot-wide window. A group of four Germans stood off to the side, unnerved by the chaos. Miguel, a veteran of Third-World procedures, pushed his way through to the counter and began demonstrating his fluent Italian. "Please hurry signoré," Miguel moaned through the window. "My friend and I have not eaten in days."

The man behind the counter seemed unsympathetic. "Please, signoré, we have just come from the Sahara Desert by bicycle. It is a very long way and we are starving."

A crowd began to form around Miguel. In response, he told the group about our Sahara crossing. While he spoke, he intermittently moaned the words, "signoré, mangiaré . . . mangiaré signoré." The piteous pleading made it seem as if we would die of starvation in minutes.

The crowd, now sympathetic to our cause, demanded the clerk process our passports first. The harried clerk, unused to a mob with a unified voice, shuffled for our passports while speaking in conciliatory tones to Miguel. In minutes we had our money and were running to our bikes with food in mind.

"Being a professor," Miguel whispered to me as we left, "I'm naturally inclined toward theatrics."

SATIATED by a one-hour stop at a roadside café, we cycled east on Strada 113. There were other priorities besides food. I had been cycling with defective bearings since Algeria, so I needed to find a bike shop that could repair my bottom bracket. Miguel wanted a smaller chain ring, considering the Sicilian mountains we'd have to cross. At each small town, Miguel asked about a bike shop.

"Next town," was always the answer.

After three or four such replies, my bottom bracket seized again and I was forced to walk. Miguel cycled ahead to find a bike shop while I lingered behind, walking up hills then coasting down the other side. I came upon Miguel hours later, waiting for me at the top of a hill. "I'm told there's a repair shop in the town down below," he informed me, and we coasted down to the small village together.

The repair shop was nothing but an open-sided hut, occupied by a toothless, white-haired mechanic. I showed him my bottom bracket and demonstrated that my pedals wouldn't turn. The old man said something in Italian and I turned to Miguel.

"He speaks a strange dialect. I think he said there's nothing wrong with your bearings."

"But my pedals won't even move."

"He says you can go a long way on those bearings."

Miguel asked the shopkeeper for tools so that we could do the job ourselves, but after a few red-faced shouts by the old man, Miguel shook his head. "He said if he tells you the bike works, then it works," Miguel translated.

We left the shop in disgust. The bitter old man followed through the door and screamed after us until we were out of earshot.

"What was the guy screaming about?" I asked while we walked to the next town.

"It was hard to tell. He went into a Sicilian dialect. Something about Mussolini and Fascism."

We found a modern repair shop in the next town. The mechanic removed my bottom crank and turned the bike on its side. A pile of powder and twisted metal poured out, remnants of what once were round metal bearings. The mechanic looked at me in disbelief, but his expression soon changed when he charged me forty dollars for the five-dollar part. Miguel and I tried bartering with the mechanic, but it was no use. I left the shop with eight dollars in my money belt.

Night came and we set up camp on a Sicilian beach of manila sand. We shared a pot of coffee while I cooked dinner on my camp stove. Miguel didn't carry a camp stove. He packed such a sparse array of gear that I was shocked he made it across Africa at all. He had no tent, no camp stove, no tools or spare parts. This was the cyclist who had beaten me across the top of Africa, a poorly supplied, fifty-five-year-old professor.

But I soon learned generosity was a trait of Miguel's to rival his perseverance. Lacking the price of the ferry to Greece, I now had no way to retrieve the $1,000 awaiting me at the American Express office in Athens. Miguel solved my problem by loaning me $200 in cash. I was to pay him back when I arrived in Greece, where Miguel would be staying for fifteen days before returning to Spain. I was reluctant to accept. We had known one another for less than two days, and Miguel was planning to take a train from Reggio, which meant we would have to meet later in Greece. I would have only a short time to make our rendezvous, since Miguel was due to depart for Spain in two weeks.

But I was grateful. The loan would save me from a detour to Rome. Miguel gave me his address in Greece, just east of my port of entry, and I assured him I would meet him there to return the loan within a fortnight.

SEPTEMBER
Taranto, Italy

SICILY SLIPPED AWAY with our eastward advance along the northern coast. At times we found ourselves high on a cliff gazing down upon tiny towns set white against the green land. The next moment the road brought us within two feet of the Mediterranean's rolling waves. We cycled along a cliff suspended twenty feet above the shore, and I looked down into the pellucid sea. Below, black boulders near the shore defied spraying white waves, the only disturbance in the turquoise water. A nude woman swam among the rocks, arching backwards with her face glowing in the amber sun and breasts piercing the limpid surface of the sea. Her tan feet could be seen smothered by milky-white sand below the waves, pink toenails resting on limpets and sea shells.

Miguel and I parted at the train station in Reggio. I continued on alone toward Brindisi, where I planned to catch the ferry bound for Greece. I cycled more than one hundred kilometers per day for six consecutive days to ensure making Greece before Miguel was due to fly back to Spain. By the ninth day, I was outside the city of Taranto, seventy kilometers from Brindisi and three days from my meeting with Miguel in Rio. I was left with a full three days to spare before Miguel's departure for Spain.

A stone wall ran alongside the thin country lane leading to Taranto. Beyond the wall lay forest. I had passed no one all day, apart from an occasional farmer working the fields. Cars sped by at a rate of about one per minute, so when I needed to relieve myself, I climbed over the wall and did so behind a clump of trees. When I returned, the bicycle was gone. Did I forget where I left it? I sprinted along the wall in a panic, but it soon became apparent that my bicycle had been stolen. I jogged up and down the road, knocked on doors, asked passersby. I searched for hours—all to no avail.

In desperation, I ran into town and sought out the police station. But the police showed little sympathy. To them, I was just another tourist complaining about another stolen handbag. I forced my way in to see the captain, a Capitano Pasquale, to whom I poured out my story. I begged him to send out a police car to search the area.

In response, Pasquale opened up a filing cabinet and pulled out a police report. "This was sent from New York," he said. "It is a police report of the mugging of Miss Italia at your beauty pageant in New York."

"What is that supposed to mean?" Was he was blaming me for mugging Miss Italia?

Pasquale shrugged his shoulders.

"Are you going to help?"

He shrugged his shoulders again.

"Look," I tried to explain, "I'm not a rich tourist. I travel on five dollars a day. I came from America on that bicycle."

"Now it appears," sniffed Pasquale, "you will be *walking* home." The four or five police officers in the room broke out into malicious laughter.

I left the station enraged. If I hadn't left, I would have slugged Pasquale before I knew what I was doing. I envisioned my hands around Pasquale's neck, around the neck of the thief, slowly squeezing the life out of their worthless bodies.

Rage slowly turned to shock while I aimlessly wandered the streets, bemoaning my loss. It wasn't so much the gear that bothered me, but my journals and ten rolls of photographs, which I had saved through Africa to send home through the more reliable Italian mail. Gone were all the records of the markets of Morocco, the exotic medina in Marrakesh. Gone were my photos of the nomads in the desert, and bags of rainbow-colored spices in the souks of Africa. Gone were my journals of Spain and Morocco, of Algeria, Tunisia and Italy. Most of all, gone was the bicycle that had carried me through fourteen countries.

I walked through the streets of Taranto in anguish, senses paralyzed, overcome by the realization that my trip was over. I did not have enough money left to buy new gear and continue the rest of the way around the planet. I didn't think about other options. My determination was dead. My desire had flown.

Dazed, I blindly roamed the streets in the futile hope I would catch a glimpse of my gear and the thief who had ended my travels. While I searched, I went over in my mind what assets were left to me. It wasn't much: the clothes on my back and my money belt. Thank God, I still had my money belt. Inside the belt rested my passport and $200 sent from heaven by a patron saint named Miguel.

I checked into a hotel, then went to the American School of English, which I noticed near the center of town during my search for Papillon. I asked the staff to translate a letter in which I described my trip, the robbery, and any equipment I thought might be resold in Taranto. I then made 100 copies of the letter and began distributing them to pawn shops, camera shops, camping stores, newspapers, tourists—anyone I thought might come across my gear for sale. My hotel address, phone and room number were listed at the bottom of the letter. I resolved to stay in Taranto for another ten days. If I heard nothing in that time, I would be forced to return home.

Distributing flyers, talking to camera shops, bike shops and newspapers, I pounded the streets of Taranto for days. I heard nothing. My rendezvous with Miguel passed, and his address in Spain was lost with Papillon. I cringed to wonder what he thought of my unworthiness.

At wit's end, I went to the hotel bar and proceeded to get drunk. I felt as if I were in the middle of a cold, never-ending winter, surrounded by a bleak and barren landscape. My senses seemed as if they were detached from my body, as if I were watching someone else sipping my beer, sitting on my stool, watching someone else get robbed and wander despondently around Taranto.

The night grew long and I threw back enough beers to envision my return home, when a businessman who sat on the empty stool next to me attempted to strike up a conversation. Eventually, I told the man about the robbery, about the foiled adventure, and about my shattered aspirations. When I finished, my companion left the bar and returned with a red and white T-shirt in his hands. "This is my company name on this T-shirt. A little charity never hurts."

My wardrobe now entailed a pair of cycling shorts, shoes, and not one, but two T-shirts. "So, you lost your journals," he reasoned. "So what! You go to your room and write down everything you remember about Africa. There's nothing you can do about the photographs, but you can always take more in Asia."

In time, my spirits began to lift from the lowest they had been throughout the entire journey. When I finally returned to my room, my determination was rekindled. How much would it cost me to buy new supplies? Once I had a bicycle, I could buy the other bare necessities while I continued east. A few days of research were needed before I could make any plans.

SEPTEMBER
Taranto, Italy

I AROSE with the sun, then went out to begin pricing bicycles in Taranto. I still held some doubt. No one had contacted me through my letters, newspapers refused to publish my story, and finding the gear I needed to continue my journey was a dubious prospect.

Inexpensive bicycles in Italy, a country devoted to professional cycling, were not exactly common commodities. I found sleek Italian racing bikes costing $2,000 or more, designed for the country's elite racing community. There were "moderately priced" road bikes for the average cyclist, all in the $1,000 range. Mountain bikes, I learned, ran at least $700. The more I looked, the more clear it became that Italian bicycles were beyond my means. I was forced to give up my quest and search for new ideas.

Walking back to the hotel in defeat, my resolve faded. Taranto's buildings stood dingy gray in the afternoon sun. This was an ugly city, I thought. With ugly people. A man walked by carrying a baguette. City dwellers shuttled by on buses and trams. I caught a glimpse of a cyclist with loaded panniers.

I half expected the gear to be mine, but as I approached, my hopes were dashed. His name was Peter, a German at the end of a two-week bicycle tour and now on his way back to Athens where he worked as a high-school English teacher.

We talked for an hour at the roadside, and I told Peter about my trip, the robbery, and my plan to buy a new bicycle in Italy with the intention of continuing the journey.

"Come to Athens," Peter suggested. "You can stay with me until you buy a new bicycle. Gear is a lot cheaper there anyway, and I'll show you the cheapest shops."

Perhaps my luck had finally changed.

6

Greece

Holargos, Greece

I HITCHHIKED from Taranto with an Italian business logo on my back and what was left of Miguel's lifesaving $200 secured in my cycling shorts. My conscience haunted me, Miguel having already left Greece. His address in Spain had been stolen with the bicycle, so I was left with no way to reach him. I could only hold faith that he would contact me through the information I had given him, although when I would return to the States to receive that communication was uncertain.

With Peter's address tucked in my side pocket, I found a new determination to succeed, wrought from the knowledge that there was nothing left to lose. I now resolved to continue the journey regardless of the consequences. Traveling eastward was now an all-consuming dedication.

I spent my last dollar on an overnight ferry to Greece, deck class. Lacking proper clothing and camping gear, I found myself in the frigid night air wearing two pitifully inadequate T-shirts. Another backpacker traveling deck class loaned me his ground mat, but it provided little help. Around midnight, the crisp sea air awakened me in a shiver. Dragging my ground mat behind, I slipped into the engine room and slept underneath a boiler the remainder of the night.

The ferry docked in Patras, Greece's port city 100 kilometers west of Athens. I was truly self-contained now, with no bicycle or bags to cause me worry. I hitchhiked the distance to Athens then sought out the American Express office where $1,000 had been waiting for me for over a month. A quick bus ride took me the eight kilometers north, to Hollargos, where Peter resided.

His house was a small duplicate of all the neighboring houses linked end to end in long rows, each with their own meticulously manicured lawn the size of a beach blanket. A spare cot was prepared in the living room, and I readied myself for a two-week stay in the city of the Parthenon.

The following morning, Peter gave me a list of shops to visit and I spent the next three days in Athens shopping for a bicycle. I spent evenings in the Holargos cafés, updating Peter on my progress and asking advice about proper prices for gear. How could I hope to replace the equipment I had honed through fourteen countries of trial and error? In Athens, almost every tool was sold in separate shops, or found lying on a blanket in front of a fifteen-year-old street vendor. In America, I had been able to fulfill all my needs at a single shop, but in Greece, outfitting a journey such as mine would be a time-consuming process of investigation and bartering.

It took a week searching through the bike shops in Athens to find a new bicycle. Made in Taiwan, its lemon-yellow frame glowed like a neon beacon in the sunlight. The new model was twice as heavy as Papillon, with smaller wheels and fat tires, making the progress I achieved with my original bike impossible. The conspicuous color would attract a great deal of unwanted attention as well. The new bike had many failings, but it became Papillon II.

I rode the eight kilometers back to Tony's apartment, which was like discovering all the good and evil contained within a new friend. The Asian design was heavy and cumbersome, with fragile automatic gear shifters, a part that would be impossible to replace outside of Europe. The fat tires made it seem as if I was dragging something behind me, or was riding on two deflated inner tubes. I gained a new appreciation of the original Papillon, as grimy and beat-up as it was.

The bike cost me $300. The shop also supplied me with a rear rack and panniers, but carried no other accessories—no tools, no pump, no spare parts. I would have to spend at least another week finding those things, but it seemed an impossible task in the confusion of Athens' streets, vendors, and storefronts.

Peter had warned me about the poor quality of Greek products and his warning turned out to be a prophesy. The only portable stove available weighed five pounds, with no wind break, and required refill canisters which were rare outside of Europe. The used camera I bought carried the brand name "Praktica," an old, East German relic. My sleeping bag provided insulation sufficient only for a cool summer night, and my ground mat was no more than a worthless foam pad.

I spent a second week in Athens buying gear, but my worldly possessions were meager. My rear saddle bags and handlebar bag came apart at the seams after one leisurely ride around Athens. My tire pump didn't grip the tube. I needed to wrap a piece of plastic bag around the tire valve for the pump to work properly. My water bottle leaked so that every time I drank, a flood of water poured down my chest. I tried several ideas to repair the bottle, including fixing an old rubber tube to the top, all to no avail.

To those items I added a pen, pad, knife, lighter, one tin cup and a small pot. Everything I purchased was invariably bestowed with some defect or deficiency. My tent, a small blue dome weighing ten pounds, rewarded me with a broken pole and ripped seam after one use. I had to come to terms with the fact that my three-pound American tent was gone. My light-weight and compact mess kit, an item impossible to find in Greece, was gone. Items such as my state-of-the-art camp stove and Ziefel tire pump were mere memories, images of the distant West, images of another world.

Before leaving Athens, I added the Greek version of a roadside tool kit to my wanting store of equipment: an adjustable crescent wrench, spoke wrench, and a flat piece of metal to use as a tire lever. Patches, I learned, were available at gas stations rather than bike shops. The store where I bought my bike reluctantly sold me two spare cables, a spare tube, and some spokes. It would have to suffice.

With the bare necessities in hand, clothes became my next concern. I still owned only the clothes on my back; sufficient, with temperatures lingering around eighty-five degrees during the day. I added only a pair of shorts and a sweatshirt to my supplies. My plan was to acquire more clothes along the way, as the temperature dropped with the onset of winter.

I had spent two weeks in Athens buying provisions, the recipient of Peter's hospitality. Now, it was time to leave, and continue the eastward journey. Armed with my sparse array of gear, I thanked Peter for his help and camaraderie, boarded my lemon-yellow bicycle, and cycled out of Holargos.

LATE SEPTEMBER
Evia, Greece

I WAS ON THE ROAD again, and it felt as if I were finally walking after a long stay in the hospital, or waking up after an interminable sleep. Greece was new and wide and green. Sandy brown hills followed my progress, always coated by a green fur of stunted bushes. Blue-green lakes, squat shrubs bordering their shores, were backed by a pillar of rising hills. The first several days out of Athens found me visiting an archeological dig, or gazing at a monastery hidden away in some secluded glen. Most of the sites were deserted. Some were engulfed in swampy marshes, with broken columns rising out of a vast sea of reeds, as if rediscovery had awaited the appearance of some traveler to give confirmation of their existence.

I cycled past amphitheaters cut into hillsides and overgrown with weeds. Some areas were under excavation, priceless statuettes lying next to carefully placed catalogue numbers, and marble figurines standing alone, untended and unguarded. It seemed Greece held so many treasures and objects of the past that they were taken for granted. Like a diamond on a planet made of diamonds, their value was reduced by sheer numbers.

I cycled through the monastic retreat of Meteora, where ancient hermitages sat precariously atop high, pillar-like cliffs. A steep road rose from the valley up to the monasteries and the Pindus range beyond. At the base of the climb, a villager by the roadside called, "You'll never make it up there with a bicycle." I made the top, and the mountains descended into an undulating infinity.

For a change of pace, I took a ferry to the Isle of Evia, a thin strip of land along the east coast of the mainland. Landing at the southern tip of the island, I cycled its length, a distance equivalent to the southern half of Greece. At times I found myself cycling along a central ridge with the blue waters of the Aegean Sea shimmering to my right, the setting sun and the orange glitter of wavelets dominating the western skyline to my left.

Twenty kilometers west of Thessaloniki, the Aegean Sea

encroached on the land, pushing the Thrace corridor up against the underbelly of Bulgaria. Small, block-shaped houses were arranged neatly in rows, some stacked one above the other along gently sloping hills. Between towns, the well-paved road wound through glens and modest clumps of trees.

The miles dusted Papillon's wheels a powdered sugar gray when I left the suburbs of Thessaloniki behind. The road eastward from Kavala—sometimes paved, more often a white powder—rose into hills that faded into the purple haze of distance. Green scrub and the last of the dry summer grass followed along with my progress, beyond each bend and curve, each upward gradation and descent. Sheep were common, even prevalent, sometimes causing me to wait as the flocks crossed the road every few kilometers. Not far from the Turkish border, a white sign stood, printed in three languages with black, block letters: BHNMAHNE! ACHTUNG! ATTENTION! STONES FALL DOWN 5 KM FROM HERE.

A flock of sheep had gathered where the tan dirt of the road met a small lake surrounded by a lawn of cropped grass. Two cyclists, almost invisible, rested on the bank, their clothes and gear so colorless from wear and time that they looked like a pair of dusty chameleons.

We talked, and I learned the two young women were from Australia, had been on the road for over a year, and traveled well armed, with bulky, club-like branches strapped to their handlebars.

"What do you use those for?" I asked.

"Dogs," said one.

And men," added the other

Apparently, the Turks were not shy when it came to approaching foreign women, and the two had encountered constant problems with men offering them money for sex. "We're headed to England," one of them said, "or get as close as we can 'till the money runs out."

"Right now we're living on bread to save money," the other admitted. "You wouldn't happen to have any butter?"

We traded road information. I gave them my copy of *The Odyssey* in exchange for an obscure spy novel. When it was time to leave, the two Australians called after me with a warning. "Watch out for dogs near Istanbul. They're thick as flies!"

7

Turkey and the Middle East

MID-OCTOBER
Istanbul, Turkey
I ROLLED INTO ISTANBUL, its mosques and minarets towering above everything. The horizon was a collection of round domes, accompanied by spires pointing to the clouds like Roman lances. Against a dusty gray sky, the Blue Mosque hovered above them all, and where the Golden Horn cut its way into Istanbul, the Sancta Sophia stood in confirmation of the city's rich history.

There was more to see in Istanbul than my two-week stay would allow. The Topkapi Palace rose from the shores of the Marmara as a testimony to the days of the sultans. All was a testimony to history: countless ancient structures, countless bridges and bazaars, endless museums and market places. And people came from the surrounding world to enjoy these treasures, as if this place was the center of all things. Istanbul was a city alive with Brits and Greeks, Russians and Americans. It seemed the city did not belong to the Turks, but to the visitors, and to history.

I set up my tent at a local campground, then sought out the Russian consulate to apply for a visa. I waited in lines and filled out forms the entire morning. By late afternoon I had not yet talked to a single official. Finally, I reached the point, after waiting three hours in line, where only one Pakistani remained between me and the visa clerk. At that moment the man behind the counter slammed a gate shut over the window. "That's enough!" he shouted, disgusted with the never-ending line. "Come back tomorrow!"

The Pakistani in front of me went completely berserk. "Come

back tomorrow! Come back tomorrow!" He ranted and raved and beat on the gate. "I have waited here all day, then you shut the gate in my face?" In response to the Pakistani's ravings, the officials behind the gate closed two shutters and disappeared behind the security of the facade. Glasnost, apparently, had not yet reached Istanbul's small corner of the world.

With the remainder of the day free, I wandered through the bazaars in search of reading material. On a whim, I decided to find some useless trinket for sale and see how low I could negotiate the price. I considered myself a good barterer, yet always bought items of necessity, which put me at a strategic disadvantage. Perhaps I could gain some insight into prices in Turkey by bartering for something that was completely useless to me. My opportunity came when I was wandering through the catwalk-thin alleys near Beyazit camii and an eager salesman approached with a jacket.

"Buy leather jacket meestir?" he whispered, as if he were about to sell me a missile guidance system. I looked at him with indecision, the way a tourist searching for souvenirs might do.

"Only one hundred dollars. Look, real leather!" And, in an attempt to verify this last point, he held the coat over the flame of his lighter. I was not sure what the demonstration proved, other than the garment was definitely not made of paper.

"Here, sir. Try it on." He insisted upon fitting me while meticulously buttoning and arranging the jacket as if handling a mink coat.

"One hundred dollars," I said hesitantly. I don't know . . ."

"Look, meestir. *Real* leather." He put the lighter to it again.

"No, it's too much," I said and took off the jacket.

"Okay, meestir, ninety dollars." And again the lighter.

I tried the jacket on again." No, it's too heavy."

He gave me another jacket, a carbon copy of the first. I tried it on. "Still too heavy."

"Eighty dollars. *Real leather.*"

"Maybe another jacket," I asked, and, after trying several, all exactly the same and all treated to the infamous lighter test, the price came down still more.

"Sixty dollars. Rock bottom price! Look, real leather."

That was pretty good, $100 down to $60, but I thought I'd lead him on a little longer. Walking away was always a good last-ditch ploy to lower the price. I walked away, he followed.

"Okay, meestir, you are good bargainer. From my heart I *give* you jacket. Fifty dollars. My cost only."

That was it I figured, as low as he would go. I decided to break the sad news.

"I have no need for the jacket," I told him finally, and walked away, sincerely this time, but still the salesman followed. I had hooked him by the amount of time spent in serious bartering. Now there was no escape.

"Forty dollars meestir, only forty."

Once again I explained my cruel game, and again he followed.

"Thirty dollars, meestir! Real leather for thirty dollars."

By then all I wanted to do was get away, so I sprinted around a corner and tried to hide in the crowd. While I fled, I felt a tug on my arm. "Twenty dollars, meestir? Real leather!" I saw him reach for his lighter and I quickened my pace.

Still he followed. In one last attempt to rid himself of the jacket, he grabbed me. "Okay meestir, here." and he put the jacket in my arms. "Take it. Fifteen dollars." I was actually tempted to buy the thing, but considering my mode of travel, it would have been more of a hindrance than a help.

Finally I began ignoring the man, a tactic which had the effect of intensifying my pursuer's efforts. In desperation, I ran through a side alley in an effort to escape the leech-like salesman. He didn't follow, although he did shout after me. From a fading distance, I thought I heard the words, "Ten dollars meestir . . ."

Later, while finding my way through the bazaar, a man grabbed my arm as I was passing his shop. "Buy leather jacket," he whispered. "Only one hundred dollars!"

LATE OCTOBER

the Anatolia Mountains

A WEEK IN ISTANBUL, waiting in endless lines, lost in a sea of paperwork, and that to secure two visas. Syria and Egypt were the only countries neighboring Turkey willing to allow me across their borders. But where to then? By blindly cycling south I ran the risk of encountering another dead end: Saudi Arabia, the Red Sea, Sudan,

Libya. Iran and Iraq had already denied me visas.

Although the southern route represented a significant detour, I was left with no other option but air travel, and that was a despicable option. I decided to leave for Syria with all possible speed. The warm Mediterranean summer was coming quickly to an end, and the high passes of central Turkey awaited.

The weather turned cold my last day in Istanbul, and the sky, a burnt gray, confirmed the start of winter. Snow began to fall when I entered the Anatolia foothills, and I found myself bartering for winter clothing while shivering in short sleeves. A thousand years of practice had given the Turks their superior bartering skills, but in my case a child could have sensed an advantage. The bulk of my Turkish lira went to buy a pair of long pants and a sweatshirt. With my thin sleeping bag and quickly decomposing tent, the clothes were of little help. I was compelled to seek out a hotel for the night.

Two dollars bought me a room, but hotels in the Anatolia region were not places of room service and carpeted lobbies. They were places to sleep for the night. Most were nothing but a square building subdivided by curtains into small cubicles. The cubicles were exactly the size of the one cot provided. Wool blankets served as central heating, but I still found it necessary to add my sleeping bag to the combination for comfort. After five nights staying in mountain hotels, I quickly learned that peeling my inner layer of wet clothes off and setting them aside for the night left me with a frozen stiff sweatshirt the following morning.

The shops in the Anatolia foothills were almost as Spartan as the sleeping accommodations. Dirt floors prevailed, a wooden board serving as the counter. Pencil and paper was Turkey's equivalent of a cash register. The shelves set in the walls were, at first glance, overflowing with stock, but with closer scrutiny it was clear that they held very little food. Old electrical wires, rusted car parts, miscellaneous crumpled pieces of newspaper and yellowed paper bags littered the shelves. The only food for sale was *ekmek*, the local bread, similar to a round burrito shell. The bread was so thin that I was forced to carry fifty sheets to see me through a single day. *Peynir*, goat cheese, was the only other staple consistently available in the region.

EARLY NOVEMBER
Nallihan, Turkey

AS I MOVED farther south into Anatolia, the mountains seemed to prey upon my weaknesses, targeting the failings in my equipment. The dirt road tilted upward at an incline so drastic that I was able to make only forty kilometers of progress. With the onset of night, I began preparing my camp in a wooded area off the dirt track. I spent two hours collecting wood and another hour setting fire to the frozen logs. Sleep came sporadically due to the cold. Freezing rain fell after dark, and the melting snow leaked through my tent walls to leave me shivering until morning.

I crawled out of my tent at dawn. Snow had colored the landscape white. Everything inside my tent was wet; my sleeping bag, my clothes, socks, spare sweatshirt. My fire from the previous night was nothing but a steaming mound. In an attempt to return some feeling to my limbs, I heated a cup of water on my camp stove and rolled the tin cup up and down my arms. Periodically, I reheated the water on the stove, then sipped, then rolled. Without that last bit of fuel to warm my numbed hands, rekindling the fire would have been a difficult task, and fire became a necessity.

I began rebuilding the dead logs. Everything that could be used for fodder was frozen: twigs, leaves, grass. I made a collection of dead branches and created five separate piles. The first was withered grass, moss, leaves, and toothpick-sized twigs. The next four piles contained branches of increasing size, from toothpick up to pencil width, then large limbs and logs. My panniers provided a windbreak, with a lit candle tucked behind. My spare inner tube was cut into two-inch squares stacked next to the candle.

Using the candle, I thawed the moss, grass, and leaves, then built a pile to produce an ember. A flaming piece of rubber draped on the pile served as fire starter. One toothpick, two toothpicks, slowly added, slowly thawed, grudgingly burned to life. Slowly, with care, I added one toothpick at a time. Too fast, and the frozen sticks would douse the embryonic flame.

When a tiny core of glowing embers was ready, I built a tepee of toothpicks on top, then draped another square of rubber. I added larger sticks, slightly bigger than a toothpick, then larger—one stick every few minutes. Rubber squares needed to be added at intervals to help thaw the wood. It took me an hour to build up to pencil-sized twigs. Another hour, and a full log finally went on the fire.

When the fire no longer needed tending, I gathered enough frozen wood to create an eventual blaze. I bathed my face in the heat of the flame, then rotated my limbs like a rotisserie near the warmth. A fire in these snow-filled mountains was all things desired throughout a cold traveling day. It was comforting warmth to heat a cup of coffee in the morning. It was a glow to dry wet clothes, and stave off darkness in the night. Sometimes, it beat off the effects of hypothermia, and sometimes, it meant salvation.

With my gear dry, I doused the fire and cycled deeper into the mountains toward Ankara. The dirt road became ankle-deep mud. The gray winter sky poured out its rain and sleet. Cycling was impossible. Pushing my bike, the kilometers went by slowly as rain saturated the ground. I was reduced to stopping every few yards to clear the brake pads of clinging mud. Four hours of effort, and I had traveled twenty-six kilometers.

My night was occupied with a familiar routine: build a fire, stay awake from the cold, rekindle the fire, dry wet clothes. I set out in the morning in the worst weather the mountains could offer. The temperature was slightly above freezing, with a steady, ice-cold rain turning the dirt road into mud. Snow would have left my skin dry, but rain seeped through every layer of clothing. Within minutes my clothes once again were drenched, and the warmth of the morning fire was a memory.

Near the summit of a 2,000-meter pass, the rain changed into sleet, turning the mud road into a semi-frozen stream, turning my hands into numb stumps and my clothes into muddy rags dangling in a winter driven wind. I dropped into a lower gear before I was forced to walk. Short of the top, I stopped to drain my stove of whatever fuel was left. It wasn't much. It took twenty minutes to restore feeling to my fingers before the gas cut out. My feet were still numb.

Wind drove the sleet into my face. I rode with my head down to absorb the needling impacts. My feet felt like blocks of wood, and my face was warped by the cold into a permanent grimace. Battling a headwind, I used my palms to shift down to my lowest gear, then numbed my mind, put my head down, and cranked.

A heat-sapping three hours later, I arrived in Nallihan on the main road to Ankara. The rain pelted the ground at an angle, and the once-dirt road had been transformed into a watery quagmire. I stood in front of the local hotel, ankle deep in mud. A wooden door swung in the wind, revealing an inner lobby. This was my first glimpse of the interior before the manager stopped me at the threshold. Pointing to my mud-caked shoes, the man denied me entry.

I was spent from the day's ride. Traveling on was impossible, but I had not yet learned enough Turkish to

argue my case. The effort of mime required an energy and concentration that had long been spent in the day's exertion.

"May I be of service?" a voice came suddenly from behind. A man wearing a thick fur coat approached from across the street. Realizing my condition, he persuaded the hotel owner to give me lodging.

"I am the doctor here," the man announced, after negotiating a price for the room. "My name is Canin. I will come to check on you later."

Leaving my mud-spattered saddle bags on the bike, I took my gear into the hotel. The plastic liners inside my panniers were filled with a brew of sepia rain water leached with sweat, and all my clothes and equipment were inundated with mud. Despite my best efforts, I left a brown trail from Papillon all the way up to my cubicle door.

The interior of the hotel was nothing but a central room ten-feet square surrounded by the usual curtains and cots. But there was one thing unusual about this particular hotel. In the middle of the main room stood a cast-iron stove which illuminated the lobby with a soft yellow light. I gingerly moved my gear inside then, piece by piece, set my clothes out to dry by the heat of the coal-burning stove.

I filled my tin cup with coffee and placed it on the top hot plate, then I thawed my numb hands in the orange glow. My two sweatshirts slowly dried while the coal exchanged its life for fire, until I felt the burning embers deep within the pit of my mind, and thoughts of snow and mountains were subdued by the warm reality of the present.

When Canin returned hours later, I still was drying my shoes in front of the stove. The effort of the past week had left me drained, but I accepted Canin's offer to guide me around the town and show me the sights. There wasn't much to see. The main attraction seemed to be a local café set above a tier of houses, where we met two of

Canin's friends. My three hosts ordered lamb chops, thick chunks of skewered beef, blocks of yellow cheese, tomatoes in olive oil, and diced melon to accompany *raki*, the Turkish equivalent of ouzo.

The staples of my diet for the past week, ekmek and goat cheese, were nowhere to be seen. The others watched me as I availed myself of their hospitality, but Canin and his friends did not eat. They had come to drink and talk, and, perhaps out of courtesy, left the food for me.

In time I felt rejuvenated. The raki oozed into my mind to join the warmth left by the coal stove, and I felt as if I had found a safe haven where I could fully recover from the wind, rain and cold.

My hosts, all three doctors I discovered, asked the standard questions about my journey. I answered with more interest than usual, considering their generosity. Muymey, the eldest of the three, described medical school and the state of health care in the country. I asked him how much schooling was needed to become a doctor.

"Six years," he told me, "plus one year of medical service in the east—our commitment to the government."

"Why the east?"

"Life is very hard in the east. They live in poverty and there are many illnesses and diseases."

"And after the east?"

"We go where the government tells us."

"So, you never relinquish your commitment to the government?"

"We go where they send us," Muymey returned, as if my question was nonsensical. To them, it was a set way of life, a set system. In Turkey, there was no other way.

"Do you mind going where the government sends you?" I asked. "No," answered Muymey, who seemed to be the group's spokesman. "When we decided to become doctors, we knew there would be travel."

Muymey already had fulfilled his year in the east. The other two, having recently graduated, were awaiting their assignments. I asked Muymey what it was like in the east but he seemed unwilling to reply, as if I were somehow disparaging his country. Turning to a new subject, I asked if they made good money as doctors.

"Not good, not bad," replied Canin.

"How much?" I persisted.

"Three million lira every month."

One hundred fifty dollars a week for a doctor traveling at the government's whim, with one year in the harsh east. But that wasn't a bad wage in Turkey, where bread costs about fifteen cents and a hotel two dollars a night.

We left the restaurant at midnight. The three refused to let me pay the bill, even though I had eaten all the food. On the way back to the hotel, Muymey gave me a tour of his office, where he showed me what may have been the only computer within a hundred miles. I had asked the three about Turkey's weather, and everything I wanted to know was available. The climate became gradually warmer to the south, soaring into the eighties near the Syrian border. I printed out the new information then returned to my hotel, where I slunk around the sleeping tenants with a lighted candle and discretely distributed the rest of my wet clothes around the stoked coal stove.

MID-NOVEMBER
the Syrian border, Syria

FROM NALLIHAN, it took me ten days through descending mountains to reach the Syrian border, where I found the usual border guards anxious to relieve their boredom with my arrival. One of the customs officials wanted to test-ride Papillon, but his legs were so short that he ended up flailing his feet in the air without touching the pedals. A junior guard aided him by running behind and pushing by the seat, but whenever the guard let go, the customs official would fall flat on the ground. This did not deter the others, who each rode the bike in turn, while I was subjected to a one-hour immigration check.

The area south of the border supported no towns or villages, providing a military buffer zone between the two countries. As a result, I went without food for the entire day. The first Syrians I came upon were two Syrian women washing clothes in a streambed.

"Yacol?" I asked, remembering my Arabic from Africa. I expected to be shown a place to buy supplies, but instead they led me back to their hut in a small village. They motioned for me to join five Arabs who were sitting on the floor smoking cigarettes.

· The women disappeared into the kitchen, returning minutes later with a large tray laden with mutton and cheese, bread and hummus, along with some items I did not recognize. A steaming pot of tea was set by me. I waited for one of the Arabs sitting with me to start, but learned they had already eaten. The entire tray was solely for me.

The following days in Syria showed me similar generosity. I was fed by the villagers four days in a row, and was offered a place to sleep on two occasions. A vendor selling oranges offered me a bed. The baker gave me lunch. I stopped to buy food at a local market and the owner brought me to the back of the store and fed me, served me coffee, then insisted I stay the night. I sat like an honored guest in the middle of the living room, the women bringing food and tea, while friends and family members periodically arrived to ask familiar questions. It seemed I was the entertainment, not due to any innate skills of my own—more like the side show coming to town.

LATE NOVEMBER
Damascus, Syria

I CYCLED ever south. Unable to find supplies, I was at the mercy of the local people. To acquire food, I learned to cycle into the center of town where the villagers mingled. When they realized I was a foreign traveler, I usually received an offering of food. Sometimes, I was reduced to knocking on doors and begging. The generous Syrians would accept no money—offering was useless, even taken as an insult.

Three days of cycling brought me to Damascus, where my priority became researching possible routes east. As in the past, I found the attainment of visas to be a time-consuming, money-draining and maddening affair. The former Soviet countries rejected me, as they had done in Istanbul. I was rebuffed again by the Iranians, the Saudis and Iraqis.

With Jordan the only country willing to issue me a visa, my last remaining route was south, to Aqaba, then a ship around the Arabian Peninsula to Pakistan. If that hope failed, there was no other option but to fly over Iran.

My new plan set, I left Damascus and continued south toward the Jordanian border. I reflected on the unexpected kindness of the Syrian people with the miles toward my last night's camp in Syria fading behind me. Even the overbearing presence of Assad's government could not cast a shadow on the generosity I had encountered throughout the country.

The prospect of accomplishing the final kilometers to the border caused me to continue cycling after night had fallen. I pitched my tent about 100 yards off the road, after blindly barging through the brush and thickets which dominated the landscape of southern Syria. I fell asleep with the knowledge that Jordan was ten kilometers away, my last hope for a way east.

I WAS JOLTED FROM SLEEP by an earthquake. Something was violently shaking my tent. I pushed my head through the tent flap and was grabbed by strong hands, then flung against a tree. Four men stood over me, two of them wildly hurling gear from my tent. I was being robbed.

An Arab the size of a gorilla tore the money belt from my waist then shoved me to the ground. My passport was theirs. They took my camera, began packing the tent. In a panic, I could think of only one thing. Stall and argue until the four moved away from Papillon, then quickly unlock the bike and ride before they could react. It was a plan born of instinct, thought through in seconds. My gear would be sacrificed, my passport, my money belt. It was my only hope.

The thieves gathered up the last of my gear and pushed me toward the bicycle. I was shoved to the ground when I resisted. As long as the key remained hidden in my cycling shorts, I had some bargaining power. The four turned back toward the tent, and at that moment, I had my chance. In one frantic motion I unlocked the bike, threw the chain on the ground and ran through the brush with every sinew of strength. I didn't look back. I ran until I was able to jump on the bike, then I pedaled through the brush in a single-minded effort. I heard my pursuers crashing through the thickets behind me and knew, if I could make the road, they would never catch me.

But the road was 100 yards away, through undergrowth and brambles which slowed me down. Barely short of the road's edge, the smallest of the four caught me and knocked me off the bike. I looked up to see a station wagon waiting at the roadside with an open back hatch. While I was on the ground, my assailant dragged Papillon over to the car. The other three were still running toward the road. I had to wrestle the bike away from this one Arab before the other three arrived.

I rose up, ran over to the car and grabbed Papillon, but there were only a few seconds to spare. We were still struggling when the remaining thugs burst from the thickets. I felt I could have overpowered the small Arab, but with the others closing in, I was outnumbered. The Arab and I stood in a stalemate, each clinging to one side of the bike. The other three began to encircle me.

Once again, I was surrounded.

"Get in the car!" one of the Syrians shouted. The sudden use of English was like a slap in the face. I suddenly realized, I wasn't being robbed; I was being taken prisoner! The terrorists forced me toward their car. Panic-stricken, I released Papillon, barged through the smaller two Arabs, and fled down the street screaming. I felt weak from the earlier struggle and the largest man was right behind me, bounding along in angry pursuit. In my weakened condition, I lacked the strength to sprint. Desperate, I tried to stop an oncoming car. The driver saw what was happening and swerved past in an act of sheer cowardice.

There were no other cars in sight. All four kidnappers were now in the chase. In terror, I ran down the street hoping to flag down another car. I was bereft of energy. My pursers gained.

A van approached just when my legs failed. Mercifully, it came to a stop in answer to my pleas. There were three large men inside dressed in business suits. At the sight of the van, the attackers stopped.

I pleaded through the window, hoping at least one of the Arabs understood English. If they drove off, I would try to cling to the window. After I recapped the horrifying incident, they let me into their car. My saviors seemed to be businessmen, all young except the driver.

The older Arab asked me to repeat my story. My attackers huddled together a short distance away, yet they refused to run. Were they afraid the businessmen would notify the police if my gear wasn't returned?

The driver demanded the return of my passport, and the thieves obliged. Why the man possessed such power over the thugs I didn't know and didn't care. Nor did I care that the thieves still had Papillon. I only knew that I was safe, in the hands of competent men. We drove away, and the passenger next to me in the back seat turned, speaking in fluent English.

"There's something we must explain to you," he said. "Those people you ran from are with the government."

"Government?"

"Yes, they are police, of sorts. Like your CIA."

"Secret Police?"

"Yes. They are Mukhabarat, government police. We must follow them to their base for questioning."

"Questioning! Wha- why do we have to go? Just let me out here with my passport and I'll walk to Jordan!" I was stammering, in a state of shock.

"We cannot let you out," the driver replied. "You see, we are with the government also."

I was dead. In my hysterical state of mind, I imagined they would find me in ten years, buried in some unmarked mass grave, or old and mindless in a dark cell like the lepers in *Ben-Hur*. I had been fighting with the Syrian Secret Police! Why didn't they show their I.D.? Didn't they have guns?

The elder Syrian driving the van saw the unmitigated panic in my face and smiled, not a smile of sadism but a friendly smile of assurance.

"You must not worry," the young Syrian next to me said. "We are not with the police. This man is a famous judge," and he pointed to the silver-haired driver. "He wants to help you. When the judge gets involved, usually nothing happens."

It was the word "usually" that haunted me while we drove to the police station. The judge, in an attempt to assuage my obvious terror, continued to assure me that everything would be all right. The more he assured me, the more worried I grew.

When we arrived at the police compound, the judge and his aids marched ahead of me in a display of confidence. I was taken away by the arm and put in a cell. I languished for hours, mentally numb, physically defeated. I wrung my hands and paced the room, mumbling over and over again, "usually nothing happens . . . usually nothing happens . . . usually nothing happens."

When the judge finally came to see me, I was a collection of nerves, terror, and slight hope. My mind was running through so many scenarios that I felt as if I had been punched in the stomach, physical fatigue brought on by mental anguish.

"They say you were camped next to a military installation," I heard the judge say though my mental haze. "They say you were taking photographs. They are developing the film now. If nothing shows up, I feel confident you will be released." I was taken to be questioned with the judge by my side, his hand on my shoulder.

The interrogation room was large, with at least twelve functionaries standing against the walls and one ranking official sitting at a central desk. My camera sat open on the desk. The film was gone. The judge's aids were in separate, dark corners of the room, speaking rapid-fire Arabic in an attempt to sway some of the lesser officials, while the judge spoke to the head man at the desk.

Hours went by. I was repeatedly asked the same questions by a succession of bureaucrats, each taking their place in turn at the central desk. Higher ranking dignitaries continued to appear until, much to my relief, the most senior official seemed to be a close friend of the judge.

The judge sat down next to his friend in a high-backed chair and spoke in calm Arabic, like a pasha casually dictating the order of the day. My attackers, seated together in the room, suddenly scattered to opposite corners. At length, the head official stood, then rained down such a tirade of Arabic upon the assailants that I knew I was free. I knew the judge and his assistants had worked their magic to prove that even in Syria, justice existed. Albeit selective justice. Without the divine intervention of the judge, my fate might have been much different. I was reminded of the part luck played in the success of my journey, and was left with the feeling that my luck came in the form of some benevolent guardian angel.

The judge arranged the return of my bicycle and camera, then walked me outside the gates of the compound. Loud reprimands could be heard taking place inside. No doubt my attackers were being scolded, not for the arrest, but for foolishly stumbling upon the judge.

"If I were you," the judge advised after we had cleared the gate, "I'd get to Jordan as fast as possible. I won't be there to protect you if those police decide to pick you up again after their reprimand." Then he and his aids climbed into their van and drove away.

I was two feet outside the gate of the Syrian base, and discovered that my tires had been slashed. Once again I was overcome with fear.

I envisioned the original four thugs tracking me down before I could reach the Jordanian border, dragging me out into the desert, and insuring that I would never be heard from again. I rode the entire five kilometers to the border on completely flat tires. When I finally changed the tubes, they were folded in thirds inside the tire, and my rims were dented and damaged.

Safely across the Jordanian border, I reviewed my situation with a more rational mind. Although I was grateful for having escaped the Mukhabarat unharmed, the experience was not without its effects. I carried no spare tires, so I was forced to find a way to repair the originals. Half my gear was left strewn about the scrub of the Syrian desert ten kilometers north of the border, and the Syrians had confiscated all my film of Turkey and the Middle East, as well as my unused rolls. The only photographs to survive of my entire journey were those from Europe. All others had been stolen by thieves, or by governments.

DECEMBER 2

Aqaba, Jordan

I SPENT MY FIRST DAYS in Jordan collecting my nerves while I cycled toward Aqaba. Winter reached its way into the Middle East as November came to an end. A cold, driving rain prevailed with my southward advance. I made my way along the coast of the Dead Sea, the lowest point on the face of the Earth. From those shores, there was nowhere to go but up.

A Mediterranean climate prevailed in southern Aqaba, which struck me as a city of tourism and beauty. The Red Sea supported water skiers and scuba divers, fishermen, sailors and swimmers. Cafés lined the shore where tourists lounged underneath umbrellas and sipped their beer from tea cups. Since public drinking was frowned upon in Jordan, yet tourists wanted their alcohol, a compromise was made by serving pitchers of beer in tea pots and providing the patron with a tea cup. The authorities turned a blind eye to this obvious charade.

In Aqaba's markets bordering the shores of the Red Sea, I found new tires to replace the slashed ones, but Aqaba was yet another trap. The Pakistani embassy informed me that a visa was not required for Americans, but how to get to Pakistan?

There was no way to travel eastward from Aqaba. No passenger boats plied the Arabian Sea to Karachi. The only available boats traveled to Sinai. After stating my case at all the shipping offices, I achieved no success in securing passage on a freighter.

I went to every travel agency in Aqaba asking for ideas. Due to the ongoing turmoil in the Middle East, travel through Saudi Arabia was restricted. Every official at the Saudi embassy met me with the same refrain, "You may wait forever for a visa, only to find you've been declined."

None of the agencies, embassies, or bureaucrats knew if passenger boats traveled from Egypt to Karachi, either from port Said, Alexandria, or Suez. The only other options were to sneak across one of the borders with no visa, or take a plane from Amman, an option I looked upon with disdain.

DECEMBER 4
over the Arabian Sea

THE RESEARCH, roadblocks, and frustrating complexities in pursuing a way east were as extensive and mind numbing as all the combined detours I was forced to take over the past months. After pursuing the slightest prayer of a chance east, it became clear that all possibilities were prolonged dead ends. A plane flight over Iran was imminent.

I boarded the plane in a dejected and demoralized mood. I was frustrated with all the roadblocks, and dejected that I had wasted time and money by continuing south in the false hope an avenue eastward would present itself. All that, then to be forced into the despicable option of air travel—an option that made me feel I had somehow lost a personal battle, that I had not tried hard enough in pursuit of an eastward path.

With the plane descending toward Karachi, I pondered the simplicity of having traveled what, on Papillon, would have taken two months. And Air Jordan was much more sensible toward Papillon than was my original carrier from Newark. They didn't require boxing, turning of the handlebars, pedals removed or bags detached. Simply wheel the bicycle aboard in Jordan. Wheel it off in Pakistan.

8

The Red-Eye Runaround

I ARRIVED IN KARACHI at four o'clock in the morning. The process which brought me by plane from Aqaba to Amman, then to Karachi, left me with a mind-numbing fatigue known only to those travelers who ply the roads of the Third World. The serpentine immigration line twisted before me in a haze, ending at the all too familiar window, one-foot square, behind which sat the unavoidable bureaucrat calmly engaged in doing nothing. After an hour, my turn came at the center of the hub and the official said, "Passport." I handed over the document and wondered how many times I'd heard that word, said in exactly the same way by ever-more apathetic officials.

He flipped through the pages several times, then broke the chain of predictability by saying, "Visa."

"No visa. American," I said, attempting to explain that Americans did not require a visa to enter Pakistan.

"Visa?" the official insisted, pointing to my Egyptian visa. "I don't have a visa," I replied.

"Visa?" he persisted, pointing to my Syrian visa.

The charade went on for a maddening ten minutes, while I continued my futile attempts to explain what I'd been told at their embassy in Amman. Finally, the official lifted his head from the pages of my passport and said, "No visa?"

"No, no visa." The mental duel had worn me down. It was 4 a.m. and my mind was slinking into a threshold between light and dark, preparing to shut down.

After much confusion, I was led to a large white room encircled by plastic chairs. There were other people in the room, but those were the only details I was able to absorb. The problem with my visa was my main priority. I talked to the head immigration official who informed me that Americans did require visas, and that I was to be detained until they could decide what to do. The official took my passport and assured me that I would have a temporary, three-day visa within hours, then I would be allowed to proceed to the embassy in Karachi to secure a proper visa.

I convinced two of the guards to let me retrieve Papillon from the luggage room and change money at the airport bank. They allowed me to go, under guard, since an agreed-upon bribe was awaiting them once I held some coveted Pakistani rupees in my hands.

That accomplished, I took my place on one of the hard, plastic chairs and contemplated my cycling options from Karachi. My plan was to cycle along the Indus River into northern Pakistan, then over the Karakoram mountains following the ancient Silk Road, gateway to China. Once there, an entirely new set of difficulties would confront me, but I didn't allow myself to plan that far ahead. My eyelids began to droop, and I was unable to think beyond the comfort of my plastic chair.

I awoke six hours later, at eleven o'clock. With a clear mind, it was easier to take in my surroundings. The room was large, about seventy-meters square, with no features to distract from its austere whiteness save the plastic chairs, which lined one half of one wall. About thirty other people of various nationalities occupied the room. Some looked Indian, some African. Others were Southeast Asian. A few were asleep on collapsed cardboard boxes, but many sat huddled in corners as if sick or afraid. One old man meditating on his cardboard mat was dressed in a flowing, pajama-like *dhoti*. His black face contrasted sharply with his long gray beard, which rippled over his dhoti to touch the floor. I saw no Westerners, only impoverished Third-World fugitives. The entire scene was like some huge, indoor refugee camp.

The one exit to the immense detention area was an archway ten-feet wide, beyond which stood the immigration office. Two guards stood at the threshold, which made me wonder where they thought anyone was going to go. The only way out was through the same immigration line that sent me into limbo, and limbo was where

I remained—not yet officially in Pakistan but surely outside the borders of Jordan. I was, bureaucratically speaking, between two countries—floating somewhere over the Arabian Sea.

Concerned by the fact that I had not yet been given my three-day visa, I went to the door and asked the guards for information. They directed me through the arch and across the hall to the immigration office, where I found a rotund official behind a cluttered desk. He was not the same man who had seized my passport many hours earlier. I asked him about the status of my visa.

"Who are you?"

"What do you mean, who am I? You guys are supposed to have a visa for me!"

I explained the situation for the second time in twenty-four hours. How I'd been misled in Jordan. How the official from the night before had taken my passport to obtain a visa. How I had fallen asleep.

When I was finished, the fat man leaned back, held out his hand, and said, "Passport."

"I don't have it! I just told you I gave it to the official this morning!"

"What official?"

"Don't you know?"

"Okay, go sit down."

"You will take care of my visa?"

"Yes, go sit down now."

I went back through the arch to the detention area and looked again at the other occupants in the room. My heart sank when I realized that some of them had been there at least overnight and showed signs of having taken up permanent residence. I approached the old man in the dhoti, still sitting cross-legged on his box and, through mime, discovered he was from Bangladesh. I pointed to him as if to say "you," put my head in my hands to indicate "sleep," then pointed to his cardboard box, hoping he would understand my mime for "You sleep here . . ." I held up one finger, then two, and so on to ask, "How many nights?"

He understood. Slowly, he uncurled all five fingers on both hands to indicate ten.

"Ten?"

Before I could clarify he showed another ten, then five.

"Twenty-five days?" When I flashed the same number back for confirmation, the Bangladeshi nodded his head. He had been there twenty-five days.

"Yes, he has been here twenty-five days," came a voice from behind me. It was one of the Africans.

"You speak English?"

"Yes, my name is Sa'id, from Somalia."

"How long have you been here?"

"Fifteen days. So have all the others. At least fifteen days."

That was enough. I stormed back to the immigration office in a tirade, screaming to the fat man that my situation was the fault of their own embassy in Jordan. He leaned back, his double chin rolling over his neck.

"You are a liar," he said and put his hands behind his head. I flew into a rage, screaming, flailing around the office in an attempt to explain what had transpired in Amman.

"You are a liar." He said again, once I had finished. "Our people in Jordan would not tell you this. You have come to this country illegally."

The same line of conversation went on for a seeming eternity, until the only reply I could get from the fat man was, "Go sit down." No matter what I said or how I said it, the inevitable reply was, "Go sit down." Finally, like a man who has had the wind knocked out of him after a long fall, I went and sat down. That was the last time I was allowed in the immigration office without a bribe.

I spent the rest of the day talking to the Somalian and learning the rules of our indoor detention camp. The only amenities were water and access to a toilet. In order to get food, we were forced to bribe the floor sweepers, who came around periodically to relieve us of our rupees. Whenever someone acquired food or tea they would ration it out in minute portions to everyone in the cell. Now that I was one of the group, a relatively rich American, it fell upon me to feed the detainees—a task I took up without the least bit of regret. The Somalian split the cost with me, but the two of us and one tourist from Tunisia were the only ones with any appreciable, therefore extortable funds.

In the course of my conversations with Sa'id, he revealed some of the missing pieces of the bizarre detention camp. "Except for the three Bangladeshis," he told me, "we are all here for no visas. They are here because they were traveling with forged passports."

"How does a person get out of here?" I asked, looking at the others who seemed resigned to a long stay.

"It's hard. You have to buy a plane ticket, but they won't let you go to the ticket counter. I was able to bribe my way to the phone and call a friend of mine in Karachi, who bought me a ticket to Malaysia. I actually flew out of here to Malaysia but I didn't have a visa for there either, so they sent me back."

"Why would all these people arrive with no visas?" Was it possible misinformation was that prevalent?

"Well, all the Somalians left because of the civil war. Myself—my property was taken, so I ran. No one will give Somalians a visa because they're all trying to leave, and are mostly poor."

The others, I learned, were in similar situations, either fleeing a war, or poverty, or an oppressive government.

"Can't your embassy help get you out of here?"

"No, I tried. Somalia being such a poor country, my government doesn't care. My friend is the only one trying to help. When he calls me here they let me talk to him because he says he's from the embassy. Without a bribe, that is the only other way to use the phone. The others here are poor, so they are not allowed into the office."

THE REST OF THE DAY passed with no success in reaching the phone. I would first have to learn where to place my bribes in order to succeed. It would be difficult, since the guards knew I had money, and they would be sure to get their ill-gotten share before I would see so much as the office door.

Before going to sleep, I distributed what little gear I owned among the refugees. None of them owned blankets, some lacked shoes, so any clothes I handed out were used as blankets, pillows, even foot coverings. I was impressed with the ingenuity of one Ethiopian, who wore a T-shirt around his legs at night.

The next morning, I began to learn the bribe-path to the phone. By midday, I had distributed enough rupees to gain access to the immigration office, where the fat man took the largest payoff of all.

I then faced my next problem. I still did not know the telephone number of the American embassy.

"What's the number of the American Embassy?" I asked the man behind the desk.

"I don't know."

"Information? Telephone book? Operator?"

"Go sit down."

It was clear that I would have to try another approach. I wrote out a dozen notes describing my situation and slipped them to any Western travelers brave enough to step out of the immigration line in response to my pleas. The notes requested them to contact the American Embassy immediately.

I paid a floor sweeper to get me the number to the embassy, but, after gaining access to the office phone through bribes, I discovered he had given me the wrong number. I never saw that floor sweeper again.

Time and again I bribed various people for the proper telephone number, only to discover the number was false. On the fifth try, I was able to get through to the Japanese embassy which, after hearing my desperate plea to contact the American Embassy on my behalf, promptly hung up. Dejected, I went back to the room and sat next to Sa'id.

"This place is like prison!" I said.

"It's worse. At least in prison you can have a bed and a shower. Here, all you get is 'go sit down.' I'll tell you, if it weren't for my friend on the outside trying to help me I would be here forever."

The Somalian's apathy emboldened me to storm into the immigration office and once again demand the number to the U.S. Embassy, upon which I was told to "Go sit down."

My only hope, it seemed, was with the notes smuggled out to other travelers.

THE NEXT DAY AND A HALF continued in the same manner: constant wrong numbers, setbacks, and failed negotiations. Much to all our surprise, the Tunisian was able to extricate himself by paying a bribe equal to the price of his plane ticket back to Tunisia. His entire negotiation had gone on since I arrived in Pakistan, and I watched with vested interest.

My third day in captivity, we were visited by three doctors from Immigration Health Control. The visit was significant for me, since I was able to elicit a promise from one of the doctors to get me the elusive embassy phone number.

Later that night, the doctor returned and, without saying a word, handed me a slip of paper. It was late—around 10 p.m.—but I was able to bribe my way to the phone with the last of my rupees. Expecting the lack of success I had encountered so many times over the last few days, I was stunned when the voice came through.

"American Embassy . . ." A U.S. Marine manning the telephones answered, and was appalled by my detention. Although most of the diplomats had left the embassy for the evening, the Marine assured me he would do everything in his power to see me free before the night was over.

"I'll need the number there," he said. He wanted to keep me informed and, if possible, have the American Consul call me back. There was a number, but the guards wouldn't give it to me without a bribe, and I was out of rupees. The Marine asked me to describe where I was located, then told me to do anything safely within my power to call him back with a phone number. I returned to the room and told Sa'id about the phone call. I explained that I needed the number for the office phone but was out of rupees.

"I know where the number is written down," Sa'id whispered. "I saw the guard look it up when I was in the office once. If I can get into the office, maybe I can see it. It's in the open right by the phone."

The Somalian gained entry to the office with a fallacious complaint about stomach pains. He returned with the office phone number. Sa'id loaned me some rupees and I was able to use the phone by handing them over to the grinning official. I gave the Marine the office number and, five minutes later, the American Consul called me back.

Within an hour, the U.S. diplomats arrived in force. The Pakistani officials were noticeably shocked at the response, since none of the Third World governments had ever reacted with such vehemence. One nervous official asked me why I hadn't told them how famous I was, thinking only a celebrity would warrant such a reaction.

The adjoining hallway suddenly was awash with Pakistani

bureaucrats, and I was ushered out to speak to the American delegation. One man from the Drug Enforcement Agency asked all the questions. He was a towering man with a Texas accent, and his presence intimidated the Pakistanis. But his concern toward me was not to gain my release, only the possibility that I might be smuggling drugs.

After he heard my story, confident there were no drugs involved, he turned his attention to the Pakistani bureaucrats with specific questions about the other detainees. At length, the Texan set his briefcase on the ground and opened it up. A phone attached to a small wire folded out like a children's pop-up book while he grabbed the adjoining receiver and spoke the simple words, "Everything's all right here." Then he folded up his briefcase and left, taking most of the American contingent with him.

The three delegates left to defend me became surrounded by Pakistani officials after the departure of the Texan. The Pakistanis allowed only one of the three American delegates inside to negotiate my release, and I later felt grateful that person turned out to be Vice-consul Howard Banks. Mr. Banks, as I learned, was not a professional politician, not a man there to further his career or agenda. He was a man who saw another man in need, and I believe he would have changed places with me if he possessed the power. Mr. Banks negotiated not only with enthusiasm, but with a stark honesty and straightforwardness uncommon in diplomatic circles. He asked questions that conveyed a basic concern for the rights of a human being, regardless of social or political status.

Throughout the course of the negotiation, Mr. Banks was alone, surrounded by at least a dozen lingering Pakistani higher-ups. He was armed with nothing but his wits. He explained to me that he wielded no real power, only the hope of conversation. Somehow I admired that. Just as I had negotiated the sands of the Sahara alone, I felt that he was now negotiating the desert of Pakistan's political system alone, and stoically.

While the dealings progressed, I was continuously summoned to the office, then returned to the detention area to face questions from over a dozen detainees, all of whom saw me as some sort of symbol—one person who could defeat the system for the honor of all. The embassy sent a man in with food, two boxes of cookies, which I gave to the other refugees.

The detainees grew restless. While I was bounced back and forth to the immigration office, they began to cheer, catcall and shout for my release. In an attempt to keep them quiet, a cart of food was wheeled into the detention room while I was answering questions in the immigration office. One of the Pakistani officials ordered me to calm the refugees down.

My attempts produced the opposite effect. In an act of bravado and self-sacrifice, the refugees marched out of the room, arms folded across their chests. They were staging a hunger strike until I was released. The display was in full view of the embassy officials. It was the first time I saw my Pakistani captors sweat. Banks, seeing the political advantage of the moment, demanded that I be flown back to the United States at the expense of the Pakistani government. It was they, he argued, who allowed me to board without a visa in Amman; therefore, it was their responsibility to fly me back.

I was both shocked and horrified when the Pakistanis began to acquiesce. I did not want to return to the States, or be flown back to Jordan, where I would face the same roadblocks that had landed me in Karachi in the first place.

"Wait," I said, well aware of the fact that I was about to ruin the present advantage. A world map dominated the wall behind the fat man's desk. I glanced at it to see where the closest airport was outside of Pakistan.

"Fly me to Bombay," I said on a whim." I'll pay for the ticket."

After several more hours of negotiation, it was decided I would be given into the custody of the U.S. Embassy under the condition that I would be flown out of Pakistan within three days. I collected my scattered gear from the other refugees with a promise I'd do everything within my power to get them out. Some of them handed me letters to post. Others gave me a telephone number to call. I would at least be able to establish contacts for them outside the cloistered detention area, as well as relay the valuable office phone number.

A Range Rover with U.S. government insignias took me to the Holiday Inn, where I was expected to remain until the embassy could arrange for my Indian visa and plane ticket. Since I still possessed no Pakistani visa, I was not allowed to leave the Holiday Inn located next to the consulate. I was also expected to pay $200 a night for the room, an expense well beyond my means. But Mr. Banks, in another display of diplomatic genius, introduced me as "the famous American cyclist," a celebrity worthy of consular rates. I was charged fifty dollars for the room and my bicycle was gingerly placed behind the front desk, where it was guarded with pride.

Over the next few days, I was subjected to the most disorienting display of wealth and decadence in memory. Here was a cultural reality beyond my recent experience. One day earlier I had slept with refugees who were using cardboard boxes for beds and begging for food. The next day, I ate in the hotel café, alongside men in business suits and hotel guests complaining about cold food. Next to the café stood two restaurants which served delicacies that I hadn't seen since leaving America: steaks, salad, lobster, fine wines. Two floors above, next to a luxuriously ornamented whirlpool and sauna room, lurked an indoor swimming pool where the elite of the world romped and played.

As usual, my mode of travel helped me adapt to the environment. Even though I walked around in tattered clothes that blended uneasily with the business dress of the rest of the clientele, I was not looked upon as a troublesome vagrant, but as an eccentric celebrity. Papillon attracted a good deal of attention in full view behind the desk, and it seemed as if everyone in the hotel knew of "the famous American cyclist."

My growing notoriety was at a peak my second morning in the hotel. I awoke to a knock at the door. I opened to find the hotel manager and a smartly dressed public relations man.

"Mr. Scott?" the manager asked.

"Yes."

"Famous American cyclist?"

"Uh, y-yes."

"Please, there is a photographer downstairs who would like to take your photograph."

Mr. Banks was called from the embassy and the four of us posed with Papillon. Banks could hardly contain his laughter over how his money-saving introduction had escalated. He seemed to derive great satisfaction in causing me to burst into laughter by making comments through the side of his mouth as we stood rigid, facing the camera.

Banks was beside himself when the photographer asked me how many medals I'd won—information for the article. The story would appear in five major newspapers and magazines.

The following evening, my last in Karachi, Howard and his wife treated me to dinner at the consular restaurant, a place set up specifically for overseas American diplomats. The menu was completely American, a commodity Banks thought I'd appreciate before entering the starving lands of Asia. The dinner was in part to celebrate the bizarre meeting of two Americans so far from their home, and in part to acknowledge a letter I had written praising the American officials in Karachi.

"The letter was sent all the way to the top," Banks said. "Usually, all we get are negative comments."

In the morning, I was escorted to the embassy to pick up my passport and visa. I found that, there too, I was looked upon as a kind of celebrity. "The cyclist from the airport," was all the explanation necessary. Everyone already knew the details.

Banks showed me what he described as "your file." Inside was a copy of my passport, a copy of the letter thanking the embassy officials, a report detailing my detention, and a letter I had written on behalf of the other refugees. There was also a fax from London which had arrived after I was released from detention. It was from British Foreign Affairs and read: "An English national traveling from Karachi has informed us of an American detained at Karachi airport . . ."

On the document, the word URGENT was marked in large red letters. I remembered the Englishman referred to in the report. Of all the people I had slipped notes to, he seemed the most appalled at my predicament and promised repeatedly that he would report my dire circumstances to the proper officials.

We made the rounds at the embassy, where I was constantly applauded as some sort of modern-day American hero. Howard drove me to the airport where it was his duty to be sure I left Pakistan. We exchanged addresses and he promised to send me the newspapers when the articles appeared.

Somewhere over the Arabian Sea, while the plane careened toward Bombay and cast its shadow across the cresting waves below, I reflected upon the international camaraderie that helped me jump over hurdle after hurdle. The judge in Syria, the Venezuelan Miguel, Howard Banks—all sent to me as if by divine intervention.

I savored my considerable good fortune, praying the trend would last, while the plane slowly descended toward India.

9

India

I SHUFFLED through the crowded Bombay airport, a dozen thoughts flashing through my mind. I would have to begin my education in one of the worst places in any country—a popular point of entry. The prospective guides, hotel touts, and money changers all knew what the phrase "fresh off the boat" meant. For them it meant easy money from wealthy Westerners. For me it meant finding my way around the city with no concept of proper price, cultural norms, or a word of Hindi in my vocabulary. Other than the vague concept of "east," I didn't even know where I wanted to go.

I looked beyond the glass doors of the protected airport lobby, and my worst fears were realized. In the parking lot, Western tourists were being mobbed by groups of money changers, taxi drivers and desperate guides, all wrapped in a shroud of poverty beyond anything I had yet seen. And there were hundreds of them. To compound my difficulties, customs had let the air out of Papillon's tires in search of drugs, and one of the tire rims had been damaged on the plane. How would I, beleaguered by a lame bicycle, possibly be able to get away from the airport without losing half my gear?

Before pushing through the glass doors, I battened down my panniers, making sure nothing was loose or detachable. Two feet beyond the doors, my neon-yellow bicycle attracted every onlooker within a hundred yards.

Nimble hands rifled through my panniers to a chorus of, "Guidemeestir! Taximeestir! Change money sahib!"

111

I bounced around the crowd before noticing a small opening back through the glass doors. I pushed through the mob, then continued straight past the glass doors and back into the airport. The crowd was stopped at the threshold by airport security.

There had to be a better way. At least if I could acquire a map or directions to a cheap hotel, it might be possible to hire a taxi and make a quick getaway. I went to the tourist information booth I'd passed my first trip through the airport and asked about directions to an affordable hotel.

"Oh, we can find you very cheap hotel, sahib," the man behind the counter said. "No need for directions. They will send a car to pick you up."

"That doesn't sound like it will be cheap to me." My concept of cheap and most Western travelers' concept of the word were two very different ideas.

"Look," the dark-skinned man said as he produced a catalog listing perhaps 100 hotels. "There are many hotels here. We can find you one." He flipped through the pages. "How about this one? On the beach, indoor pool–"

"How much?" I interrupted, knowing the place would be beyond my means.

"One hundred dollars."

"Too much."

"This one then, fifty dollars."

"I want to pay in rupees." I knew from past experience that any hotel displaying its rates in dollars was usually out of my price range.

"How much do you want to pay?"

"Two hundred rupees or less." At an exchange rate of forty rupees to the dollar, I could afford five dollars per night until I learned enough to hit the road again. If India was anything like the other countries, five dollars was an exclusive enough price to ensure that I would be among native professionals and backpack-type tourists.

"Two hundred rupees—let's see." The persistent tourism official quickly flipped to the back of the book. "The farther you get from the beach, the less the price. You don't care about beach?"

"I don't care about beach." I wondered how much of a beach could exist in this swarm of humanity anyway.

"Ah, here's one. One hundred seventy-five rupees . . . pool . . . outdoor bar . . . covered patio."

I glanced at the picture in the catalog. It seemed too picturesque for the price.

"They'll send a car?"

"Sure. They will come right to this booth and get you."

That would solve the gauntlet problem, at least. "I'll take it."

The hotel sent a Suburban, and I was escorted past the disappointed mob. At the last minute, two persistent guides grabbed the bicycle from my grip, quickly threw it through the open back hatch of the Suburban, then promptly demanded money for their services. I could see India was going to be a test of patience.

The hotel was exactly like the picture in the catalog. An external patio provided shade next to the pool, with an outdoor bar beneath a thatched awning, giving the entire scene a Caribbean aura. Surprisingly, I was the sole resident. Perhaps I had found a place too expensive for the locals yet not exclusive enough for Western tourists. I decided to stay three days, while making short trips into the city in pursuit of my Indian education. I needed maps. I needed a rudimentary Hindi vocabulary, and, most important, I needed a plan. Blindly heading east would eventually put me up against the borders of inaccessible Myanmar, or the forbidden underbelly of Tibet. A few days of research seemed inescapable.

DECEMBER 12
Bombay

SINCE MY CHIEF TASK was to find maps, my first foray into Bombay was in search of India's tourist bureau. Cycling through Bombay proved to be a difficult task, revealing mass poverty coupled with overpopulation. The streets were narrower than those in the States, with myriad converging alleys, paths and walkways. Vehicles traveled in all directions, as if someone had taken them up in a huge dice shaker and spilled them randomly into the square. The motorists drove as if they held a total disdain for any living creature, with the exception of Brahman cattle, and a few of those sacred animals rambled through the streets, passing naked children squatting in ditches alongside the road. Cyclists wove their way through the chaos. Hundreds of them, and as many rickshaws. Car horns blared as if they were new toys in the hands of children on Christmas day. Finally, there was me, one tender-footed Westerner with virgin Western ears.

Five miles of cycling through the city and its chaos brought me to the tourist bureau. I told them of my plans to cycle across India. They gave me a few brochures about the Taj Mahal, then sent me to the West India Auto Association, where my plan was greeted with enthusiasm. The Auto Association equipped me with detailed road maps, a route plan from Bombay to Calcutta, road information by the kilometer, town locations, city maps, ascents, descents, hotels, and more. It was the most detailed information I'd received of any country, including America. The accuracy of the maps however, and my own ability to stay true to the route plan throughout India, remained to be tested.

During my time in Bombay, I learned the beggars' routines, proper prices, and a few words of Hindi, until my preparations to leave Bombay were complete. I checked out of the hotel while an English couple who had arrived the previous day were leaving with luggage in tow. They had just flown in from England and I assumed they were on their way to Agra or Delhi or some similar tourist destination.

"What's next on your agenda?" I asked.

"We're going back to the airport," the girl said, tensing her face. "We're flying back home. This place is disgusting."

"You can't judge all of India solely by what you see in Bombay."

"We're going home!" the boyfriend shouted. "These people are all thieves. They charged us a hundred dollars for a taxi ride from the airport. By the time we realized the value of a rupee, it was too late. Naked children. People shitting in the streets. My God, it's terrible."

I thought about suggesting a hotel closer to the beach, but decided against it.

"Good luck," he told me, "but you'll never make it across India on that bicycle." And, as if to accentuate his point, he added, "Never."

DECEMBER 13
Ghoti, India

I WAS FINALLY traveling east again, and to celebrate the rewards of cycling, India's scenery rolled open before me. Banyan trees interlaced their warped branches throughout the dust and scrub beyond the road, like vigilant sentries guarding the mysterious lands to come. Green river valleys and rolling hills were interspersed with rice paddies and small clusters of grass huts. Half-clothed farmers in drab, earth-worn dhotis, legs covered to the knees in rice paddies, carried collections of pots, crops, and livestock on their heads. They stopped from their duties to stare when I sped by in an attempt to avoid the usual crowd of onlookers.

Domestic buffalo wandered at will across the green fields or plodded knee-deep through the rice paddies. Some carried loads of grass so enormous that the lumbering animals looked like magical moving piles of hay, the beast itself totally hidden by the load. Others pulled carts or plows, and still others roamed carefree through the streets. In one village, I came upon a naked child squatting in the middle of the street while molding a pile of buffalo dung—India's version of Play Dough.

The food, I found, was not as varied as the scenery. The places that catered to passing travelers, the *dhabas*, consisted of an open fire pit. That was it, no chairs, no tables, no forks or knives. At all the dhabas I experienced, the selection was simple: *dahl* and rice. After three days in India, my taste for dahl had already deserted me. The dish is comprised of lentils in a gluey sauce the consistency of pea soup, and is eaten by mixing the dahl with rice then rolling the conglomeration into sticky, pea-soup rice balls. As a way to alleviate the monotony of eating the same thing every day, the Indians had developed a hundred ways to spice the dish. My routine became green, spicy dahl for breakfast, yellow, caustic dahl for lunch, and the acidic brown variety for dinner.

The dhabas that cranked out dahl like a factory assembly line were not restaurants as thought of in America. Some consisted of nothing but wooden boxes made of rotted wood, with room for one cross-legged cook and a small fire. Patrons walked up to the open end of the box, paid five rupees for their dahl, then squatted on the ground while they ate. Some dhabas were more elaborate, made of mud bricks with a hay roof and enough space inside for a dozen squatting patrons. Some used clay ovens—others, open fires.

The highest scale dhabas were larger, made of wood, and provided several *charpoys* out front. These body-length rope beds were simply constructed, with four small tree trunks nailed into a rectangle supported by four short legs. Rope was crisscrossed inside the rectangle to produce a hammock-like cot. The charpoys functioned as tables, chairs, and cots for the transient clientele. At night, they were rented as beds to passing travelers.

The man who cooked the food at the dhaba, and in essence ran the place, was the *chowkidar*. He was usually dressed in pajamas and covered with dirt, fire soot, and cow dung from the dried cow-dung patties used as fuel for the fire. My impression was the word *chowkidar* meant "manager" or "caretaker," since it was used to describe the people who ran the low-rate hotels as well. Those who ran the higher-class hotels, such as my five-dollar hotel in Bombay, used the English word, "manager."

Smaller villages usually offered a quiet dhaba, but buying supplies in some of the larger towns became a frustrating ritual. The crowds at the roadside dhabas were so oppressive that I found it easier to pack away whatever food was available, then eat later, at my own convenience. At each town, my Western features and neon bicycle attracted every curious villager like a magnet, so I was forced to stock up quickly and leave before I became smothered. In the town of Ghoti, I stayed too long. I walked along a row of outdoor food stalls and the crowd grew like a rolling snowball.

I was soon hemmed in by a swarm of humanity, unable to escape, unable to move, barely able to breathe. Questions in Hindi were shouted in my direction until the mingling shrieks turned into one loud wail. Barging my way toward the edge, the crowd followed along, leaving me always at its center. The mob swelled to well over 100 while more and more townsfolk entered the milieu. I felt like a monkey in a cage, forced to suffer the stares of curious zoo patrons.

A shout of English rose above the din as a translator forced his way through the swarm. Unable to reach me, he was left flailing his arms in the air and screaming from ten rows away.

"The mayor," I thought I heard him scream." The mayor requests you join him for tea." He turned to the throng and announced in Hindi what must have been something like, "The Mayor will have tea with the monkey." His statement was followed by a huge cheer from the multitudes.

Helpless, I was swept off by the villagers toward the mayor's house. Once there, I was shoved hand to hand onto the porch, where the mayor sat sipping his *chai*. It soon became obvious the mayor spoke not one word of English, nor did he harbor any concern for my well-being or curiosity about my trip, my intellect, my existence. The invitation by the mayor was an underhanded technique to raise himself up in the eyes of his townspeople. It was his way of saying: "Look at me, my subjects. I am important enough to have tea with the white man, and you, simple townsfolk, are not."

My theory was supported by the fact that we remained on the porch, as a spectacle to the others, rather than retreating inside to the relative peace and quiet of the house. If before I felt like a monkey in a cage, now I felt like a monkey dancing to music, and the mayor was the organ grinder.

The crowd of spectators grew even larger while I drank my chai. After all, where could I go? Vendors began selling tea to the onlookers. Eventually all the kiosk owners were there, peddling their wares to what must have been the entire population of the town. I scanned the fringes of the audience watching for someone, anyone, to leave. Some did leave, only to return with half a dozen friends and family members. I began to suspect that people from neighboring towns were arriving. I was the equivalent of the World Series, and the vendors were hawking their version of popcorn and peanuts.

Endless glasses of chai passed my lips before the mayor stood up and began what promised to be a long-winded speech. This was my chance. While the mayor focused the crowd's attention, I grabbed Papillon, drove through the thinnest part of the milieu toward the back of the house, then cycled down the main street in an all-out sprint. Behind me, a swarm of brown bodies clamored for bicycles when they realized their entertainment had escaped. A fleet of bicycles sped after me, through the town and along the thin dirt road beyond. Thanks to the design of the Indian bicycle, combined with the cycling technique of the average Indian, the villagers were able to keep me in sight for less than a kilometer before I disappeared over the rolling hills. The one-speed Hero bicycles proved no match for Papillon's twenty-one gears.

DECEMBER 15

20 km north of Nashik, India

THE INCIDENT with the mayor prompted me to take a detour off the main thoroughfare and head into the wilds of central India, hoping that the population would become less dense. The map I had acquired from the tourist bureau in Bombay listed all the national parks in India by representing their locations with an icon. Parks known for tigers were depicted by a tiger's head; those known for wild elephants, an elephant's head, and so on. I planned my route across India by intersecting as many of these icons as possible, thus avoiding population and increasing my exposure to nature, campsite availability, and peace of mind.

As if to support my decision, I was blessed with a peaceful campsite set on the banks of the Godavari River where I bathed before nightfall. But even remote areas of India supported people. I awoke late the following morning to find the villagers gaping at the blue dome, my tent, which had sprouted in their field during the night.

I had encountered the same problem in the past when a village was close by. As a result, I developed the habit of getting up before sunrise to avoid the curiosity. But I was too late at the Godavari campsite. The crowd watched me in silence, like the audience at a matinee, while I performed all my morning duties. They watched me urinate next to a tree. Relieve my diarrhea behind a mound of hay. Roll up my sleeping bag. Brush my teeth. Pack my tent. When I tried to talk to them, they opened their eyes wider and dropped their jaws, as if their entertainment had begun a tap dance.

I made my escape into the town of Nashik, a town that implanted itself in my memory as a mass of trucks, cows, children, bicycles, and humanity, with a few bleating goats adding their cries to the milieu. Children sat naked along the dusty road, naively unaware of the perpetual traffic jam they created with the assistance of a few wandering farm and jungle animals. Broken down trucks stood along the road, surrounded by mopeds, cars, bicycles, whose owners saw fit to make repairs on the main thoroughfare rather than push the vehicle off to the side. One truck driver had scattered the pieces of his dismantled engine from one side of the road to the other. I hoped, by making my way toward the tiger icon on my map, that scenes like the town of Nashik would become less frequent.

DECEMBER 22
Ajanta, India

THE LANDSCAPE became increasingly forested, and I chose ever more lonely side roads in my progress east. Unfortunately, leaving behind the truck drivers meant leaving behind the places where they ate, so I made due late in the day with the only roadside shack available. The dhaba itself was much the same as many of the others I'd seen, but surprisingly, the food was more varied and abundant. I sat down on one of the rope charpoys used as a table during the day. The leather-skinned chowkidar laid a board across the frame to serve as a tray, then he shuttled out five separate dishes. I was given potatoes in hot mustard and the inescapable dahl and rice, as well as *roti*, a thin, tortilla-like bread. Mutton stew came later, and a mixture of nuts with names to confound any Westerner's memory. Throughout the meal the chowkidar continuously refilled the dishes, which gave me the rare chance to satiate my hunger, but also gave the curious locals time to swell into a mob. While the swarm of onlookers became increasingly unbearable, I resorted to watching the only mammal that didn't stare back: the chowkidar's pet pig, which was chained to a nearby tree.

The villagers formed a circle around me when I paid for the meal. I ran down the street and ducked into a tea house to escape the scene—much to the chagrin of the tea house owner, since my entourage had no qualms about following me inside. I asked for a package of biscuits amidst echoes from the forty or so people who had surrounded me. The owner was so taken aback by the mob, chanting "biscuits, biscuits," that he tossed the biscuits to me over the throng and motioned for me to leave before I could pay. I beat a hasty retreat out of town, and the Indians clamored for their Hero bicycles.

I cycled on with a line of cyclists trailing after me like a bending serpent.

"Biscuits! Biscuits!" the chant rose from behind. The riders dropped to a dozen—then ten—then eight—while I picked up the pace into a set of rolling hills two kilometers east of town. The chant grew fainter, until I was alone on the road once again.

A rugged thirty kilometers through semi-jungle followed my encounter with the mob. I neared central Maharashtra, and the landscape was transformed from sparse patches of forest to a thicker, more dense jungle. Parrots fluttered through the canopy overhead when I cycled beneath their treetop perches. Black-faced macaques showed themselves for a brief glimpse. An animal I did not recognize, a lynx or a small mountain lion, scampered through the undergrowth.

A sculpted cliff extending the length of the horizon opened up from the forest. My tourist information from the travel bureau listed this landmark as Ajanta, a series of rock-hewn caves constructed by Jains and Buddhists over a period of centuries, only to be abandoned and lost to the memory of civilization. According to my brochure, an English hunting party re-discovered the forgotten caves in 1943 while tracking tigers. It was a vision the explorers must have marveled at when the land was pristine.

Today, a broken-down hotel run by the local government stands next to the caves, like a collection of slums rotting next to a priceless palace. No tourist was foolish enough to stay in the hotel, which my travel guide described as having "feces flowing out of the bathroom onto the floor." No one, that is, except for me. Since Ajanta was a one-day stop for the tourist bus, most people moved on to the finer hotels of Aurangabad, but as a bicycle traveler, I did not have the luxury of traversing 100 kilometers for a place to sleep.

Evening came to Ajanta, and a soothing transformation enveloped the atmosphere. The tourists left on their buses; the small kiosks which served them were buttoned up one by one. The shopkeepers moved on to nearby villages. The hotel remained empty except for me, one chowkidar, and a staff of one small boy. Darkness crept through our tiny piece of jungle, and the boy began closing heavy wooden shutters over the windows as if to shut out some powerful and lingering threat.

Settling in with my candlelit book, I was overcome with a pervasive feeling of aloneness. Not loneliness, for it wasn't an uneasy feeling, but a secure one. The sound of parakeets and peacocks seeped through the wooden shutters, rising over the chatter of macaques resting in a cluster of trees outside my window. I felt a peaceful sense of belonging. The jungle was not a threat, but a comfort. I put my book aside and listened, awash in a serenity of mind and spirit that eased any cycling worries. From the soothing calm of my isolated piece of jungle, all past hardships seemed to fade into insignificance.

DECEMBER 25
Chagaon, India

THE DAYS out of Ajanta brought me through Maharashtra and close to the southern border of Madhya Pradesh. Although I cycled into gradually less populated areas, mobs still pestered me as I passed through the occasional village. One of my lesser concerns was the fact that Christmas was almost at hand. Considering the poverty of the area, my celebration would once again be a somber one, with dreaded dahl playing no insignificant role.

I reached the village of Chagaon on Christmas Day, expecting to stock up with roti then cycle into the jungle to set up camp. A wide, rectangular building, like a toppled tombstone, stood at the end of the road where the warped branches of banyan trees signaled the town's eastern edge. I thought the squat structure might be a hotel, but a hotel in such a remote area was a desperate hope.

Inside, a clerk behind the counter assured me that I had indeed found a hotel, built in their small village to serve the pilgrims arriving at the nearby temple, which was one in a series of holy pilgrimage sites throughout India. Of course, according to the clerk, only the rich could afford their rates. Most of those undertaking the pilgrimage slept by the roadside, or on a dhaba charpoy for two rupees.

I bought a five-dollar travel respite by reserving a room in the hotel for a night. The ground floor held a surprisingly elaborate dining room which, although I was the only resident of the hotel, the clerk assured me would be serving dinner. My room set, I went into town to prepare for what I hoped would be a rare holiday meal.

The town's main strip seemed like a cross between the American old west and the simple economy of Asia. A dirt road bisected clusters of small huts and shops, ending abruptly at the edge of town to leave a receding landscape of rolling plains and broken forest.

The stores were nothing but wooden boxes connected side by side and open at the end facing the street. Every town had a box devoted exclusively to betel nut, the palm nut chewed by a tenth of the Indian population that produces the often-seen red lips, red spittle, and red-toothed smile. Some cubicles carried the chewy delicacy known as *paan*, a combination of various nuts and candy rolled in a betel leaf. The rest of the shops were similar, each selling only one item. There was the cigarette box. The rum box. The chai box. There was the battery box. The rusty nail box. The bicycle parts box peddled old, rusted and worn Hero bike parts. There was the sandal box, and the pajama robe box. There were boxes that seemed to sell nothing but wrinkled paper bags and worn, crinkled photos of the local temple.

The hair-cut box was like all those I'd seen since Bombay, a three-sided room big enough to hold one chair and a barber, with the open side facing the street. The shop was set beside the other stores along the town's main strip and looked little different from the paan shop down the way, or the betel nut and cigarette kiosks next door.

With my thumb and forefinger, I showed the barber the length I desired then went through my usual mime act while he cut my hair. Soon, the entire village gathered in the street around the open end of the shop to watch an American get his hair cut. It wasn't long before the barber gathered a hint of what my life was like in India.

Since I had already conveyed the details of my trip to the barber, I relied on him to relay my story to the curious crowd which had completely blocked the side of the shop and overflowed into the street. At first the barber was polite with his replies, but after he heard the same question a dozen times, he became more and more irritable, until finally he was screaming one word answers, then dismissing the questions outright. Eventually, he was left pleading with the crowd to leave his shop.

I arrived back at the hotel just as the restaurant was opening for dinner. Much to my relief, the villagers did not follow me from the barber shop. I sat down in the deserted dining room and attempted to mime the following question to the waiter, put as simply as possible: "If you were to have a feast on a special occasion, what would you eat?" The waiter had a complete lack of understanding. It seemed the date December 25th conveyed little meaning in this Hindu society.

I tried again, using the Hindi for "to eat." "You," pointing at him, "khana," pointing at the menu.

No success.

Another man was brought to my table. Through a combination of Hindi, English, and mime, the same question was posed. Still no.

Another man—no.

A short, bald man who spoke English arrived on the scene. With his coarse voice, he explained that he was the head man, and seemed amenable to the idea of planning my menu. In fact, after the request was translated to the others, they all seemed interested by the project. The cook was called to my table where he—along with the head man, waiter, and manager—began a heated debate over the composition of my Christmas dinner. While the discussion progressed, the head man would occasionally break from the group to ask me a technical question. "Do you like chicken? Spice? Do you want soup?"

Another cook came out of the kitchen to join the conversation. Even though they did not understand the purpose of my feast, they nevertheless attacked the problem with a religious fervor.

In time the decisions were over; the menu was constructed. After a few minutes my drink was served, a glass of chai in the absence of wine. The food came soon after and was served in waves: roasted mutton, chicken masala, pickled mango, vegetables and curry. The tide of food overburdened my small table, overwhelmed my senses, washing over my tongue, my teeth, my mind. Another glass of chai was delivered. Someone found a bottle of wine, a miraculous discovery I was told. The television set was turned on and I invited the staff to join the meal. Thoughts of dahl and roti and camps in the jungle were but distant daydreams.

Ultimately, the food stopped flowing and my dinner came to an end. I sat, watching music videos from Bombay, with a drum-tight belly and a comforting feeling of satiation.

In the dim light of the dining room, the head man walked over to me with a grim look on his face. I felt sure the issue of payment was about to be discussed. He bent down as a father would in explaining something to a child, then offered me his hand. "Good Christmas, Sah!" he said, with a sincerity that accompanies matters of religion. He shook my hand, smiled, then left me to reflect upon a holiday in which he was the outsider. He had known the meaning of the feast all along, and he had helped provide the most unique celebration I could have imagined.

DECEMBER 26
Anjangaon, India

ALTHOUGH I LEFT CHAGAON early in the morning, I was able to make only sixty kilometers by nightfall. The surrounding jungle became more dense with my eastward progress, and the road became increasingly difficult to negotiate. By midday the road had deteriorated into a barren track comprised of two thin, tan ruts compacted by intermittent oxen traffic.

But the track was the only thing barren in the landscape. The road bent over every curvature in the terrain, becoming obscured by a tangled forest of brown trunks that rose into the thick overhead canopy. On either side of the path, sparse vegetation lost itself to areas of dense jungle, where patches of sunlight intervened to bathe a valley of undergrowth.

The trees themselves were new to an American's senses. Some, the most intriguing, showed twenty feet of straight trunk before their warped and weaving branches sprawled out sideways at first, then toward the ground, the sky, and back. Many of the first branches were leafless, but at the top, where sunlight illuminated a green canopy, the trees became more alive. Other varieties looked like flowers in the jungle, beginning with a ten-foot stem only to produce a perfectly round, green bloom at the top, like a dandelion in full seed.

I set camp in a clearing next to a choked stream, full and turgid, pressed by the surrounding jungle. My campsite was surrounded by wildflowers of all colors, with a banyan tree at the far edge. At the base of the banyan, enormous roots warped themselves into the detritus around a tepee-shaped gap.

I laid my sleeping bag against the roots of the banyan and scanned the surrounding jungle. Macaques swung and chattered in the tree tops, and birds—red, green, orange, with trailing feathers—perched and gathered around my small clearing. Just before I fell asleep next to my campfire, a group of hyenas trotted out of the trees to entertain while they dodged the light from dying embers.

JANUARY 1
jungle road, India

I AWOKE thirty kilometers away from the nearest chai house. When

124

I finally accomplished the distance, the crowd became so suffocating that I drank my tea while walking in circles to evade the entourage, who by then had formed a processionary circle behind me. These mobs were especially difficult to take in the early hours of the morning, before my wits were bolstered by a few cups of tea.

I moved farther into central India, and the towns disappeared, leaving nothing but jungle in my path. Only small clusters of huts existed, and I was hard pressed to find the food I needed for a day's ride.

My map showed a village a few days to the east by the name of Kanha. Next to the village, a tiger head was imprinted on the map, along with the letter "T" to indicate a tourist attraction. I decided to make a detour to Kanha in the hope it was a wildlife preserve catering to tourists where I could find food and rest in comfort for a few days.

My immediate concern was finding enough food to get me to Kanha. The previous day I had eaten only three sugar balls given to me from a dirty glass jar off an old man's dusty shelf. The man insisted there was no food in his three-hut village and I believed him—at least none he could afford to give away. Cycling on, I stopped at a group of shacks. Across the road stood a relatively large wooden building which seemed strangely out of place in comparison to the mud huts and surrounding jungle. I peered through the door of one of the huts in search of food, when a man came out of the building across the road.

"Hey, you there!" he called out in English. "You there! Do you speak English? Come over here!"

He seemed unduly excited. When I walked over to him, I discovered why. He was the doctor he said. Not just *a* doctor but *the* doctor—the doctor for the entire region. I had stumbled upon his home base, located in the village solely because it was the geographic center of his region.

"You are the first English speaker I have seen in months!" he said gleefully. "And the first foreigner ever in this village."

"Ever?"

"Since I've been here—five years. And I've asked the locals; they've never seen a foreigner in their lives."

The doctor brought me some food, and we talked on the front

steps. My need for an English-speaking companion was as great as his, especially one who traveled widely and knew the area.

"This is a very poor area," the doctor told me while we ate." Poorest in India. I am the only doctor to serve all these people. The poverty is bad enough, but the geography makes it even harder to do my job. Villages are spread throughout the jungle. Sometimes it takes days to reach a certain area."

"Do you see many diseases?"

"Oh yes. Mostly malaria, snake bites, parasites, and I do treat my share of rare diseases."

"What should I do if I get bit by a cobra?" I thought I knew the answer to this but it seemed prudent to get an expert's opinion.

"There's not much you can do if you're alone. A tourniquet is about it. Unless you have antivenin, of course. What are you taking for malaria?"

"Nothing."

"Well, it's not really the season yet but I'll give you some prophylactic medication. You'll need it eventually."

Before I left, the doctor filled my bags with various medicines and gave me some roti to pack away. "You won't find much extra food in this area," he cautioned.

JANUARY 2
jungle road, India

THE ROAD EASTWARD through the jungle was nothing more than a dirt track, with lesser trails periodically forking off into a tangle of thickets and trees. I was following what I thought to be the main track, but at times it was difficult to tell whether I was on the right path toward Kanha or if I had taken an inadvertent detour.

Around midday I came upon a woman carrying a basket on her head. She was walking down the path with her back turned to me. In need of directions, I cycled up behind her and asked, in Hindi, "Is this the road to Kanha?" The woman took one look at me and my yellow bicycle, dropped her basket, and raced off into the jungle shrieking in fear.

Later in the day food took priority over directions. Arriving at a group of shacks, I asked for "khana," hoping to find some food.

The man pointed down the road and stated proudly, "One hundred kilometers."

It was then I realized the surprising similarity in the pronunciation of khana, to eat—and Kanha, the village. There was obviously some subtle pronunciation difference hidden to the Western ear.

"No, no," I said, trying again with my hand to my mouth, "khana, khana."

"Ha-gee. Kanha. One hundred kilometers."

"Nahin, nahin, khana, khana, khana." I tried a variety of pronunciations.

The man scratched his head and said, by then quite unsure of himself, "One hundred kilometers?"

"Dahl?"

The man gave me some roti and I went on my way, confident, at least, that I was on the correct road to the village.

I found no food the remainder of the day, which forced me to cycle past nightfall in the blind hope of finding something to eat. At night the jungle gave off a blackness unlike anything exuded by plains or mountains, for the jungle allowed no moonlight, no starlight to reach its floor. It became my belief that the jungle oozed blackness out of its own being, out of the collective essence of the trees, the leaves, the branches. A dimly lit wooden hut became apparent, casting an orange gloom on the surrounding trees. Inside, three men lurked in the shadows. One man, tilting on a wooden stool with his back against the wall, brandished a rifle.

"Dahl? Khana?" I pleaded toward the dark innards of the hut.

"Move on," said the man with the rifle, in English.

"All I want is something to eat."

"Move on!" the man said, with more of an "or else" tone.

The three were some of the Naxalites I had been warned about, a terrorist organization operating out of the jungles of northwest and central India. I decided it would be prudent to move on.

An hour later I came upon another single hut, this one brightly lit by a roaring fire set inside an outdoor cooking hearth. At my request, the man heated up some rice. There was a charpoy out front which he offered for the night but I refused. The excessive attention and curious crowds of late caused me to crave privacy, and I intended to camp in the jungle after filling my empty belly.

I gave the chowkidar two rupees for the rice, then I moved down the road a few kilometers and trekked off the path into the jungle. The existence of the man's hut may have meant a village nearby and I didn't want to be awakened at first light by the multitudes admiring my tent. I set camp quickly, even in the dark. I had done it so many times I no longer needed my eyes. Within minutes I was sleeping easily inside my synthetic blue dome.

It seemed as if I had just fallen asleep when a loud cry jolted me awake. I sat up and listened in the darkness. Something was crashing toward me through the jungle. Brush and branches snapped like twigs. Whatever it was, it was big, larger than a man. The creature did not care what heard it coming. Ten feet from my tent, the sound stopped, and the night went silent again.

Was that breathing I heard? Suddenly, a spine-quivering wail shuddered the tent walls. A long, high pitched moan followed, infusing fear into the core of my imagination. That was the sound from a movie I once saw as a child. *The Legend of Boggy Creek* depicted a rampaging big foot that tore through a small town, killing several people before disappearing into the woods. The beast outside the thin walls of my tent was my childhood monster, with the same moan and the same night-shrouded anonymity.

The animal thrashed in the shadows, just beyond the embers of my dead fire, and with each bellow my tent walls shivered in tune with my spine. The creature came near, then slowly crashed off into the distance, its long, heavy footsteps becoming gradually more dim. Still, the departure of the beast gave me little solace. I remained awake half the night in child-like panic.

JANUARY 4
Kanha, India

I AWOKE EARLY from a sweat-ridden sleep then cycled eastward through a valley of trees and tangled undergrowth. Kanha came into view when the sun was just rising over a distant mountain range. A clearing opened up from the jungle revealing five low buildings made of red brick. The buildings encircled a central pavilion and a fire pit area, where backyard lounge chairs—some with umbrellas attached, some in the reclined position—suggested that vacationers were afoot. Black-faced macaques bounded along the brown tile roofs while, in an adjoining field, twenty or so spotted deer casually grazed amid the grass and wildflowers. No human beings were in sight.

I searched through the compound for signs of life, until three Indians in Western dress emerged from one of the buildings. They were engaged in conversation and didn't notice me at first. When I approached, they stopped in surprise.

"Where did you come from?" one asked.

"How did you get here?" another asked.

"I cycled here . . . with this," I said, pointing to Papillon.

"Cycled here? How long did it take?"

"Well . . . the last village I remember is Warúd, five days from here."

"Where did you sleep?" They all seemed horrified.

"I slept in my tent. In the jungle."

"Are you crazy?"

"What'ya mean?"

"Don't you realize you just cycled through miles of the Bengal tiger's habitat?"

When I saw the tiger head on my map, I had the idea they'd be in some kind of enclosure, or huge walled-in preserve. Once again I was looked upon as an eccentric celebrity due to the accomplishment which I attributed, rather than courage, to my own ignorance and wandering ways.

The three Indians occupying the camp were Pradeep Naravanee, a retired army captain from Delhi and the head of Kanha Camp; Raj Sankaran, a farmer and land owner from Haryana; and Vijay Venkatesh, an ex-construction worker and wanderer from Hyderabad. The three ran the camp with the help of one cook, one waiter and a boy who cleaned the rooms. Experts about the park and its wildlife, their job was mainly to drive the tourist-laden jeeps through the park while acting as guides and naturalists.

This information I gathered in the first fifteen minutes of conversation. They also admitted that the camp was not designed for individual tourists. Groups booked an entire tour in advance, their stay at Kanha Camp only a part of the overall package. After some discussion, the three decided to make an exception in my case. It was deemed unsafe to send me back out into the jungle, a fearful prospect now that my misconception about fences had been put to rest.

A price of 175 rupees per day for room and board was agreed upon and I was shown to one of the small, well-kept rooms, each equipped with a modern toilet and shower.

I had been searching for a place to stop and rest for a month, perhaps work. I wanted a secluded place, a relaxing place. Most of all, I wanted an inexpensive place. Kanha would have been the perfect candidate, but for a price of six dollars per day, I could only afford two days at the camp.

But even a short two days away from the rigors of cycling seemed to me like a small holiday. Since the next tour group wasn't due for another week, the park provided the perfect atmosphere to catch up on bike repairs and delve into one of the books I had traded for in Ajanta. The pavilion held a small library, including the book *Lord Jim* which I fantasized could be read in two days with a bit of luck and privacy.

My room arranged, I removed *Lord Jim* from the shelf and retreated to one of the lounge chairs surrounding the central fire pit. This was one of the few times I felt comfortable leaving the bicycle out in the open, unlocked. After all, who was around to steal it? And if they did, where would they go? A table was placed under the pavilion as I read, and the cook, Monish, began setting up for dinner. By evening, the steamer Patna had sunk and I was awash in chicken curry, relaxing at the dinner table alongside Raj, Pradeep and Vijay.

"We have three jeeps," Pradeep told me while we ate, the sounds of the jungle pressing in upon our well-lit pavilion. "When tourists are here we take them out twice a day; once from sunrise until noon, and again from four to dusk. No one is allowed into the park at night."

"How do you find the tigers?"

"Sometimes we get lucky and see one from the jeep," explained Raj, "but usually the elephants find them."

"Elephants?"

"There are elephants that roam the park. The mahouts track tigers and when they find one, the elephants surround it. The tiger won't move when it's surrounded. Then we drive the jeeps to the nearest track and the elephants pick us up and take us to the tiger."

Suddenly I was desperate to see a tiger, but I knew the price of a full-blown trip into the park was well beyond my meager financial means. Instead, I decided to satisfy myself with a few quiet days discovering Joseph Conrad.

After dinner, Raj built a fire in the central pit, while Vijay produced a bottle of Old Monk dark rum. By the time darkness had fallen, the moon was high overhead and conversation flowed liberally, oiled by the bottle of Old Monk. Tiger stories abounded. The time there were seven at once, all feeding on the same kill. The time there was one right across the river, feeding on a buffalo for two days.

"And this one Japanese bloke must have taken a thousand photographs!" Raj said, oblivious of the Japanese stereotype.

MY SECOND DAY in Kanha went much as the first. Monish, who insisted upon calling me "Sah," served me breakfast while I sat in a lounge chair watching the sun rise over twenty spotted deer grazing in a meadow of grass and wildflowers. Since tourists were a common fixture at the camp, the usual curiosity toward Papillon was somewhat diminished. I was left in peace with Joseph Conrad. By the time Lord Jim arrived at his jungle paradise of Patusan, the four of us were again sitting around the blazing fire, sipping from a fresh bottle of Old Monk. It was my last night at the camp. I would be forced to leave the following day due to lack of funds.

The campfire dialogue was subdued, a discussion in Hindi concerning Pradeep. I discerned the words for "leave" and "New Delhi," among others.

"Is Pradeep leaving?" I asked in English. As a courtesy, the three switched to English.

"I have to go to Delhi for a month," Pradeep told me. "My wife is having a baby and last time she had a miscarriage. There were complications." He stopped to take a sip of his rum and gaze into the fire. "She's nervous about it, and I want to be there for support."

He turned to Raj and Vijay. "Have you found anyone to drive the third jeep yet?"

They hadn't.

"All we need is a driver, remember," Pradeep explained. "We can have one of the park guides go along with him."

Then I heard myself say something through the fire's smoky haze and a rum-induced reality.

"I'll do it!" I said. "I'll drive the jeep."

They all stared at me for a time, until Pradeep asked, "You can stay a month?"

"I'll need room and board."

"Can you drive?"

"Of course."

There was a short discussion before Pradeep stood. "That's it then. Tomorrow I'll leave for Delhi."

With the last words in Hindi, I could barely comprehend what was happening. Within the space of a few minutes, I had secured a month in my own jungle hideaway, my Patusan.

JANUARY 14

Kanha, India

THE FOLLOWING MORNING, Pradeep boarded a train bound for Delhi and Vijay took one of the jeeps to greet the next batch of tourists at the nearest rail head, Mandla, a day's ride north of the park. Meanwhile, Raj and I drove into the park with the other jeep and began my education. Safety was the first lesson: never get out of the jeep. But I wondered how much protection the jeep offered if we were to encounter a tiger or one of the one-ton bison that roamed the forest. They were not the sturdy enclosed vehicles like modern Suburbans. They were more like old World War II issue, with no windows, no doors, and wide open sides.

"Don't worry," Raj assured me. "The tigers see us as one large animal when we're in a jeep. They won't attack an animal that large."

Throughout the following week I learned my way around Kanha, and how to track tigers with the help of pug marks, alarm calls and other methods. I learned the Hindi names of all the inhabitants of the 480,000-acre preserve. Barasingha, or swamp deer, were closer to the size of a moose than a deer. The much smaller spotted deer, known as chital, were the main prey of the park's tigers. The preserve also held massive Indian bison, as well as leopards, jungle cats and swamp bears. There were so many species of birds that even Raj didn't know all their names.

A tourist information center located in the middle of the park furthered my education. Inside were the usual pictures with descriptions of each jungle inhabitant, pieces of bone, discarded antlers and other artifacts. Buttons beside each animal's picture produced the corresponding mating and alarm calls. The alarm calls were important in tracking tigers since, when heard in the jungle, the sound meant a predator was nearby.

I walked around the center pushing buttons, learning the calls I hadn't yet identified in the park, until I came upon the swamp deer. A button was marked "mating call of the barasingha." I pressed it. Out came such a terrifying moan that I inadvertently took two steps back. It was my childhood bigfoot from Boggy Creek. I had been kept up that night camped in the jungle, petrified, by a deer.

BY THE END of my first week in Kanha, Vijay still hadn't returned with his batch of tourists, and the only animal I had yet to see remained the elusive tiger. Raj decided to take me into the park along with the cook, the waiter, and the room cleaner. "Whenever I take the staff, we see a tiger," he promised. "The staff is good luck!"

The sun dipped below the treetops when the five of us sped out into the jungle. Raj drove down the main dirt track then veered off toward prime tiger country. He took us past the barasingha swamp where the huge beasts stood, seaweed dangling from their antlers. We drove past the glowing silver pond, like a postcard, with leafless trees seeming like scaly old men dancing, their fingerless arms raised to the sky. We searched until the leaves of the sol trees turned golden in the half-light of dusk, until night was almost upon us; it was time to return. We left the park and entered the surrounding protected jungle known as the "buffer zone," an area I had cycled through on my way to Kanha Camp.

Suddenly, Raj slammed on the brakes as hushed, urgent Hindi rose from the staff in the back of the jeep. Standing before us, half on, half off the track, loomed a massive tiger. The majestic cat stood, frozen at the sight of us, with his head turned in our direction and his hindquarters planted, unseen, in the thick jungle undergrowth.

Raj inched the jeep forward, slowly, taking care not to scare the animal away. With our slow advance, the tiger hunched down, as if he were hiding from us there in the middle of the track.

Raj moved the jeep up, inch by inch until, at length, we were sitting beside the tiger. If I had stepped out of the open jeep, I could have touched the beast.

There seemed to be something basic in the meeting, something primordial. It was an ancient confrontation, prey facing predator. I was gripped by some latent urge to flee, commingled with an irrepressible wonder and awe.

The animal stood with an undisturbed dignity, and, after a time, I no longer thought of him as a beast, but a work of art. Here was a Goya in the middle of the jungle, an inspiring yet haunting requiem. Still, with all his majesty, whenever I looked into the tiger's eyes he became a beast again, and some suppressed instinct welled up from ancestors that knew only to fight or flee.

The tiger's eyes seemed to understand that thought. They always followed, like a painting I once saw as a child that I kept circling around as if I could somehow outwit the painter. The tiger's eyes could not be outwitted.

We waited, looking into the jungle's essence, and in the end it wasn't the tiger that left but us. Darkness had fallen and we were forced to leave the park. Reluctantly, we moved off, and it seemed we had entered a world of haze, where everything moves slow, and dreams grasp for a tenuous hold in reality.

The others felt the same. I could see it in them. the same look of bewilderment, the same wide-eyed half smile, the same hurried speech as if we could explain what we had seen. Raj had seen many tigers, but the feeling was always the same. And to see one that close, from a jeep, rather than high on the back of an elephant was rare indeed.

Raj had been right. The staff was lucky after all.

When we returned to the camp, steeping in a silent catharsis, Raj built a fire and cracked open a bottle of rum. Before long we were drunk, whether from the half-empty bottle of Old Monk or from the vision the jungle had honored us with hardly mattered. What mattered was the jungle had blessed us, and it felt good to be alive.

Eventually, Raj was delving into his endless warehouse of jungle tales, this time about the legendary K.K. Sengupta, tiger hunter and international diplomat.

I took a mouthful of rum. It was a luxury to have drink, I thought, and rare to be surrounded by warmth and security, among friends. The rum flowed as freely as the fire, and the conversation. A warm rush permeated my limbs when I joined the discussion.

"Who is this Sengupta anyway? Is he still alive?"

"Oh, he's still alive," explained Raj, "although he's over eighty now. He used to hunt tigers around here in the days of the Maharajas. Got a bungalow just near here."

"Can we go see him?"

"Go see him! Why, he is most revered. The hospital in Baihir is in his name. He built it!" But Raj was carefree and adventurous, not to mention drunk. We were soon in a jeep careening toward Sengupta's bungalow. Darkness sped by the open jeep while the thick night wind wrapped our rum-filled hearts in its warm embrace. Visions of the earlier tiger sighting were still in my mind, close enough to touch, hands shaking when I snapped a photo in the twilight shadows of the sol trees.

When we pulled up to the bungalow, I was astounded. The jungle parted to reveal a sprawling, immaculately manicured lawn as long and green as a football field. The "bungalow" was an expansive, ranch-style house with two sprawling wings attached to a central, two-story section. On top of the house rested an anomaly in this Third-World wilderness—a shining white, space-age satellite dish. The entire property was bordered by a lazily flowing stream, beyond which the jungle once again reigned supreme.

We parked the jeep in a circular driveway similar to those in old, English movies, always leading up to an ostentatious mansion. We walked the few steps up to the door. Raj nervously knocked then took upon himself a look of unmitigated terror, as if Vishnu himself were about to appear through the threshold. His fears, it turned out, were allayed for the moment, since the door was answered not by some deity, but a dark Hindu servant dressed in a creamy white, buttoned-down server's jacket and long white gloves tucked under the pressed, creased cuffs.

"May I be of service?" he asked, in English—perfect, James Mason English.

"Raj Sankaran from Kanha Camp to see Commodore Sengupta." Raj sounded brave. His voice hardly wavered. I wondered if I would have been as confident knocking on the door of an American official of equivalent weight. The dapper servant led us to the parlor, then went to inform Sengupta of our presence.

While we waited, I studied the photographs that adorned the walls and mantle of the palatial fireplace at the far end of the room. They were photos, many in black and white, of Sengupta and his wife at various stages in history. One showed the two in the wilderness, holding rifles and dressed in jungle khaki, a dead tiger at their feet. They looked like young Hollywood stars posing for a movie billboard. Raj examined a photograph on the mantle of Sengupta with his arm around another man.

"You see this man in the photo," Raj said in astonishment. "That's Rajiv Gandhi!"

Just then the servant returned and said, "Please have a seat on the lawn."

We were escorted outdoors to a ten-foot-wide fire pit which contained a raging fire. Elaborate lawn furniture surrounded the pit, all on the near bank of the sluggish stream. Across the water, the firelight attempted in vain to pierce the dancing shadows hidden behind black jungle trees.

A second servant arrived pushing a liquor caddy. "Do you take soda or ice with your Scotch, sir?" he asked. Ten or so bottles rested on the cart, a half gallon of Johnny Walker Red dominating the display.

"Uh . . . ice." I hadn't seen Scotch in a year.

A half glass of Scotch later, Sengupta himself came out. A stout man, he was helped by his wife, a cane, and two servants. Yellow firelight glistened off the server's silver tray while Sengupta poured himself a tumbler of Scotch. All was dark except for the circle of flickering light around the fire pit. The dim glow deepened the creases of age on Sengupta's face, making him seem rugged and jungle-wise. A peacock called from beyond the river.

Raj, perhaps as a way to justify our presence, told the Senguptas of my trip while exaggerating to the point of embarrassment.

"My goodness," said Mrs. Sengupta when Raj had finished his overblown introduction. "You must be awfully brave!"

In response, I recounted Ben Archer's memorable line, "I can't figure out if you're brave or just crazy!"

Laughter, and the following liquor caddy, served to thaw the atmosphere, and we all relaxed.

The Scotch continued to flow while Sengupta told us of his tiger-hunting days, about building a hospital in Baihir, and about this house in the jungle he loved so much.

"When I built this house, there was nothing else here," he recalled." No camps, no park, no tourists—only jungle. The nearest town was Baihir, back then only a few huts in the jungle."

I had cycled through Baihir on my way to Kanha Camp. It was well outside the boundaries of the park.

The rest of the night washed over us with the voices of history echoing through the fire. We were invited to stay for dinner, which we ate with knives and forks while watching an English soccer match on the satellite system. Just as Sengupta was a blend of English education and Indian ideals, so was his house a reflection of the West. Inside, I felt as if I were back in America, yet outside lurked the jungle and the eyes of the beast.

When it came time to leave the Sengupta's, Raj and I had entered a new world. If the sight of the tiger earlier that evening had raised our consciousness to a new plane, changed our understanding of where we belonged in the circle of life, then we left Sengupta having risen even higher. We drove back through the night in peace, the air thick with whispering memories.

Back at the camp, while lying in bed, I tried to grasp the entire day with my mind. The day seemed like a week. A week that would linger in my thoughts as a cherished treasure of India.

JANUARY 26
Kanha, India

TIME WENT BY easily at the camp while we made our twice-daily forays into the park with the tourists. During our nightly gatherings around the campfire, I began to notice a few glaring differences between Raj and Vijay.

Raj was a stocky, bearded man who came from a hard-working farm in Haryana. Although he was a Brahman and a landowner, he still had a country innocence about him, a friendliness that reminded me of Midwest America.

Vijay, on the other hand, hailed from Hyderabad, a large city. He was articulate, clean shaven, and had spent his life engaged in various business ventures. Vijay acted as the business manager and accountant for Kanha Camp and the affiliated tourist agency. He possessed a sharp intellect and quick wit, but he was every bit as friendly as Raj Sankaran.

On occasion, Aman, the head ranger of the area known as Mukki Range, joined us for a late evening cup of chai. We talked about the park, its history and its wildlife. I learned that Kanha actually meant "red clay," a substance that abounded in the area. At one time there was a village within the present boundaries of the park named Kanha, after the red clay upon which it was built. When the park was established, the villagers were relocated *outside* the park, along with those from another village named Kisli. The park then took on the name of the two relocated villages: Kanha Kisli National Park.

The days passed, and silence deepened at Kanha Kisli. Vijay left to gather the next batch of tourists, so Raj and I were alone at the camp once again. That night Aman came to share our fire, and I welcomed him with my usual questions about the park. With hot chai brimming in our cups, and the fire warming a chill night wind, I asked the ranger what precautions I should take when cycling through tiger territory.

"You shouldn't worry," he assured me. "Tigers and leopards rarely will break into a tent, but you should build a small fire anyway; that will keep them away. Your real worry is wild elephants. Never camp in an area with elephants. They'll trample over you without even knowing you're there.

"But you are at some risk while cycling," he warned. "Tigers are not altogether nocturnal; they may hunt at night to avoid man. They seem to be the most active at twilight and sunrise. You should not cycle during those times."

His comments brought a few questions to my mind. I asked the ranger what happened if a tiger killed some livestock, or worse, if a villager killed a tiger.

"You have just hit upon the most controversial subject in the whole region," he explained. "First of all, it's extremely rare for a tiger to venture out of the forest and kill livestock. If one does, and a villager shoots the tiger in defense of his animals, then the law is on his side. He's justified. If a tiger kills livestock outside the park, the owners get compensated, usually far more than the domestic animal was worth. "It is far more common for a villager to engage in fraud, where he illegally takes his herds into the park to graze. A tiger kills an animal. The villager shoots the tiger. Then, knowing what he has done is illegal and that he will get no money for the lost animal, he drags both carcasses outside the park to make it look like it happened there."

I asked Aman how he knew where the kills actually took place. "We investigate. It's fairly easy to tell. Sometimes we have to do toxicology on the animals. One old trick is for a villager to take one of his animals into the park, usually one that is old or sick, poison it, then wait for a tiger to come along and eat the poisoned animal. When the tiger dies, the villager drags both carcasses out of the park then puts a bullet hole in the dead tiger to make it look like it was shot. That way, he plans to get compensated more than his sick animal was worth and he gets rid of a tiger at the same time."

The night faded away with the dying fire. Our conversation became more subdued, and I took the opportunity to ask Aman for permission to cycle through the protected area of the park. The idea had been gnawing at me for days, but I knew there was little chance of gaining the clearance necessary for such an excursion.

"What about the pilgrimage?" Raj interjected before the ranger could answer.

"You can go on the pilgrimage," Aman conceded.

"It's for the villagers who used to live in the park," Raj said.

"There's a sacred lake in the park," Aman added. "When we moved the villagers out, we promised them they could go to their lake once a year."

"And you're saying I could cycle along with them?"

"That's right, but there will be rangers posted at all the side paths. You would only be allowed to go to the lake and back."

That was better than nothing. Before we turned in, Aman wrote up a form giving me permission to cycle the pilgrimage route, then he advised an early start. "The villagers leave at sunrise."

FEBRUARY 4
Kanha, India

THE DAY OF THE PILGRIMAGE, I awoke before sunrise. The cook had heard about my excursion and was waiting with a breakfast of *parathas* and a packed lunch. It was 5 a.m. when I arrived at the main jeep track leading into the park. A lowered gate and a guard hut stood at the entrance. There was no one waiting except me. Perhaps the villagers had already left. I showed the guard my pass, the gate was raised, and I began toward the sacred lake alone.

Ten minutes later, I came upon the first turn-off that led deeper into the jungle and away from the lake. No rangers were posted. I knew the trails well enough to realize the path led north, and if I took it I would be able to cycle across the entire park. I took the path.

I knew that Bligh Lodge, a camp run by English tour operators, lay on the northern edge of the sanctuary. My plan was to cycle across the park to Bligh Lodge, spend the night there, then hope for a ride back to Kanha Camp the following morning. The idea that had been growing since my arrival at Kanha was suddenly a reality.

By midday, I knew why I desired so much to enter the park by bicycle. On Papillon, I became part of the park, part of the ecosystem, traveling under my own power while subject to the same forces of nature that dominated the animals in the jungle. And the animals reacted to me as a part of the whole. Chital sauntered past and around me, as though I were some new breed of bison harmlessly grazing along the track. Bison cocked their heads when I rode past, but never ran or became threatening. To them, perhaps I looked like a chital. Wild boar dashed around my wheels, as if playing some new game with a new two-wheeled animal. The ride was unforgettable.

At noon I climbed a large cliff, atop which teetered a boulder similar to the erratics left by glaciers. I ate my lunch sitting on top of the boulder and watched the confined jeep-loads of tourists clatter along the track far below. Whenever passengers noticed me perched atop my boulder, the jeep would stop and all binoculars present would be turned and trained on my position. What an irony I must have presented to these animal watchers, who had come from America seeking tigers only to find a fellow American eating lunch on top of a cliff.

I laughed when I thought about it, when I thought about the difference between cycling and driving. I laughed when I thought about the mountain bike magazine in London and the refrain, "Better you than me." What would they have given for this story?

I arrived at Bligh Lodge with the sun still high on the horizon. Since everyone was out tiger hunting, the place was left tended by two young college interns.

"The owner of the lodge takes college students to help a few months of the year," one of the girls said.

But I wondered how much they had learned. When I explained my situation, and that I needed a place to stay for the night, they insisted I would have to ask the boss when he returned with the tourists. Their response seemed a bit callous to me. After all, what was the alternative? To cycle at night through the jungle? They didn't seem to comprehend the dangers that posed.

I further explained my situation, saying that I was an employee at Kanha Camp. Not impressed, one of the girls flicked her hair and turned to walk away.

I knew there was an elephant left at the lodge by a man who had ridden it across India. He had mentioned the journey in his recent book. I went to the shed where the elephant was housed and watched him for a while, feeling sorry he was left in such an unfriendly place. In the lodge library, which was similar to the one at Kanha Camp, I found the man's book, signed by the author. I wondered if my hosts even knew the signed copy was there, or if they cared.

At sunset the jeeps returned bearing tourists and the lodge operators, but they treated me no differently than had the two girls. When they discovered I was from Kanha Camp, they received the news as if I had revealed that I was carrying typhus. Exasperated, I mounted Papillon and started pedaling back to Kanha Camp while the sun set behind Mukki range.

I cycled well into the night, stopping many times to assure myself that I was on the correct trail back. When I heard the roar of a distant tiger, beyond the blackness, I knew what it was like to be a part of nature, to feel its fear. I knew what it was like to be a chital.

A warm fire greeted me when I finally arrived back at the camp. Vijay had returned with his tourists and was sitting with Raj and another Indian I did not recognize. The tourists were nowhere to be seen. Half expecting someone to be worried about me, I approached the fire and was greeted with nonchalance, handed a cup of Old Monk, and beckoned to a chair next to the gentle fire. Vijay introduced me to the new arrival, who he described as "the tour bus driver," a small, spindly man with gray hair and the light skin of a Sikh. Like Raj and Vijay, he was friendly to the core. I sat down and the three resumed their Hindi conversation, no doubt tiger stories I'd already heard a dozen times. When I caught the words "khana" and "Kanha," followed by laughter, I knew the new man was being treated to the "lost American cyclist" tale.

When the Old Monk ran out, Raj went to bed, followed by the bus driver who complained of the long drive from New Delhi. Vijay, who had not partaken in the camaraderie of the fireside ritual for some time, produced two one-liter bottles of beer and joined me by the fire. He laughed when I told him about Bligh Lodge and the tiger's roar in the night. We both laughed. It was laughter at the knowledge of fear tucked safely away behind the warm glow of fire and friendships.

After some time, when the fire died to that medium glow that turns all things a dim orange, I asked Vijay how he, once a city dweller, came to be running a jungle camp. Vijay took a long pull at his beer then gazed into the fire, as if he were hesitant to explain the matter.

"I used to work in construction," he finally said, "in Hyderabad—subcontracting." He paused again to watch some sparks scatter toward the black sky, then began haltingly, hesitantly. "I had a partner. My best friend. He was an expert marksman. Guns were a hobby with him. One day we were on a construction site and he spotted a snake wiggling out of a nearby water pipe. He got his pistol from his truck and hit the snake in two shots." Vijay raised his eyebrows in remembrance of his friend's marksmanship.

"We all took turns with the pistol. I hit the mark in four. No one else hit the snake in under ten shots." Vijay stopped and sucked on his beer. There was a wet glimmer in his eyes reflected by the orange flame.

"The next day," he continued, "some Naxalites came and demanded my friend's gun. I guess that's how they get their guns, by threatening common citizens. My friend wouldn't give it to them so they beat him up, then broke into his truck and took the gun and the permit."

Vijay didn't look up. He leaned forward with his forearms on his knees and was forced, involuntarily it seemed, into bitter remembrance.

"Unfortunately, two guns were listed on the permit—the revolver, and a rifle he kept in the rear of his truck. When the Naxalites saw the second gun on the permit, they came back the next day and demanded the rifle. My friend refused again, and again they began beating him. I was with him this time and I had my gun. My friend's blood was everywhere."

Vijay was in a trance, trapped somewhere deep within his own thoughts.

"So—I walked up—and shot the Naxalites—dead."

He seemed to emerge from the memory then finished the story matter-of-factly.

"If I stayed in Hyderabad, the Naxalites would have tracked me down and killed me, so I went to work in Malaysia for a few years. Then I came here."

The story was finished. I looked at my friend in disbelief—friendly, gentle Vijay. The story seemed so anomalous to his personality that I was inclined not to believe him. But in the weeks to come I would have the story confirmed by several people, including a private conversation with his ex-partner who visited the camp one weekend.

FEBRUARY 8

Kanha, India

THE NEW TOURISTS turned out to be a group of bird watchers from America, led by a professor from Cornell University, John, who was compiling a soundtrack of the bird calls of India. John was a young man, in his middle thirties, whose arms were constantly filled with a menagerie of sound equipment and reference guides. The largest of his many bird books was the size of a bread box.

He was accompanied by an older gentleman who "was a fighter pilot in Burma during the war," and was promised by the professor that he would see "at least three owls this trip." There was a second professor along, Walt, who had recently finished writing a biography of Mozart. He was accompanied by his wife Mary, a scatologist. The group also included a few reserved travelers who spent much of their time inside their rooms.

We saw no tigers that first day, but dinner offered some lively conversation by well-educated tourists. John discussed the birds they'd seen that day over his opened bread-box book, while the others eagerly checked off the new bird sightings on their "life lists."

"There are two types of birders, 'listers' and 'watchers,'" John explained to me. "Listers try to record as many birds as possible in their lifetime. It's like a competition. Watchers do it more for the love of nature." He went on to describe his recordings for Cornell University and his extensive travels in that pursuit. I described my trip to the group and some of the birds I'd seen but couldn't identify by name.

"Just think how many birds you could have listed by now!" Mary mused.

"Yeah, but all the books he'd have to carry!" pointed out the fighter pilot.

The night air was refreshingly cool while we ate a dinner of chicken curry underneath the open pavilion. The only walls to hold up the heavy wooden roof were several sturdy tree trunks, leaving the surrounding grounds open to view. A few chickens scratched and plucked in the scrub near the central fire pit. They were dinner. Kanha Camp's lack of a refrigeration system was solved the old-fashioned way, by buying live chickens and letting them wander around the camp until dinner time. The chickens were killed when needed. But the Indian chickens didn't look at all like those in the West. They were scrawny and of various colors, like interbred dogs. At one point in our meal, Mary noticed some of the chickens pecking about in the scrub.

"Look!" she called to the others, then ran off to get her binoculars. The other bird watchers saw the exotic looking chickens and did the same. Soon, the group of birders were standing at the edge of the table gazing at the next evening's dinner. John sat with his head in his hands, too embarrassed to reveal the mistake.

"I hate to tell you this," I whispered to the old man still sitting next to me, too tired to run off with the others, "but that's what we're eating for dinner."

"Do me a favor," he whispered back, "don't tell my wife!"

After dinner, for the first time in my stay at Kanha, some of the tourists joined us around the fire pit. The scrawny bus driver for the tour group was there, along with John, Walt and Mary. John had his recording equipment out and was wandering around collecting sounds with a directional microphone the size of a baseball bat.

"Watch this," he said, turning on a recording of an owl he'd just captured on tape. The owl, hearing itself, flew near the fire to investigate and perched in a tree ten feet away from us.

"It's a male owl," the professor explained, "coming to see what another male is doing in his territory." Someone went inside and woke up the fighter pilot so he could add the owl to his life list. The old man walked out, bleary eyed—saw the owl for a split second, said "Okay," then walked back inside.

"I think I understand the definition of a 'lister' now," I said to John, who suppressed a quick smile in the presence of the others in his group.

THE FOLLOWING MORNING Vijay drove me to Mandla, where I boarded a train to New Delhi for the purpose of renewing my visa. My time at Kanha had been so relaxing that I couldn't see breaking it up by taking a third-class coach as many bargain travelers did. Instead, I spent the money and went first class, which gave me an entire cabin shared with only one other person, a forest service bureaucrat. The first-class train ride included three meals a day served by a waiter, the morning paper delivered with tea, and a feeling I was some prestigious Agatha Christie character on an intriguing, private mission.

My time in Delhi, where I remained a week, was dominated by two trips a day to Delhi's Mecca to Western travelers in Asia: Wimpy Burger. I found enough time between lamb burgers to renew my visa, secure a visa to Nepal, and travel the heavily touristed "golden triangle" which encompasses some of the most sought after sights in India.

My plan was to cycle to Nepal, then attempt to enter China through Tibet. Since traveling eastward, through India, would eventually lead me to inaccessible Myanmar, I was forced to travel north, to China, in order to continue east.

The return train stopped at Mandla. I hitchhiked to Baihir, then was given a ride in the K.K. Sengupta Hospital ambulance to Kanha Camp. "No Problem, don't worry," the driver told me before he shuttled us into the jungle, in answer to whether it was common practice for the ambulance to double as a taxi.

Back at the camp I found the birders were gone, replaced by two Canadian women in the midst of a spontaneous tour through Asia.

"We go wherever feels right," they told us. "Wherever the wind blows."

Those carefree travelers stayed three days. After that the days dissolved away at Kanha Camp, amidst elephant forays into the jungle, tiger sightings, a spectacular leopard encounter and nights around the fire.

In Africa, I met a traveler who, after describing some of the earth's wonders he'd seen, said, "I can't imagine a person dying without first experiencing these things." Kanha Kisli was such a place for me.

A month to the day after I first cycled into Kanha, Pradeep returned and invited me to stay as long as I wanted. I stayed another fifteen days. When it came time to leave, the three gave me their home addresses. "You are family now," they told me. "You can come and stay with us whenever you want."

Vijay was taking a group of tourists to Bandhavgarh, a park 100 kilometers north of Kanha. He asked me if I wanted a ride and I accepted. At least I would have Vijay's company for one more day. We drove out of the camp and away from the sol forest, and I inwardly said farewell to forty-five days in paradise.

FEBRUARY 19
Bandhavgarh, India

WE ARRIVED at the small village after dark. Rather than camp in the jungle, I shared Vijay's room in the local hotel. Late in the evening, I strolled out along the pungent back alleys of Bandhavgarh. The streets were dark. The only light came from the occasional dhaba, with flames burning inside to cook the meals of late night wanderers. Some dhabas hoarded their light and aromas behind tattered curtains, and some had no doors at all, sharing their culinary wealth with the streets.

It was always the loudest and most crowded dhaba that served the best food, just as the most trucks at truck stops in the States indicated the better restaurants. But in Bandhavgarh, a village in the middle of the jungle, the dhabas were not crowded and rarely noisy. The one I wandered into was no exception. Its attraction was the warm and loving light given off by the heat of the cooking fire, forcing the night to stay outside.

There were only four people and the chowkidar inside. The four consisted of the skinny bus driver for the tour group, who had been at Kanha Camp, and his helpers. They sat by the fire, Hindi wafting through the glowing air, the smell of curry permeating the mud-brick walls, and cow-dung fuel stacked next to the food pot.

"Come," said the bus driver, recognizing me." We have a chicken in the pot. You will share it with us."

The price of a whole chicken was 100 rupees, the equivalent of dining at the Ritz to villagers in these remote areas.

I declined the offer. I knew the meal was expensive for them, even though they were sharing it among four people.

"You must," the bus driver insisted. "Here, pull up a chair." He moved a chair over to the only table in the dhaba.

"I'll eat with you," I said, "if you let me pay." One hundred rupees represented less of a monetary strain to me, even though I had become accustomed to the value of a rupee.

"Nonsense," the bus driver said, and that was the end of the discussion. I ate my chicken curry with the chowkidar's flat-faced puppy on my lap, the sound of Hindi drenched in the scent of curry, and the ubiquitous glass of chai, smooth as the sounds of Asia.

FEBRUARY 27

Varanasi, India

I SAID FAREWELL to Vijay at sunrise, then set out from Bandhavgarh toward Uttar Pradesh. The road improved as the jungle was left behind. Sol forest slowly transformed into occasional clusters of trees, while the road surface graduated from packed dirt to pavement. Northward loomed India's flat *terai*, a great, green expanse, once forest, now a band of cultivated land extending along the northern length of the country. Beyond that: Nepal and the great Himalayas.

Varanasi was the first large city I encountered after my time at Kanha Kisli, and by the time I arrived my supplies were in such a depleted state it was a marvel I made it at all. I had no patches left, no spare tube or tire, and my Indian tire was paper thin. I still carried no proper tools, spokes or cables, and I had long since abandoned the hope of replacing my hopelessly damaged camp stove. But in Varanasi, India's sacred city on the Ganges stalked by tourists, it might be possible to find the parts I sought. Yet, when I entered Varanasi, I began to realize it would take some time to learn the labyrinthine streets of the sprawling market places.

The guidemeestirs that pervaded every touristed area in Asia accosted me when I walked deeper into the city. My usual philosophy was to shout "No thank you" as loudly and rudely as possible, then walk off at a brisk pace. The guidemeestirs were usually stunned for the proper amount of time to allow a fast getaway. But this time I needed a guide, especially if I were to find the necessary supplies without lingering long enough to become an Indian citizen. I stopped when a voice in perfect English caught my ear through the babble of screaming guides.

"Do you need a hotel?" the prospective guide asked me, but I preferred to find hotels on my own. When taken to a hotel by a guide, the price was increased to provide the guide a kickback.

"No, no hotel . . ." I replied, about to explain my list of needs.

"Come," the guide interrupted, "I will take you to the hotel where the other cyclist is staying."

"Other cyclist?"

"Yes, he is English—like you. I took him there yesterday. He had all the baggages like you have."

"After you," I said, upon hearing the highly reasonable rates.

I was given a room on the second floor next to the other cyclist. A weather worn, beat up mountain bike laden with the dust of India was chained to the banister directly across from my room. The cyclist was out, so I chained Papillon next to the other bike then explained my needs to the guidemeestir.

"Don't worry sir," my fluent guide said, after I gave him a list of the things I needed. "We will find these things, though it will take all day I think."

True to his word, the guide orchestrated the shopping and bartering throughout the streets of Varanasi with the skill of a master. We found everything except the tire. It was only after we finished our search for supplies, when the sun was dipping into the Ganges, that I realized I had made a crucial mistake. In my excitement over seeing another mountain bike at the hotel, I had committed the cardinal tourist sin. I had failed to set a price for the services of my guide *before* the service was rendered. Now, the guide could name almost any price he wanted, and bartering would be much more difficult for me, if not impossible.

I saw one way out. Throughout the course of the day, my guide had repeatedly pointed out all the wine shops in the area. Could it be my friend had a passion for wine?

"I'll tell you what," I suggested when the list of supplies was complete. "I'll buy you all the wine you can drink for guiding me around today." At thirty cents a bag, how could I go wrong?

"A deal!"

I was shocked. The next minute we were sitting in a bar ordering wine bags.

The night progressed, and the guide's friends joined us, then the guide himself began buying rounds. A highly unusual act, I thought, for one who made his living as a guide. But I soon discovered my friend was a man of many talents.

"Me and my friends have a blues band!" he told me through a wine hazed slur.

"Blues band. In India?"

"Sure, we love James Brown."

One of the group produced a harmonica, another began drumming on the table with his hands, and the guidemeestir belted out a Hindi blues song. They were surprisingly entertaining. The entire bar crowd gathered around to listen.

The night marched on, marked by music, plastic wine bags, and new found friendships. I dared the thought that perhaps my guide was unique in Asia—a person who offered his services for the sake of helping others rather than for money. Still, I remained skeptical. I had been fleeced too many times to let my guard down completely, so when my host asked if I wanted to take a boat ride on the Ganges, alarm bells went off in my mind.

Boat rides down the Ganges were the main tourist attraction in Varanasi. It was there, atop the *ghats* on the banks of the sacred river, where Hindu bodies were burned for the ashes to be scattered upon the water. But I knew from researching the excursion that, during the day, the act of burning was staged for the tourists. It was at night, away from heathen eyes, when the real burning took place. That was why tourist boats were not allowed to ply the Ganges at night. It would surely cost me a fortune if my host could accomplish such an illegal act.

"How can we do this?" I asked. "It's illegal."

"Don't worry," guidemeestir said.

"He can do it!" the harmonica player said, nodding.

"How much?" I asked.

"It will cost you nothing."

Hard to believe. My alarm bells were ringing at full force. But I felt emboldened by the wine, and in one of those frivolous decisions a person makes after a few bags of wine, I agreed.

The two of us stumbled down to the banks of the river, where a fleet of rowboats sat idle, waiting for sunrise to bring paying tourists. The boat drivers were asleep in their shacks along the river, which did not deter my drunken friend. He began clapping his hands and shouting in Hindi, rousting an army of confused, bleary-eyed boatmen out of their waterside shacks. I felt sure we would be attacked when the guide barked out his orders. Instead, a senior boatman came kowtowing, motioning us to his boat.

We were rowed out with the full moon glistening off the Ganges, fires from the distant ghats lighting the banks where writhing and bending shadows danced. Scattered ashes added a haze to the rising moon. Wrapped in a wine-filled elation, I felt the scene was worth a thousand rupees.

Then the guidemeestir passed out. I knew it was a ploy to stick me with the bill. The entire night had been an elaborate con; the boatman was no doubt the guide's friend, and would demand a fortune to keep our illegal act quiet. I was ripe for blackmail.

"I'm not paying!" I told the boatman after attempting to wake up the guide. "He said he would pay; I'm not paying!"

"Oh, there is no paying sahib," the boatman said, calmly.

"How can that be?" I asked, still skeptical. "We woke you up in the middle of the night."

"No sahib, my boss said no pay."

"Your boss?"

"Yes sahib, this man is my boss," the boatman said, and pointed to my unconscious guide.

"He is your boss?"

"Yes, Sahib, he owns all the boats on the Ganges."

I had been socializing with the boat baron of Varanasi. I finally realized, he had guided me out of simple kindness after all.

I ARRIVED back at the hotel at sunrise and slept until noon. When I finally awoke, I found my next-door neighbor crouched down, analyzing Papillon.

"What happened to your front tire?" he asked when he saw the large Indian rim and worn front tire.

I explained my situation. I told him about the Syrians, about the Italian robbery that left me with no spare parts.

After my explanation, the cyclist gave me one of his two spare tires. "I always carry two," he said, "because it's impossible to find these in Asia."

His name was Bob Sacks, from Michigan, where he worked as a carpenter six months a year. The other six months, winter months in Michigan, he spent mountain biking through foreign lands. He had traveled to the shores of Africa and the mountains of South America, the continent of Europe and the great expanses of Asia.

He made a good companion as we explored the streets and back alleys of Varanasi, until the sun cradled the horizon like a half-moon. We walked, exchanging travel tales and cycling information, and I reflected upon the past months in Asia. It would be difficult to leave this exotic city, one of my last in India. Nepal waited to the north, three days' ride. India had shown me much, from her overflowing cities to sparsely populated jungle. I would miss Kanha Kisli and night time campfires; dinners at sunset and wildflower fields. I would miss open jeeps and bungalows, rum-wrapped evenings and Goya in the jungle. When sleep came at the end of a Varanasi day, I knew I would miss this city on the Ganges. I knew I would miss India.

APRIL 5
Delhi, India

THE FOLLOWING MORNING I set out north, toward the tiny mountain kingdom of Nepal. I cycled through the terai that bisects northern India like a great green swath. The road that rose into the foothills of the Himalayas, from the sea-level terai, took me through ever increasing gradations in altitude. I cycled through terraced foothills tilled by Nepalese farmers who had learned in their vertical world to use every last inch of fertile space. In the distance, the whiteness of the Himalayas rose up above brown, arid mountains encircling the green terraced fields. Cycling to Tibet would entail reaching that whiteness, then traveling beyond it, through the highest mountain range in the world.

Kathmandu was a town of tourists and comfortable hotels, of relaxing restaurants and veteran travelers. The streets were thick with pagodas and shrines, with holy men wandering among beggars and hawkers and guidemeestirs. There was poverty as well, in half-nude children urinating in the streets, one-armed beggars with skins of dirt. It was a poverty that had so pervasive that I barely noticed it anymore. To me, it was like part of the scenery: a tree, a building, a park bench.

I spent several days in Kathmandu, applying for visas and permission to cycle over the Himalayas into Tibet. My research faced me with some disturbing facts. China refused me a visa unless I booked a package tour to Lhasa, tours which traveled by plane to Tibet then back to Nepal. Individual travel in Tibet was forbidden.

Could I sneak across the border? This was commonly done by trekkers, usually by following local donkey trains through the Mustang Valley. The problem for me was—unlike the tourists who trekked across the border, met the locals, then hiked back—I would have to continue across the length of China, one of the largest countries in the world. Without a proper visa the task would have been impossible.

When my options in Kathmandu dried up, I cycled westward, to Pokhara, hoping some solution would present itself in Nepal's second largest city. If Kathmandu was Nepal's bustling capital, then Pokhara was the country's relaxing hideaway. Less crowded, at 884 meters in altitude the town was surrounded by white mountains. Phewa Tal lake shimmered near the west end of town, with quiet and relaxing cafés lining its shores. The streets were filled with backpackers, mountaineers, and cycle tourists, all casually strolling along in a town that must have represented a short respite from adventure. Pokhara seemed to me an oasis where people came to rest and rejuvenate after cycling through Asia, kayaking a river, or conquering a mountain peak. And with the variety of food available, Pokhara was a culinary haven in a sea of Asian dahl.

I checked into a lakeside hotel for four dollars. From my open balcony, Phewa Tal lake glittered across the way, and white mountains illuminated the skyline to the north. The manager of the hotel agreed to lock my bike in the storage room while I searched on foot for a way through to Tibet. The following day I applied for trekking permits, rented the gear I needed, and walked north out of Pokhara. After ascending an endless staircase of stone, earth, and mud, I arrived at Sarankot, a scenic lookout point 1,500 meters straight toward the sky from Pokhara. The climb took three hours. Since I had started late, I reached the top at dusk. Far below, the lights of Pokhara were just blinking on to challenge the night, like an island of tiny fireflies glowing in defiance to a sea of black hills.

The following morning, I was greeted by another view: The Annapurna massif stretched out in a white panorama to the north. It took me ten days to reach those mountains. Ten days of rhododendrons blazing rose red on mountain riverbanks—ten days of snow and ice and avalanche zones surrounded by the pristine Himalayas. The trek ended at Annapurna base camp, an area surrounded by eight of Nepal's highest peaks. Of the one hundred or so trekkers who started for the camp from Pokhara, only six made it to the top. The rest were turned back by Sherpas due to unusually high avalanche risk. A group of nine Germans had perished in an avalanche days earlier. The five who made it were the only ones willing to wait several days in camps along the way until the danger subsided.

The base camp stood at 4,100 meters, an altitude which showed me the folly of attempting to sneak through the mountains into Tibet. By the time I arrived back in Pokhara, my options were fairly limited. It wasn't until a mountaineer suggested I enter China through Pakistan, where overland travel was permitted, that my plans began to change.

That had been my original plan, before being deported from Karachi. It never occurred to me to return to the country. I spent an additional week lounging about my hotel while taking advantage of all the Western amenities the small city offered. When the time finally came, it was difficult to leave Pokhara's luxuries behind.

I boarded a train and started back to Delhi. Within a week I had the visas, and was cycling toward Pakistan for the second time in four months.

10

Back to Pakistan

IT FELT GOOD to be cycling again, although I would not recommend the stretch between Amritsar and Lahore to any fellow cyclists. The area consisted of dust, squalor, disease, pigs, rampant crowds, and marauding bands of children.

Before beginning the long, winding stretch northward to the Chinese frontier, I needed to overcome my first small obstacle: the Pakistani border. It wasn't long ago that I had been deported from the country. Did they keep records of such things? Was my name present on some blacklist only to precipitate another stay in immigration detention, and this time indefinitely? If so, how could I explain my situation to Howard Banks after having promised to leave Pakistan for good?

Another factor worried me. According to all the literature and travel information I had accumulated over the past months, the border was closed to overland travel due to fighting in the area between bands of Sikhs, Muslims and Hindus. My travel guide made the circumstances seem dire indeed: "Depending on the political situation in the Indian Punjab you may be able to take a bus from Delhi to Lahore in a convoy with military escort, three days in each month. There is no other way to cross overland from India."

These factors weighed heavily on my mind when I approached a vast, dusty plain, the disputed border between East and West Punjab. A single hut served as immigration processing where a lone guard sat stuffing his mouth with roti.

154

"Which way to Lahore?" I asked him in Urdu.

"Sedha," he said, pointing down the dirt road." But the immigration man is not here." The guard analyzed his roti. He never looked up, making me feel like a bothersome insect which should be casually dismissed with the wave of a hand.

"Only a few minutes," the official assured me. "Wait there."

I knew what that meant. A few minutes in Asia usually translated into hours, time I spent recovering from the effects of the constant 100 degree days of late, and exploring the immigration hut. Pasted to the far wall of the hut above a decomposing desk was a list of names headed "enemies of Pakistan." Next to the list was one mug shot, no doubt representing the supreme enemy of Pakistan. My name was not on the list.

My paranoia, as it turned out, was completely unjustified. In time, the immigration official arrived and I was stamped across the border into Pakistan, despite the fact that the border crossing was said to be impossible. It was one giant hurdle leaped in my 1,000-mile journey backward, all for the dim hope of traveling overland through China.

A short thirty-kilometer ride from the border brought me to Lahore, where I was faced with the most crowded conditions since Bombay. People stood shoulder to shoulder in the streets, and I began to suspect some Orwellian theme was being enacted around me. I was trapped like a lab rat in an overpopulated cage, deprived of the smallest piece of private space.

Traveling throughout India, especially along the Grand Trunk Road, had made me sensitive to crowds, overpopulation, and unwanted attention toward my bicycle. I felt as a Hollywood actor must feel when traveling among the public—always stared at, always a crowd of fanatics lingering around, never able to travel in anonymity. Because of this new-found craving for privacy, I put aside exploring Lahore and checked into a four-dollar hotel room. There, in the Spartan room, my experiences of the teeming city became a ninety-cent dinner of chicken, rice, and roti brought from the market by a small boy, the clatter of bicycle rickshaws jerking by on the streets below, and the sound of Urdu seeping in from the hallway.

FROM LAHORE, the Grand Trunk Road stretched north over the flat terai, carrying with it an unwavering flow of Pakistani life and culture. Each of three separate lanes supported its own unique segment of traveler. The outside lane, semi-paved with asphalt, was pock marked with deep craters and ravines—impossible for cycling. This lane was made more difficult by the trucks that weaved down the road dodging wandering cows and goats, animals that conveyed little respect for the trucks' sole ownership of this fastest lane. Inexorably intertwined throughout the clamor and chaos, throughout the low bass pleas of the fleeing cows and screeches of black faced macaques, was the blare of the dreaded klaxon. This Asian version of the truck horn produced a sound many times louder than those found in the Western world. It was a sound to make the body cringe, eyes squint, and head bow in an autonomic response.

The next lane was loose dirt—or more accurately, dust—conveying pedestrians and cyclists. Those on foot carried the odd pot, basket of chickens, or hay bundle on their heads. Some were garbed in bright colored saris, while many drab, gray dhotis of the more impoverished villagers dotted the scene. The latter were tied up around the thigh, a style considered low class and vulgar in the more bourgeois cities.

The cyclists who formed their own flowing, unbroken contingent of the northward migration occupied the edge of this second lane. They bounced down the road carrying anything from television sets to families of four. One cyclist looked like a huge haystack teetering along on wheels, with the rider and bike hidden beneath the pile; others cycled in bare feet and rags, their bikes in the last stages of disrepair. Some bikes had no tires, and many were missing certain, one would think indispensable parts. Pedals for instance.

Although I began in the cycling lane, I found it was not the lane I preferred. Since the animals chose that winding milieu of natives as well, I found myself dodging pigs, goats, and cows, as well as teetering haystacks and children defecating in the road.

The lane I preferred was the third, the buffalo lane. These huge, domesticated animals grunted along towing carts laden with the commerce of Pakistan: potatoes, hay, grass, dust. The wheels that carried the produce wore deep ruts paralleling the road and arching over the countryside like a set of train tracks extending northward. That was where I took my place, one yellow bicycle in an endless procession of creaking carts and plodding buffalo.

I intended to follow the buffalo tracks into Rawalpindi, where the Grand Trunk Road veered west toward Peshawar and the Khyber Pass. My route led north, along the ancient Silk Road, over the 5,000-meter-high Khunjerab Pass and across the massive Karakoram Mountains bordering China. This last-chance overland route to China was a risk, both physically and politically. The physical dangers were obvious: The Karakoram Highway stood as one of the highest thoroughfares in the world—known for landslides, glacial encroachment, and altitude related illness. The road claimed 500 Pakistani lives during its construction, one for every one-and-a-half kilometers of the passage.

An even greater obstacle for me was the political situation. I learned that tourists were forbidden to bring private transportation into China. The reasons seemed rather complex, overshadowed by bureaucratic and cultural issues. Only a few hundred "open" cities existed in China, cities where a tourist hotel had been constructed, the population educated, and a bank established to exchange foreign travelers checks. The rest of the country was off limits.

Tourists were allowed to travel between open cities, but only on public transportation. That insured the traveler would not be able to explore anything outside of those sanctioned cities. Private-hired cars were frowned upon and then allowed only with an official government escort. Traveling by bicycle was expressly forbidden. According to my best information, a traveler arriving at the border with a bicycle would have it confiscated. But those obstacles were small, and weeks away, compared to what lay directly ahead of me. Before confronting any of the political issues, I would first have to cycle over one of the largest mountain chains in the world, a journey that might take months.

I still did not know if travel was restricted in the northern reaches of Pakistan. Western hostages had recently been killed in the Indian section of Kashmir, an area which stood directly in my path, raising the possibility that I would once again face a dead end. In time, these questions would have to be answered. And the only way to answer them, was to go north.

THE ROAD CONTINUED over the flat northern plains through the town of Jhelum, then Rawalpindi an effortless 114 kilometers beyond. Rawalpindi lies at an altitude of 500 meters, although the gradual incline made that a shocking realization. I stayed one night in the city, and that time was used to take stock of the repairs I'd have to make before entering the mountains. One of my main concerns was a bent rear wheel. I attempted to straighten the rim using my rudimentary tools, but a new rim was the only permanent solution.

My chain was too short as well, a result of all the broken links I had been forced to remove over the last months. Since the short chain eliminated many gear combinations, the replacements were critical for the mountainous terrain ahead, but with a Hyperglide, ultra-thin chain, the chance of finding links was minimal.

Some of my other problems had been haunting me for months. Twelve broken spokes bent into shape behind the freewheel was a temporary solution that made it impossible to true the rim. As in England, I was left searching for the freewheel extractor tool necessary to make the repair. In addition to those problems, many of the chainring teeth were broken, warped, or eroded, and all the cables were frayed and ready to break. Succeeding in the mountains would be impossible without proper repairs. How to find the tools and parts to effect those repairs was a question I would ponder for many days to come.

FROM RAWALPINDI, the Grand Trunk Highway flooded north into Taxila, where it finally split westward to leave the Karakoram Highway alone in its quest toward China. The prospect of leaving behind the mass of humanity flowing over the Grand Trunk Road bent my body and mind toward reaching that fork.

I stayed in a youth hostel in the town of Taxila for two consecutive nights, exploring the archeological digs surrounding Taxila by day, and exchanging travel tales in the evening with the only other occupant of the hostel, a mountain climber from Japan. The morning of the third day I set out for Mansehra, 100 kilometers north, over the ever-rising foothills of the looming mountains. The road, a densely packed gray dirt, tilted upward at a constant ten-degree angle. At times, a thin strip of pavement stretched along the center, flanked by two dirt paths pockmarked with ruts. At times the road deteriorated into loose dirt and stones, causing me to be thankful for Papillon's fat, gripping tires.

The Karakoram foothills squeezed the road thin around them. Their smooth black tops rolled over the horizon like blunt mounds of dirt patted tight on the beach. Mounds gave way to sheer cliffs when I cycled through the bottom of a steep, thin trench.

In Abbottabad, I left the last track linking the Karakoram Highway with the Grand Trunk Road behind. North of the link, traffic thinned and the incessant noise and pollution of the past diminished to a bearable level. For the first time since leaving Amritsar, the air was clean and free of exhaust. I stopped for the day in the small mountain town of Mansehra, where the Silk Road began to tilt into the Karakoram at a frightening angle.

There were two possible roads northward from Mansehra. The first, a jeep track following the Kaghan Valley, ascended over the 4,500-meter Babusar pass, open to four-wheel-drive vehicles only six weeks of each year in late July and August. Villagers at the higher altitudes along the valley abandon the area between November and May because of snow.

The second option, continuing along the Karakoram Highway, would take me over the 5,000-meter high Khunjerab pass. Both routes offered the same technical difficulties. Where would I find the cold weather gear necessary to see me over the pass? How would I carry all the gear needed? Could I cycle over the pass quickly and avoid too many nights camped in the snow? A one-day layover in Mansehra was required to answer some of those questions.

I spent the day in a fruitless search through the tiny town for bicycle parts. Information was scarce. No one knew which was the safest road north. But the chowkidar at my hotel spoke fluent English, and his relatives had once lived near the Babusar pass. Now, his relatives were dead. An avalanche had closed the pass only weeks before, killing villagers and destroying towns. The way was impassable.

That new information left one remaining route. I would leave town along the Silk Road, toward the ancient Indus River.

Batagram, Pakistan

I ROUNDED A BEND out of Mansehra, and the foothills continued their endless pursuit toward the sky. At first the road stretched onward as packed, brown rock, with cliffs rushing up on either side supporting damp, green patches as if a moss had suddenly invaded the wet scenery. Waterfalls poured from the escarpment above, over the road, then into the Indus river down a long and precipitous ravine.

Three times throughout the day falls flowed over the dirt track, causing me to dismount and walk through knee-deep water that bisected the Karakoram Highway. I stopped and bathed under the third fall, which had created a modest lake preventing much of the sparse Silk Road traffic from passing.

Few vehicles attempted the passage on such a wet day. Logging trucks were able to inch through the pool. They shuttled past me the entire day carrying wide, century-old trees. Donkey trains weaved their way up the mountainside and around the temporary blockage. Those few vehicles, and Papillon, possessed the means to continue upward into the mountains.

My travel guide informed me that, "from Mansehra the road meanders down to Batagram." Nevertheless, the first thirty-five kilometers out of Mansehra were up, followed by a sixteen-kilometer descent. Since the guide was designed for bus travel, the road information was not as detailed as I would have liked.

The guide did have one short entry about travel north of Batagram, an area known as Indus Kohistan: "Some locals advise visitors not to go into the hills alone. The police advise them not to go at all, and tell stories of assault and robbery (and a lone woman said to have been raped near Dasu) . . . it's worth noting that solo travel off the KKH in Kohistan is not 100% safe."

The town of Batagram stood as testimony to the foreboding advice of my travel guide. The local population took an unusual interest in my gear. Rather than curiosity, the people seemed to take note of my cheap German camera and dead radio. Valueless, but how were they to know? Nor did the villagers speak English, and they were unwilling, or unable, to speak Urdu. To add to my discomfort, I found the beds at the local hotel infested with fleas, a discovery which came to me around midnight.

I AROSE LATE due to fatigue and a fitful, flea-ridden sleep. The unfriendly population in Batagram unnerved me, so I left quickly without buying supplies. My legs were tight from the relentless mountain ascent, causing slow progress in an unusually small gear. Ten kilometers north of Batagram, the road curled around a bend, with a cliff rising up from the left and a steep drop into a gorge to the right.

A gang of Pakistanis stood at the top of the fifty-foot cliff, rocks in hand, hooting and catcalling with my approach. Rounding the bend, I found myself directly below the group. They let loose with a barrage of rocks that pelted the ground around me. A loud clang told me the frame had been struck. Straining against the pedals, I gained speed up the hill, but the steep incline and the confined nature of the road gave me no escape. The rocks continued to batter the ground. I winced with a sharp pain in my back. Another rock had found its target.

The next bend in the road brought more rocks. Hostile bands of teenagers roamed the countryside to the north. At each bend in the road, each village and dhaba, I was pelted with rocks by waiting Pakistanis attempting to add some entertainment to their secluded lives. By noon, eleven separate gangs had bombarded me with rocks. They seemed to think of it as a joke, as a sport, as a giant video game in which I was the prize. To them, I was not a human being, I was a passing blip on a video screen.

Cycling north, the locals grew more malicious. A group of teenagers dislodged a boulder from the cliff above, missing me by a few feet. I glided down a small decline. A band of twenty Pakistanis ran out to block the road, slinging rocks with my approach. I was hit, and sent sprawling over the handlebars into the dust.

Looking up, I saw the bicycle lying several yards away, while my tormentors advanced, rocks in hand. I was left with no defense. I rose up and ran over to the leader, isolating him from the others. He dropped his rock and ran away. His accomplices hesitated for an instant, allowing me to scramble to the bicycle and cycle off. The remaining gang members pummeled me with rocks when I sped away.

Weak from lack of food, arms and legs cut and scraped from the fall, I cycled on. Around the next bend another mob rushed out of the scrub to block my way. Instinctively, I put my foot out and shoved one of my attackers to the side, creating a path to freedom. My momentum caused the man to go tumbling across the road.

The earlier crash had bent several chain links, and on the next ascent my chain snapped. I could not afford to lose another link, so I was forced to spend a half hour repairing the bad one. Coming into Thakot, the weak chain link snapped yet again, prompting me to stop and make the repair. Due to my short chain from removing bad links, I was already reduced to a limited selection of gears.

A small village came into view, where I decided to make more permanent repairs. Asking around town, I was refused food, refused gasoline for my camp stove. A gathering of delinquent teenagers added another dozen stones to my woes when I cycled out of town.

Exhausted from the day's events, and in fear of being discovered by a hostile mob, I set up camp in a well-hidden nook off the road. In all, twenty-four gangs had pelted me with rocks in one day. I could only hope the population would become less hostile in the territories to the north.

MAY 3
Shatial, Pakistan

I STOPPED to cook my lunch in the afternoon and saw no one, the first privacy in recent memory. I watched the river, far below, in its slow serpentine path toward sea level. Above, the mountains waited to reveal their inner reaches. A shaggy white mountain goat clambered among the sere brush of the cliffs, where sand and shale on the near embankment made a gradual descent to the river. The Indus, a clay-colored gray, cut the far bank into a vertical canyon carved with ripples from changing water levels. The Silk Road carried me out of Pakistan's Northern Territories and into the Northwest Frontier Province bordering China. I made my way farther toward the snow-line which seemed deceptively close, although I was not above 1,500 meters in altitude. I wore a sweatshirt for the first time since entering Pakistan, and entertained myself on the road by watching bands of workers clear away the night's landslides. Loggers at work on the Indus far below maneuvered floating trunks about by raft.

Pines held tenuous holds on the shale walls flanking the road. My view was always obscured by some mountain, a hundred feet distant, around which the road curled. On either side, cliffs rose; the river had diverted to another course. I weaved around tan, warped pillars of earth cut by excavation into a colonnade, before the route plunged straight into a black granite barrier veering out of sight to follow the next sloping valley.

The Karakoram Highway wound around a sheer stone palisade, the track miraculously clinging to the vertical rock like a thin, serpentine shelf jutting a few meters outward toward the open air. More men died in the construction of this part of the passage than any other, having accomplished feats of mountaineering in the process. This was evidenced by the many monuments erected to those who died in the course of their duties.

Still the Silk Road rose skyward. The Indus River became the Hunza River, which flowed 100 meters below a precipice supporting a group of Himalayan bharal sheep. My first view of ice came when a massive glacial arm two-stories tall blocked the way. A tunnel had been cut through the ice to accommodate the few four-wheel-drive vehicles that shuttled tourists to Kashgar. Another turn into the interior of the Karakoram and the Hunza was gone. There were cliffs again, and once again they rose up to my left and right. Landslides covered the passage at points, and in some areas the road was squeezed like the bottleneck of an hourglass, narrowing between fallen rocks then opening up again on the other side.

Around a bend, a landslide blocked the way, three-stories high with boulders ten-feet square strewn on top of each other as if they had been spilled across the road from a dice shaker. I portaged over the blockage in three trips, only to find the track tilt higher into the Karakoram. A sign appeared just beyond the landslide. Wooden, painted blue with hand-written letters, it stood three feet tall attached to two uprooted tree trunks. In yellow, the words read, "Relax, Slide Area Ends. Have A Nice Drive."

I reached the mountain town of Shatial and sought out the safety of the nearest dhaba. I was given the usual meal of *gosht*, a staple of northern Pakistan comprised of the sinew of mutton submerged in a bowl of melted fat. Roti and gosht were so prevalent in this mountain region that they drove me to the point of nausea, but no matter how distasteful, I ate everything I was given out of necessity. I became convinced, after the past weeks, that a vegetarian could never endure a prolonged visit to the northern reaches of Pakistan.

MAY 5
KKH to Gilgit, Pakistan

DIRECTLY NORTH of Shatial the Hunza rejoined me, like a lost companion, and the cliffs that formed a wall off my right shoulder were constantly offset by a sheer drop to my left. Around a bend like the hundreds I had curled by since Rawalpindi, the brown, redundant hills opened up to reveal a horizon filled with dark and treeless bluffs extending beyond sight.

Above the horizon, an azure sky held contrasting clouds, and to match the clouds, three icy peaks, barely visible, cut into the air like gleaming lances. The distant white mountains seemed disconnected from the rest, behind the drab foothills, yet appearing higher and closer than anything within my immediate surroundings.

The Karakoram Highway angled upward the way it had done for the past month, but snow-covered summits drew me onward, like a row of pyramid-shaped diamonds in the midst of landslides, brown rock, and sere, barren ground. I had been cycling in a single layer of clothing; soon, a sweatshirt went on, then another. Snow dusted the road to either side, its brightness denied at times by the black of underlying rock. At one magical point, as if some deity had opened his hand and broken the mountains down, the foothills flattened out to leave a straight, white ridge glaring down on the surrounding land. Clouds formed over the ridge, unable to pass yet stacking up against the mountains as if to increase the height of the peaks that pushed skyward. A white-coated valley surged to the left, where an animal I had never seen before foraged for snow-covered plants. It was my first glimpse of a yak.

MAY 6
40 km south of Gilgit, Pakistan

THE ROAD continued its ascent. With the increasing altitude, my lungs strained, and the thinning air sapped my limbs of energy. By midafternoon, I was overcome by the altitude. I was compelled to set camp early under a low arching bridge, but sleep came sporadically while the night passed. Animals rustled by in the darkness, adding a paranoid fear to my misery.

I awoke to find the last of my bread inundated with ants. They had invaded every minute air pocket and the supplies were not edible. I was faced with the thought of cycling a full day with no food. Satisfying myself with one cup of coffee, I set out—then was ground to a stop 500 meters down the road in a fit of nausea. The remainder of the day was spent hunched over my handle bars, walking the slightest inclines, and vomiting.

Repairs added to the day's frustrations. Three new spokes snapped behind the freewheel. As a result, the wheel was bent against my brake pads. Had I been cycling like that for hours? Days? In my weak state of mind, I did not know. The repair took two hours. My fatigue and delirium added to the duration of the task. With fifteen broken spokes behind my freewheel, solving the problem in Gilgit became imperative.

The repair complete, I set my mind on reaching Gilgit. I did not allow myself a rest; the mental energy was there to begin only once. I counted out a rhythm of five pedals. One ... two ... three ... four ... five. After each five pedals I imagined myself in a Gilgit hotel. I let my mind think of nothing but the next five pedals. One ... two ... three ... four ... five. I suffered from nausea in the saddle but went on. One ... two ... three ... four ... five ...

Then my chain snapped.

That sent me into despair. I cursed the rising road, screamed aloud, shook my fist at the mountains and threw the bicycle to the ground. Then, that obligatory duty over, I fixed the chain and began again. One ... two ... three ... four ... five ...

MAY 7
Gilgit, Pakistan

THE STREETS OF GILGIT were wide and clean in the morning mountain air. I had arrived the previous night, at the end of exhaustion, before falling into bed at one of the local hotels. Food, and a decent night's sleep—free from the eye-opening trials of foraging animals, restless population and unpredictable weather conditions—contributed to a feeling of rejuvenation and sense of astonishment at the difference one restful day could make.

Exploring the bazaars and back alleys in pursuit of equipment to make repairs, I found Gilgit to be a surprising village. I had entered a tourist Mecca complete with airport, trekking agents, first-class hotels, and upscale restaurants. Gilgit's location in the mountains made it a perfect transit point to many trekking routes, mountain peaks, and valleys frequented by moneyed travelers. It was also the access point to the overland route to China. Here, in the middle of the isolated Karakoram range, I was overcome by an odd feeling of self-consciousness while watching the snow-white tourists who were fresh off the plane. But tourism brought the luxuries, and it was refreshing to have access to all the amenities that Gilgit offered. After endless nights camping in the cold, huddled under bridges, I suddenly found myself in a city of Western comforts.

In light of my new-found energy, I spent the afternoon exploring the bazaar in an attempt to fill my ever-lengthening list of supplies necessary to see me over Khunjerab Pass. My main problem was effecting repairs to the bike. Replacing fifteen broken spokes behind the freewheel was my first priority, but accomplishing the task demanded I first remove the freewheel. That required an extractor tool which was doubtful to exist in Gilgit. I also needed to find Shimano chain links, a tire of correct size, and spokes of correct length—rare components anywhere in Asia. I suspected that none of those parts could be obtained in Gilgit. In essence, I was caught in a trap. I could not cycle out of Gilgit until securing the proper tools and spare parts, yet those very items were not available in Gilgit.

MAY 8
Gilgit, Pakistan

I CHECKED OUT of my high-priced hotel and moved to the Tourist Cottage, a small Inn with a courtyard and garden that provided the perfect outdoor environment for bicycle repairs. It also meant two dollars per night rather than ten dollars, as well as a more travel-hardened clientele. The Cottage held a tradition of serving a community dinner for all the residents. At dinner, I met the other guests—a young Australian, born in Colombia, on his way overland to find work in England before his money ran out; a couple from Japan in the midst of a one-year tour through Asia; and a German throwback to the sixties who introduced himself as "Willie."

"I'm not really German," he said while we sipped chai. "Actually, I'm a citizen of the world, man." His statement was close to accurate, considering Willie had not returned to Germany in twenty-five years.

Over the next few days I scoured the bazaar in an attempt to fulfill some of the more difficult items on my list. A local merchant, Mr. Dad Ali Shah, had a reputation for helping travelers. He provided me with two maps of western China, but he did not know where to find bicycle parts, or if bicycle parts were available in Gilgit. I was referred to the only bike shop in town, where I described my problem to the owner.

"I am afraid our mechanic is not here," he admitted. "But we do have some tools."

The owner showed me a barren red box the size of a small book, containing a scant selection of a few wrenches and one screwdriver.

"That's it?"

The owner nodded.

"How in God's name do you maintain all these bikes?"

"We have a German man who comes in every few months with his own tools. Besides, the bikes are new, they have no need for repair yet. What is the name of the part you need?"

"Freewheel extractor tool."

"I've never heard of it."

To make matters worse, at that moment a man who was introduced as the junior mechanic entered the shop. "You're wasting your time," he said. "I've looked all over Gilgit for this tool. It is not here."

I had spent two days searching through the shops and markets of Gilgit and all I could show for my efforts was two maps of western China. While I wandered the bazaar, a feeling of defeat overcame me. I was doomed to continue my journey on a bent rear wheel. I roamed through the markets of Gilgit, searching for the slightest solution to Papillon's present state of disrepair.

As a last resort, I cycled to the airport in the hope of finding any tourists traveling with bicycles. It took several days of searching, but on the third day, I spotted two mountain bikers about to board a plane bound for Switzerland. When I introduced myself and explained my predicament, one of them reached into his bag and pulled out a bundle of ten spokes and a pack of chain links. "Here," he said, "take these. I'm flying home so I won't need 'em."

"I mid' as well give you one of these tires," the other added, offering one of the spare, collapsible tires which rested on his rear rack.

With that, the two big-hearted cyclists boarded the plane. I stood in shock for a few minutes before shouting my belated thanks, then I walked back to the Tourist Cottage with new-found hope. Even though I couldn't help reveling in my good fortune, a few hurdles remained. Tools. Removing the freewheel. Supplies. Maps . . .

MAY 10
Gilgit, Pakistan

IN THE MORNING I was struck with a few new ideas. I went back to Dad Ali Shah and asked him about the tool I needed.

"I'll check around town," he promised. "Come back later. I'll let you know what I find."

I returned to discover that his search had been in vain. "I am sorry my friend," Mr. Shah informed me, "this tool is not in Gilgit."

In desperation, I made some rudimentary drawings in the hope that someone could manufacture the tool. Showing my drawings around town for hours, the only replies I received were shrugs, apologetic salaams, and confused looks.

I went back to talk to Dad Ali Shah with one question. "Is there anyone in Gilgit who has the ability to make this part?"

"If anyone can do it," he assured me, "it would be Mr. Saleem. His shop is on the other side of the bazaar."

Mr. Saleem didn't speak English, so an interpreter was found and brought to the shop. My hopes rose when the interpreter said, "Mr. Saleem is very expert. He brought this machine to Gilgit," and he pointed to the lathe furiously spinning off backlogged orders.

Mr. Saleem did prove to be very expert. With one look at my drawing and a quick analysis of the bike wheel, Mr. Saleem knew exactly what I needed. After three hours and the labors of four employees, the part was made—a beastly looking, rough and rudimentary facsimile, but functional nonetheless. In another ten minutes, after a lengthy session of miming "chain," a chain was produced and the freewheel removed. Mr. Saleem, in that humble Muslim tradition I had witnessed on so many occasions, would accept no payment.

Gilgit, Pakistan

I SPENT MY LAST DAY in Gilgit working on the bike, while pondering the hourly cost of four American tool and die workers. I cleaned and lubricated all the bearings, added the new spokes and replaced my worn brake pads. The removal of broken links throughout the past month had shortened the chain to the point that I was forced to put on a smaller, spare derailleur bought in Greece. The Greek derailleur took away half my gear selection. Finally, the original went back in place after adding the necessary chain links.

In the bazaar, I bought supplies for the journey through the mountains. I found some items I had not seen in some time. In addition to the usual rice and roti, my supplies included one tin of processed cheese, 1/4 kilo of porridge oats, two packets of powdered soup, one jar of apple jam, and two boxes of vitamins fortified with minerals and electrolytes.

With the supplies packed, and the repairs to Papillon complete, I was confident in setting off on the high road to China once again. A mountainous 240 kilometers remained to the border, through some of the most remote areas on the face of the earth.

MAY 13

the Hunza Valley, Pakistan

THE ROAD immediately out of Gilgit began twisting through a high-altitude plateau of blue rivers and white peaks. The most spectacular aspect of the scenery was that with every bend of the road, it became impossibly more spectacular. I wound through a land of summits and sky, the sun rising over the whiteness. Sunbeams glossed the pines sending a glitter from every pristine crystal of ice.

Turning around the side of a mountain, I became engulfed in beauty beyond the ability of the mind to comprehend. Cliffs rose sharply from the road, dotted with small pines that disappeared gradually into the snow-line of each mountain. Glaciers eased their way down the cracks and crevasses, glowing blue-white in the sun. The earth seemed to rise from the surface of a silver moon, with a deep purple void surrounding all else, and blackness relegated to the distant foothills.

The simplest details were difficult to absorb. Contrasting shades and tones wavered in the air as if the land was conducting an orchestra in which only purity of color played an instrument. I was awash in the essence of nature's being, and an exhilaration of spirit I soaked up with a need that had been developed by the earth's past treasures, nurtured by the Himalaya and the Atlas, conceived by the Pyrenees and Appalachians.

In the valleys below, even the shadowy crevasses held white peaks, and above, the sun cradled a white wisp of snow, like boney white fingers suspended in a sky-framed box. Far below, in the hazed obscurity of distance, a river shimmered like wavering tinsel, thin and barely visible.

The sky itself was not immune to the altitude. Clouds warped into contorted cotton puffs around sheer-ice summits that hovered toward the indigo of space. Above one craggy peak that wrinkled in upon itself, a cloud was formed in the shape of a white lance seated in a violet sky, or an ivory tusk draped with sapphires.

I pitched camp for the night in the middle of that surrounding spectacle, on a cliff overlooking the turquoise Hunza River. My tent was protected by fallen rocks and boulders which created a fortress around me, with an open end facing the Hunza. I built a fire and watched the flames weave through each recess of the gleaming rock. My tent, a small blue dome, reflected the campfire like a summer moon. Brewing coffee sacrificed its aroma to the night air.

MAY 15

Passu, Pakistan

I ALLOWED MYSELF a two-day layover in the tiny provincial capital of Hunza before I cycled toward Passu, the next mountain refuge along the Silk Road. Glaciers abounded high in the crevasses, weeping their water down the moss-covered cliffs and onto the track. The Karakoram Highway tilted higher toward the sky, some glaciers extending tongues of ice to stretch within reach of the road. A beam of ice blocked the way, like a fallen redwood, two stories tall and impassable. But Pakistani ingenuity prevailed; a cave was cut through the blockage to create a tunnel.

Passu was a gem among towns, a tiny village set in a land of white. I arrived at dusk, and it was dark by the time I checked into the Passu Inn and secured Papillon in my room. A verandah extending from the front of the small inn faced the potholed, dirt track which had brought me from Rawalpindi. The Indus River, wrapped in darkness, hummed beyond the road. Beyond the river rose a silver moon between two white-capped peaks to create an eerie gleaming.

There was only one other resident of the Passu Inn, a traveler from Finland who had come overland through the Caspian countries. We sat on the verandah, a swaying lantern illuminating the inn behind us, while a rising moon illuminated white peaks to the east. With my companion's help, I attempted to devise a plan to see me over Khunjerab Pass. I began by drawing a map of the mountains to the north.

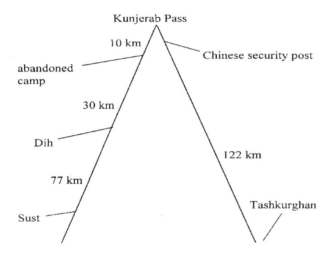

SUST WAS A RUGGED 37 kilometers uphill from Passu, 117 kilometers from the Chinese frontier and the Khunjerab Pass. Although the town was far short of the border, Sust acted as immigration and customs due to the inaccessible terrain at higher altitudes. From Dih, a police checkpost 40 kilometers from the border, the road rose 2,500 meters to the pass, a difficult ascent which would take some time. My problem was that the area between Sust and Tashkurghan supported no villages, therefore no food, no shelter. Once I left Sust, I would technically be nowhere, stamped out of Pakistan but not stamped into China for another 120 kilometers—two days at least in limbo. I hoped that the discrepancy in my passport would not cause me problems upon entering China.

I explained to the Finn that I planned to spend a day in Sust buying supplies and taking care of paperwork. He suggested that I should try to convince the guards at Dih to let me pitch my tent in the compound for the night.

I glanced at our hand-drawn map. The forty kilometers from Dih to the pass seemed like a great uphill expanse. Weather would make things difficult. Altitude presented problems. Making the pass in one day was not a certainty. If necessary, I would spend a night at the abandoned work camp. From the camp remained a drastic 17-kilometer ascent to the border, then a straight down, 120-kilometer glide to Tashkurghan. Once I achieved Tashkurgan, Chinese politics would determine my fate.

MAY ?

Sust, Pakistan

IN THE MORNING, the Finn put on his backpack and walked south. I cycled north out of Passu into a blinding snow storm. It took me eight hours to reach Sust, where I was trapped by a blizzard that raged for three days.

I spent the time searching through town for enough supplies to last me over the pass. I asked the Mountain Refuge Camp to boil eight eggs for me. I found one tin of cheese, a kilogram of dried noodles, biscuits, coffee, sugar and jam.

Through my continuing efforts to collect road information of the more northerly regions, I was referred to the Mountain Refuge's several travel logs. They contained journal entries of those who had passed over the mountains from China. Unfortunately, the information was contradictory and conflicting, some cyclists telling of a mystical "cycle permit," some being forced on buses, and a few deported from the country by force. One wrote, "If they try to put you on a bus and you just cycle away—they won't chase you."

The blizzard cleared on the fourth day, and I awoke during that interim when the rising sun hesitated to show the smallest spark above the horizon, yet yellow rays lighted the sky a dim gray. Wheeling my bike down the muddy street out of Sust, I arrived at the immigration shack where some slight confusion ensued. The shack remained locked, and the border guards who usually stood erect at the gate were lounging to the side, sipping chai. A little bewildered, I walked over to the guards.

"Exit visa?" I asked, making a stamping motion with my hand.

"No visa today," the guard said.

I was stunned. Being refused a visa after making the mental preparations for the torturous ascent to Dih was a highly deflating prospect. Besides, I had never been refused an exit stamp to *leave* a country.

"What did you say?" I asked the guard, in Urdu, wondering if I had heard him correctly.

"No visa today," he repeated.

"Why?" I asked, but was rebuffed with a blank stare. It was obvious the man did not speak English.

"There is no bus today," one of the other guards broke in, "so no visa!" The three guards stared at me with suspicion.

"I don't need a bus," I tried to explain, but still elicited nothing but blank stares.

"Bicycle," I told them." I travel by bicycle."

Incredulous stares.

"There." I pointed to Papillon lying by the roadside.

The yellow bike elicited excited stares and raised eyebrows. The guards walked over to the bicycle and began a discussion in Urdu, hands on their chins as they talked.

"Go see the man in that building," one of the guards finally said. "He is immigration."

I went to the building where I found an official who re-enacted the exact conversation the guards and I had just finished. Curious, the new man drifted out and joined his colleagues. "Go see the man in that building," he said at length, pointing to another shack. "He is immigration."

I visited two more officials in as many buildings, accomplishing nothing more than to create a Pakistani Summit Meeting around my bicycle. After much discussion, one of the lesser officials produced a key, opened the immigration office, and stamped my passport. The six looked on in curiosity as I cycled up the Silk Road.

The way from Sust was the most scenic part of the Karakoram Highway to date. The river wavered in turquoise beneath me. The Hunza began its long bend around the next white peak, and the turquoise gave way in slow gradations to a classic blue, then deep purple to match the sky. Amid this transformation—from translucent turquoise, to crystal blue and then to purple—a torrent of white water intervened to break the continuity, as if a flash of lightning had appeared amidst a perfect sunrise. It seemed the rapids spoke in words, printed in white letters, and the words printed read, "bliss."

Around a bend, encompassed by a new configuration of colors, the foaming water seemed like musical notes woven together in the fugue of white mountains, glaciers flowing from the sky, and beauty I had never before seen. Each new bend in the road was a new ascension. An ascension to a new level of art, a new level of realization, as if I had been subjected all my life to a child's finger painting then was suddenly confronted with a Pieta. With each bend in the road, thrust of a glacier, white powder gently dusted from the top of a peak, the mountains revealed nature in its purest form.

I cycled toward Dih, engulfed in ever more awe-inspiring scenery. Ten kilometers from the mountain outpost, I came upon one lonely immigration official sitting in a rickety wooden chair by a sign stating "Check Post." I looked around. One man, a chair, and a wooden sign—no hut, no food, no water. When I asked the guard what he did when it snowed, he pointed to a small overhang in the cliff. The official detained me for a few minutes, more out of curiosity than the cursory glance given to my passport, then he waved me on with a grin.

Regrettably, the mountain vistas were short lived. The view became a memory when snow began to obscure the scenery. The snow was transformed into a blizzard by a heavy wind as I pushed on toward Dih.

I arrived at the security post on the border of Khunjerab National Park after sunset. At a minimum altitude of 3,000 meters, the park provided a habitat for the rare snow leopard and the nearly-extinct Marco Polo sheep. The road through the park was reputed to be the highest public road in the world, creating difficulties for the cyclist. Unpredictable weather, altitude, and gear-wrenching ascents awaited me. Those were conditions I was ill-equipped to handle, considering the dilapidated state of my tent, but conditions that helped me negotiate permission to stay in the compound for the night.

The camp was a dismal place, with a few tents and buildings scattered along a flat part of the valley. I was grateful to be shown to a canvas tent where I spent the night quartered with two military policemen. While lying in my bunk listening to the raging blizzard outside canvas walls, I contemplated the remaining ascent. There was one stop left. At an abandoned work camp forty kilometers up the slope, ten kilometers short of Khunjerab pass, I would spend my last night in Pakistan before the final push to the top.

May 20

border post, Pakistan

I WAS NOT PREPARED for the climate. My night in the unheated tent was spent in misery. With my pitifully thin sleeping bag, I was constantly awakened by the cold. By morning, heated living rooms and hot coffee to warm the limbs were on my mind, two amenities that did not exist in such a remote mountain outpost.

The blizzard continued raging while I cycled out of Dih. Like the previous day, every item of clothing in my pack was wrapped around me. And like the previous night, warm camp fires were on my mind. All day it hailed and snowed, whipped by a fierce wind, and all day the road tilted upward. The air grew thinner with every turn of Papillon's wheels.

Contrary to several sources of information, there was no deserted work camp ten kilometers from the top of the pass. The storm had become blinding, forcing me to set up camp in a protected niche in the cliff.

I began taking precautions against hypothermia. The past few days of cold combined with an energy-sapping exertion had slowly and methodically robbed my body of heat, putting me in a gray daze in which all sounds were like echoes and all visions seemed 100 yards away. I was called upon for a clear identification of the danger, but clear thought took a conscious effort. The sweatshirts I had carried since Turkey became a blessing, and I remembered the time I almost threw them out in ninety-degree India.

Camp set, I pulled off my damp outer shirts and brewed warm coffee inside my tent to heat the interior. Using a technique I developed in Turkey, I rolled the warm cup up and down my limbs, periodically taking sips and re-heating the cup. Then I put on, in layers, every article of clothing in my pack. First a T-shirt, then a cutoff sweatshirt, another T-shirt, four sweatshirts, and my rain poncho. With socks on my hands, I changed my wet footwear for my thick Nepalese trekking socks, then slipped under my thin Greek sleeping bag.

I brewed a second hot cup of coffee with the last of the fuel that I had been rationing since Rawalpindi.

The interior of my tent was crisp, cold, but the blue walls were illuminated by an orange candle flame creating a warm glow. *War and Peace* sat open on my lap, the pages illuminated in yellow. My stove sputtered to a stop with the last of the fuel, but a steaming cup of coffee sat next to me. I slowly warmed. My cove was protected against the storm. I felt a sense of safety.

The grinding sound of gears shook me from a dull sleep. I emerged from my tent into the shrill air. A four-wheel-drive truck pulled up and two uniformed men jumped out. On their shoulders was an insignia: Khunjerab Security Force.

"This is no place for you to be," one of the rangers said. "Bad storm moving in tonight."

I looked around and wondered how much worse it could get. My cove would not have been protection enough in white-out conditions. The rangers helped me strike my carefully-built campsite, and I hoped for warm quarters no matter where the two were headed. I hadn't seen a heated building since leaving Sust, so I expected a camp similar to Dih.

They took me to an outpost consisting of a one-room brick building flanked by two canvas tents, all set in a snow field surrounded by a white-capped rim of peaks. Inside, the building was dimly lit by a cast-iron stove standing in the center of the room. Atop the stove, a boiling kettle of chai and a bubbling pot of curried *alu gobi* waited, a mixture of steamed cauliflower and local spices. Stacked just off the heat was a pile of warm, soft roti. Four guards sat huddled around the stove. The temperature had dipped to fifteen below.

"Come," the rangers bunched within the warm glow said in unison, "sit by the heat."

A chair was cleared for me where I basked in the yellow radiance of the flame, absorbing the heat of the fire. For the first time in a week, I was able to peel away some of the under layers of clothes which were permeated with a constant damp sweat. I realized I was shivering. The rangers gave me a plate of alu gobi and I ate like a ranch hand, gulping down chai and eating faster than I could chew. A short-wave radio, whining in a dark corner, declared dangerous weather conditions in the high mountains. Certainly, their outpost qualified.

The rangers, noticing my condition, set up a cot next to the stove. I hung my wet clothes on a rope over the heat and balled up under the covers of my makeshift bed. I wondered if I would have survived the night in my tent, finishing the last of the noodles I had lived on since Sust.

With the rangers, I had warmth, and a security taken for granted by most people—four strong walls standing solid against the storm. Heat given off by a wood burning stove. Warm food and hot chai. To me, those things were not necessities, they were luxuries.

I warmed into my cot and asked about the park and the remaining mountain ascent. Before dozing off, I mentioned the endangered Marco Polo sheep—the Karakoram providing their last refuge on earth.

"No sheep," one said." I fear they are all gone." The rangers had, however, recently seen several snow leopards.

I faded into sleep while listening to the whine of the radio, hiss of the stove, and whistling winds of the blizzard locked outside. The guards had taken me back down seven kilometers which I would have to re-climb, leaving seventeen kilometers to the top of the pass. " . . . but," the head ranger had observed, "With this snow, you may not be able to leave tomorrow."

MAY 21
Khunjerab Pass, between China and Pakistan
MORNING brought calm skies. I readied Papillon and started back toward the pass.

Up . . . up . . . seventeen more kilometers to the top. The air was thin and my lungs strained. Last night's blizzard had powdered the slopes with fresh snow. At 6:30 the sun rose over the peaks and played off the snow like glitter.

Up . . . up . . . rest. Up . . . up . . . rest. I set my sights on a landmark high up in the switchbacks and wouldn't allow myself to rest until reaching that mark. Then I repeated the procedure over and over again until the altitude yielded.

Ten kilometers to the top. Up ... up ... rest. Across the ravine came a sight that raised my spirits and filled my heart with joy. A lone snow leopard trotted serenely along the opposite bank of the ravine. Grey-white and majestic it made its way, then looked in my direction and sped away. Once again the silent bicycle revealed its rewards.

Five kilometers to the top. Up ... up ... rest. The air became thin and cold. Breathing was like sucking in dry ice cubes. I tried to imagine how climbers achieved 8,000 meters while expending such effort.

Four kilometers to the top. Up ... up ... rest.

Three kilometers to the top.

Two kilometers.

Top.

I stood atop Khunjerab Pass, 5,000 meters above sea level. The sun, at its zenith, glistened off the nearby peaks. Yaks grazed in a valley below, carelessly pawing up hidden weeds, and I was overcome with a tremendous feeling of exultation. I reveled in my success.

Next stop—China.

11

The Middle Kingdom

DESCENT. What a rewarding feeling after climbing time out of mind. The land all around me that was powdered white from the previous night's snow, loomed against a space-blue sky, with white-capped peaks pointing upward like gems to greet me on the horizon. Occasionally, clumps of isolated peaks strove up above the rest like lonely monoliths, testimony to the dominance of height in a land of height. It was a few kilometers of grace before the Chinese border post.

Two guards manned the secluded post, both barely beyond boyhood. I couldn't help thinking that only someone who had perpetrated some great injustice upon the Chinese People would have been stationed in such a remote mountain outpost.

"Bike?" one asked, as I handed over my passport.

"Bike." What else was there to say?

"You sell." It was a statement rather than a question.

"No sell."

You sell—fifty quai."

He was offering me about ten dollars. That sort of harassment went on for another ten minutes while the guards analyzed the visa I had acquired in New Delhi. After an hour of questioning, they finally allowed me to continue down to the immigration post in Pirali.

The thirty-kilometer descent to Pirali was like gliding through a movie set. The white-domed mountains moved by in slow motion, as if a Hollywood director was panning a camera across the landscape.

179

Startled yaks bolted while I sped by. From dens along the roadside, hundreds of Himalayan marmots, resembling rust-colored beavers with black tails, let out shrill barks when I approached. Their frog-like chorus accompanied me down the mountain.

Despite the distracting scenery, and my first prolonged descent in months, immigration and customs in Pirali weighed heavily on my mind. According to all previous information, Pirali was where I would be prevented from cycling on—either by being forced to sell my bike, deported from China, or thrown in jail. A few short kilometers separated travel fact from fiction. Around a set of white bluffs, Pirali came into view. It turned out to be nothing more than a collection of a few official buildings set in a wide section of the road. A fence surrounded the compound, with an entrance gate on the south side of town and one exit gate to the north. Cliffs rose from the fence on either side of the road, leaving no way to bypass the checkpost.

Contrary to all the rumors concerning entry into China, my border crossing began smoothly. Immigration, customs and money exchange combined took only twenty minutes. The problems began when my visa was stamped with an entry date. The official refused to return my passport.

"You must buy a bus ticket," he told me. "Cycling is not allowed."

My protests were useless. I was forced to buy a ticket to Tashkurghan and load Papillon on top of the bus. The driver was given my passport, to be returned in Tashkurghan. I was forbidden to get off at an earlier stop. It meant bussing down 120 kilometers of hard-earned descent—a demoralizing and depressing realization.

I sat, silent, angry over the lost descent, so long anticipated and now wasting away, while the bus careened down the slope toward Tashkurghan. The seats carried young tourists with backpacks, all pointing with wide eyes from the windows whenever a villager appeared at the roadside.

A group of nomads on horseback inspired the bus-load of adventurers to scramble for their cameras and begin snapping photographs through the yellowed glass. I had seen photographs of this type before, most often taken from train windows, but witnessing the practice both confused and infuriated me. Those nomads were people I could be talking with, rather than watching them go by in a blink. And they were people, not zoo animals to be pointed at, or photographed like some inanimate object. While listening to the tourists around me discussing the blur outside their windows with detached curiosity, I realized why I traveled by bicycle. I wanted to be a part of the landscape, a member of each society encountered, rather than a spectator on a passing bus.

I remained in silent frustration while watching the other tourists— among them, yet feeling apart—until I could no longer remain still. I decided to offer the bus driver a bribe. I made my way to the front of the bus holding out a ten-yuan bill while pointing to the driver's pocket, the pocket that held my passport. The driver took my money. At the next stop, another bribe saw Papillon unloaded from the luggage rack, and I was free. The bus puttered off in a flurry of smoke and fumes, leaving me alone with the Karakoram once again.

The road continued relatively flat south of Pirali, at least when compared to the harsh inclines of the central mountains. Still, slight undulations produced an overall downward trend. Isolated mountain clusters pushed skyward from the flat valleys, where untended camels grazed like free-range cattle. Hybrid yaks, interbred with cows for existence at lower altitudes, grazed alongside the camels in wild pasture land bordering the road. Himalayan marmots chirped and barked in time with my cranking pedals.

The 122-kilometer mean descent brought me to Tashkurghan, where I checked in to the deserted tourist hotel. Deserted, because few tourists entered China from Pakistan, and the few who did venture over the Karakoram invariably rode buses directly through to Kashgar.

For those tourists who passed it, the Tashkurghan Hotel was nothing more than a two-second blur in a three-day bus ride. For me, the hotel represented my first impressions of Chinese culture. When compared to the harsh Karakoram, it seemed I had entered a world of unabashed luxury and excess.

I was provided with a set of chopsticks and a pitcher of tea seconds after taking my seat in the downstairs restaurant. A petite Tajik waitress brought the most expansive meal I could have imagined after five months of gosht, dahl, and roti. Eight dishes were placed in succession on the lazy Susan that occupied three-quarters of my table: steamed rolls, sautéed tomatoes, beef and peppers, mandarin oranges, lamb and fried melon. A steaming mound of glutinous rice dominated the array.

The only other travelers to occupy the hotel joined me in this excess, a tour group of four Americans accompanied by an Afghani guide. The five had traveled from the east, and I asked them about the desert beyond Kashgar. Their reactions were all similar.

"Impossible to cycle through the desert."

"Cross the Taklamikan? Madness!"

"You know what 'Taklamikan' means? 'Desert of no return.' You'll die out there."

"There are no towns for a thousand miles. Where will you get water? Food?"

My rudimentary map of China showed towns between Kashgar and Hami, a distance of 2,000 kilometers. I showed it to them.

"I didn't see any towns," said one, while looking to his friends for confirmation.

"Three. I counted three between Kashgar and Turpan," the Afghani said.

The distance between Kashgar and Turpan was more than 800 miles. If the Afghani guide was right and only three towns existed in that distance, I would have an insurmountable logistics problem on my hands. By cycling 100 miles a day, I would come upon only one town every other day, providing the towns were evenly spaced along the way. That meant carrying at least twenty liters of water. But accomplishing that distance over rough desert roads, weighed down by twenty liters of water, would be a difficult task. I could only hope to gather more encouraging information before reaching Kashgar.

The five of us exchanged travel information until the cooks began locking the kitchen doors, then I took my leave of the group and went upstairs. The room was equipped with a bathtub, but air was all that flowed when I turned on the tap. That was a familiar occurrence in Asia, but disappointing in this case, considering the price of the hotel. My first hot bath in months would have to wait.

While lying in bed reading my volume of *War and Peace*, I contemplated the past month of mountain passes, scavenging for food, and the overwhelming beauty of the Karakoram. Any hardship I endured to see that part of the world was paid back in full by the rewards of nature. Even the lingering shiver from incessant exposure to cold over the past month—a shiver that was such a constant companion to have become a way of life—seemed a small inconvenience next to the enduring memory of those most pristine mountains.

MAY 22

Tashkurghan, China

MY FIRST DAY in China had been overwhelming. In a matter of hours, my world had been transformed from a relentless climb through the Karakoram Mountains while surviving on dahl, to freewheeling down to Tashkurghan and gorging on an eight-course meal. The culture I had grown to gain comfort with and understand was traded for an array of odd currencies, incomprehensible language, and unfamiliar gestures. If the Karakoram was the land of brute physical effort and endurance, then it seemed China was going to be the land of red tape, paperwork, and social politics.

Planning the journey from Tashkurghan to Kashgar made those problems glaringly obvious. The Chinese authorities prohibited tourists from cycling the distance, and no open areas existed between the two cities. The lone tourist destination along the 280-kilometer ride was a wildlife preserve, Karakul lake, where foreigners visited only by special permit. Perhaps if I acquired that permit, the security posts near Kashgar would let me pass.

I went to the police station with that plan in mind, but I made the mistake of bringing the bicycle with me. It generated so much curiosity that every police official in Tashkurghan guessed my intentions.

"No cycle to lake—forbidden!" became the theme of the day while each officer, from cadet to captain, tweaked and fiddled with gears and pedals.

"No, no! No cycle—bus!" I replied, while hoping I could sneak out early enough the following morning to escape discovery. I explored what little there was of Tashkurghan in celebration of my small victory, then I returned to the hotel and recruited the staff to help me compile a list of phrases in Mandarin, Tajik and Uyghur, the three predominant languages in the area. The Chinese manager of the hotel, after watching me eat with my fingers as I had done throughout India and Pakistan, insisted upon giving me a seminar in the use of chopsticks. "Only Uyghurs eat with fingers," he insisted, referring to the Muslim people of Xinjiang province.

MAY 23

road to Kashgar, China

I LEFT TASHKURGAN at sunrise, undetected by the not-so-wary local officials. The road out of town continued to descend a few kilometers, then followed a stream before the road rose almost imperceptibly. I arrived at the first checkpost shortly after sunrise, where I handed over my Karakul permit to two young guards. They seemed perplexed, but conciliatory. Still, just to be certain, they summoned a senior officer. He looked at the pass, then called a yet higher official. After some discussion, the ranking commander was summoned. He arrived looking half asleep. The head man passed me, then berated his juniors in Mandarin, no doubt for waking him up.

I had done it. With one more checkpost to come before Kashgar, my confidence was growing. The road continued to rise over a 4,200-meter pass just south of Karakul lake. Before the ascent, I had stripped down to short sleeves for the first time since Gilgit, but once the road rose toward the sky, again all my clothes went back on. Sparse vegetation and rolling, blue-black clouds crowded the summit.

A short descent brought me to the wildlife preserve, one of those newly opened areas of China meant to draw some of the burgeoning tourist market from Kashgar. The attraction was meant to be the tribal yurts set up for those who would imagine they were experiencing the rigors of native life.

But I was the only visitor, and the yurts were more like small hotel rooms than traditional yurts, complete with a night stand, reading lamp, Western-style bed, and meals served like room service by a personal waiter. Because of those luxuries, my one-night stay at Karakul Lake cost me a small fortune. I was left with little choice but to pay; I could not risk cycling away to camp illegally in front of the entirety of Karakul officialdom. I was already thankful the officials neglected to check the dates on my permit, which showed I had been in limbo for two days. I represented the ultimate Chinese tragedy: an unaccounted-for American.

My descent continued out of Karakul, 110 kilometers behind me and still going. The next checkpost came at a point where the road was bounded by two parallel cliffs. An iron fence stretched across the road blocking traffic. The only way past was through one of two small gates that swung open at the behest of the guards, who were engaged in scrutinizing passports and paperwork. Tourist buses were backed up in a large clearing south of the gates, where disgruntled Europeans and Americans on package tours milled around in sport shirts and pressed white pants.

Two restaurants stood in the clearing as well. One was a café charging prices for one cup of coffee that rivaled my daily budget. The Westerners preferred the café. A Pakistani dhaba, in all its squalid splendor, dominated the other side of the road. There, Pakistanis on their way to see Tajik relatives in China occupied their time drinking chai and eating dahl. Since the Pakistanis had helped build the Karakoram Highway, they were allowed to travel rather freely across the border.

I took a seat in the dhaba and watched the vacationers on the other side of the road, while I envisioned crossing the checkpost without a permit. Some of the Pakistanis poked fun at the Westerners in biting Urdu. I marveled at how clean the tourists looked, and I became suddenly conscious of my tattered clothes, tinged black with the soot of Asia. My dress was more similar to some of the poorer Pakistanis surrounding me in the dhaba.

After some thought, I decided to go through the gate showing my passport and any other official papers that had been forced upon me in China. I hoped it would be enough to at least offer me an opening for debate.

The line stretched through the gate. Europeans and Americans were taken aside to show their papers purchased from tour companies in the West. Pakistanis, to my surprise, were let through relatively unnoticed. A guard asked them the simple question, "Pakistani?" The reply "gee" or "ha-gee" gained a pass. When my section of the line approached the gate, I noted the fate of the half-dozen people in front of me.

"Pakistani?"

"Ha-gee."

Pass.

"Pakistani?"

"Gee."

Pass.

White-faced tourist—taken aside.

"Pakistani?"

"Gee."

Pass.

My turn came and I stepped up, armed with a feeble passport. "Pakistani?" the guard asked.

I hesitated for a few seconds.

"Ha-gee," I blurted finally—and was passed.

Had they mistaken me for a Pakistani? My skin was surely as dark as any Asian's after the past months of high-altitude exposure to the sun, and my clothes were all from India or Pakistan. I didn't stop to think it through; in minutes I was aboard Papillon completing the remainder of the descent out of the Karakoram. Kashgar and the great Tarim Basin awaited, now unobstructed by guard posts.

MAY 25
road to Kashgar, China

MY CONTINUING PROGRESS toward sea level made the temperature gradually more bearable. The road tilted downward during the last of my three-day descent, until the Silk Road deposited me into the Tarim Basin like a laundry chute. One minute I was surrounded by the foothills of the Karakoram, cycling through the river valleys that had kept me company throughout northern Pakistan. The next, I found myself on the outskirts of the Taklamikan Desert amidst a great, level expanse as wide as the boundless horizon.

After focusing on mountains in the foreground since Rawalpindi, the emptiness of the Taklamikan left me with mixed feelings of loneliness and self-conscious doubt. My goals for the past month had been at the boundaries of sight: a mountain pass, a switchback, a valley below.

I searched the almost obscure, distant horizon, and my task seemed impossible.

The only panacea was to concentrate on the sporadic buses that shuttled tourists safely to Kashgar. Military vehicles passed regularly as well, the officials showing no interest in my illegal method of travel other than a friendly wave. "He is there so it must be allowed" seemed to be the general attitude.

I pushed north through the Tarim Basin. The flat land radiated heat of 100 degrees, while the sky, hazy white from wind-blown sand, seemed like an overcast winter sky. I passed through several towns where I was told of a sandstorm brewing to the north that had grounded air traffic. "You must stop," a Uyghur truck driver told me. "Our sandstorms can bury railroad cars."

The storm could already be seen on the horizon, a rolling dark wall as if a thunder cloud had descended to the ground. Still, I had cycled through sandstorms in the Sahara; they presented little difficulty. I left the towns behind and continued into the flat expanse of the Basin. A few Uyghur cyclists sped by, traveling in the opposite direction. No traffic traveled north. The sky ahead became a rolling cloud of dismal gray, billowing southward like a mounting tidal wave. It was not like the storms I had seen in the past.

The wind rose when the sun disappeared. Needle-like specks of sand seared my eyes. I was forced down a slope off the side of the road, where I covered my head and eyes with a tattered shirt. In this manner, I advanced fifty yards before the sand found its way through the shirt. The minute I opened my eyelids, I was blinded by the wind-driven pellets.

I spent an hour devising a new idea. Before moving on, I pulled my spare sweatshirt over my head and cut two holes for eye slits. I put my sunglasses over the eye slits with the head strap extending around the shirt to hold it in place. A T-shirt went around my mouth outside the sweatshirt, like a bandanna, creating a barrier against the sand. With the new system, I was able to walk slowly, bent against the wind, using my bicycle as a crutch.

Two hours later, my progress came to less than two kilometers. I was forced to stop at intervals to clear my eyes. I knew the storm was traveling southeast, so I hoped to walk through the tempest. But, after four hours, the wind showed no sign of slackening.

Visibility was less than ten feet through the stinging sand, when something appeared on the fringe of sight. Inching down the road at walking pace, a mobile home came into view, crawled past me, then stopped. The side door opened and a hand appeared. "Hurry, get in!"

Papillon and I were unceremoniously pulled aboard. Inside, three men sat among piles of mountaineering gear and crates of Russian cognac.

"We are Russian mountain climbers," announced the man sitting on a crate of vodka. "Look, you are one big sand ball."

"You are needing of some Russian cognac I think," pronounced a second man sitting on a crate. He poured shots all around. "Best cognac in all world. This is why we bring our own."

I winced as I tasted the cognac, eliciting cheers from the Russians.

"You are agreeing with me I think—yes? Best cognac in all world."

The three men were mountain-climbing instructors at a school based in Kazakhstan. And business was thriving, as their well-equipped mobile home attested. "We have more clients now, after the breakup of the country," the driver explained. "And more places will give us permission to climb their mountains."

In that unlikely company, I reached Kashgar and my saviors deposited at the Qiniwake hotel, where I spent the remainder of the day cleaning sand from my eroded chain rings.

JUNE 3

Kashgar, China

MY FIRST FEW DAYS exploring this small city revealed luxuries beyond the realm of my experiences in the Karakoram. The contrast was difficult to assimilate, from the heated showers and hotel rooms to restaurant menus devoid of dahl baht. Roti and fingers were replaced by chopsticks and the exotic cuisine of Xinjian. The familiar hush of Urdu was replaced by the incomprehensible yet lyrical sound of Mandarin and the harsh, guttural language of the Uyghur.

Kashgar was both cosmopolitan and exotic, serving as a trading post for all those who traveled the Silk Road. Thousands of merchants flocked to Kashgar's marketplace to sell camels and donkeys, carpets and clothing, produce, spices, and cloth. The market rivaled that of Marrakesh. The thin streets, back-alley deals and rich history was reminiscent of Varanasi. There was a sense of the West as well, in the transient backpacking community, in the comfortable hotels and relaxing restaurants. With all its luxuries, Kashgar struck me as a good place to equip myself for the waiting Taklamikan.

My most pressing task while in the city was a complete overhaul of the bicycle. The brake and gear cables were all frayed at the ends and needed to be trimmed or replaced. All of the bearings in the headset and bottom bracket had become riddled with sand, creating a telling crackle whenever I pedaled or turned the handle bars. Dozens of other minor problems haunted me as well, but my worst dilemma was the rear gear shifter. Damaged in the sandstorm, it was useless, reducing my twenty-one gears down to a sorry selection of one.

I spent several days on the repairs, leaving the most difficult item, the gear shifter, for last. I dismantled the metal casing around the shifter to find sand, twisted metal, and an integral piece of the mechanism in pieces. That presented me with some problems. I would not be able to continue without gears, and spare parts in China were rare. I roamed Kashgar for hours but found no shop capable of the repair. Mountain bikes were new to Kashgar, and the few places that sold them did not stock spare parts.

I spent the following day scouring the streets of Kashgar in search of a solution. Again, I asked the owners of several shops, but none of them carried the spare part. Removing a shifter from one of the new bikes, in effect, would make the entire bike useless. For that reason, each owner quoted a price for the shifter equivalent to the full price of the bicycle. After several failed attempts at bribing mechanics, each time offering a little more money, I came to the conclusion an irresistible bribe would be needed to accomplish my goal. With my new plan in mind, I slipped into one of the shops, called the mechanic aside, put 100 yuan on the table and pointed to the shifter.

"Come back tomorrow morning at eleven," he told me in a whisper, while quickly glancing around the shop.

JUNE 7
Artush, China

AFTER TEN DAYS in Kashgar, I set out for Artush, thirty-eight kilometers to the east. Directly out of town, the road began to undulate through a series of small hills baked like clay in the desert sun. South of the road loomed the bulk of the Taklamikan desert, white and flat with the waver of hot air obscuring a curved horizon. To the north, barren ravines like lunar mountains twisted in a maze of rock canyons and brown, barren hills reminiscent of the wadis near Aqaba. Three hundred kilometers northwest, those foothills melded with the Pamir mountain range, and to the east they rose into the Tian Shan, or Fire Mountains, near Dunhuang.

A short thirty-eight-kilometer ride through dry landscape brought me to Artush, an unimpressive town with an austere tourist hotel and a populace anxiously awaiting the day tourism might flow over from Kashgar. That seemed an improbable hope, since no tourist would travel thirty-eight kilometers to see a box-shaped hotel.

The rest of the town was nothing more than a truck stop, with a mud road bisecting the few small kiosks meant to serve as shops. The only food available was *nang*, the local bread, and *lachman*, flat noodles cooked with yak meat.

The novelty of seeing a Western tourist in Artush made my one-night stay more aggravating than usual. For the purpose of satisfying Chinese curiosity, the spare keys to my room were passed to any local resident wishing a glimpse at my sand-blasted, once-yellow bicycle. Chinese strangers would periodically admit themselves into my room, stand against the wall, and watch me as if I were the local Shakespearean production. One such visitor began searching through my bags before I pushed him back out through the door. In the struggle, he knocked over my glass containers of jam and coffee which shattered on the floor. Barring a return to Kashgar, the supplies could not be replaced until Aksu, 468 kilometers away.

JUNE 8
Taklamikan Desert, China

MY MAP SHOWED a town eighty kilometers east of Artush called Batsabishe. The town did not exist. Since my water-carrying capacity was only five liters, I was forced to wave down trucks for water by standing at the roadside with upturned water bottles while holding my hand up in the halt position. Three times throughout the day I repeated the same procedure, and all three times the very first driver stopped to fill my bottles.

By midday, I had gone through ten liters of water. The sun became so oppressive that I was forced to seek shelter under a bridge, where boredom gripped me until well into the afternoon. I analyzed the desert and watched what little wildlife dared challenge the Taklamikan's soaring temperatures.

Small black beetles scurried in the shade of the bridge. They became my afternoon entertainment. I was dismayed to see one beetle take a sharp turn just inches from the shade and run out into the bleached desert. A minute later, the beetle took another turn, ran under the shade of the bridge, then began digging where a minute drop of water had fallen from one of my bottles. Out of sheer boredom, I made a pool of water in a concave rock and set the beetle on the edge. The beetle drank its fill then scuttled away into the sunlight.

There was no life east of my afternoon bridge. No black desert beetles. No shade trees. There was sand, and baked dirt. There were tufts of brown weeds. There was heat. The sky turned violet with the sinking sun, and I cycled into the canyons that pierced the foothills two kilometers north of the Silk Road. I set up my tent then built a fire from some dry desert scrub scattered throughout the canyon. Yellow light from my fire reflected against rock walls, as the crackling of dry twigs added a comforting tune to the night. The last of my coffee salvaged from the hotel floor brewed next to the fire, permeating the air with its aroma. I leaned back against a canyon wall. The glow slackened from fire red to orange.

JUNE 9
desert camp—300 km west of Aksu, China
WITH 300 KILOMETERS remaining to Aksu, the first major town on the desert crossing, I made a checklist of the cities to come. The route plan looked daunting when complete.

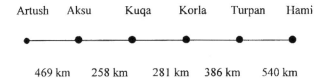

Artush	Aksu	Kuqa	Korla	Turpan	Hami
	469 km	258 km	281 km	386 km	540 km

Small towns about 100 kilometers apart were depicted on my map between the major cities, but none of them larger than Batsabishe, a town which existed only in the minds of cartographers. I could not be assured of finding supplies between cities. Turpan, the goal that drew me onward, was said to be a restful oasis beyond 1400 kilometers of dry desert sand.

The first miles of the desert crossing brought me through a barren landscape of brown dust and dry rock. Small clumps of gray weed awaiting summer rains stuck up like broom bristles through the rock. The road continued as a flat, baked and broken concrete highway arching over the horizon, then deteriorated into packed, brown dirt. Dust sucked up by hot air from the desert floor clung like searing powder to wet skin. The temperature hovered at 115 degrees Fahrenheit.

On the horizon, a colorful blob became apparent in the shimmering air, like a figure standing behind distorted glass. It seemed as if I was peering through a rippling pond with the thick, wavering air exerting its influence to obscure the view. The road became a hard, gray macadam while the vacillating image solidified. Two cyclists appeared, riding toward me, their panniers bulging with camping equipment, travel gear, and water jugs. The two looked at me, amazed, and stopped to dismount. It was the same amazement that struck me in meeting two cyclists in such a dry, dreary place.

"You know how far to Artush?" one of them asked.

"About two hundred kilometers."

"Like this?" the other questioned, waving his arm at the dry landscape.

"Like this," I assured them. "And no water. I had to wave down trucks to refill my water jugs."

The cyclists, two Germans, had ridden down from Allmatah, Kazakhstan, over the Tian Shan mountains and into China. We talked for a short time, dripping sweat onto the steaming pavement. I gave them my Pakistan travel guide for a map of Aksu and a hand-drawn copy of their U.S. military map of the Taklamikan. A testimony to satellite technology, the map showed the tiniest detail, including nuclear testing sites, flight paths, defensive positions and more. It was not the sort of thing to be caught with at a border post.

Just as the Germans had attested, the road eastward became pockmarked with potholes. The horizon constantly teetered with an uneasy glimmer. Several military and official vehicles passed me without interest, one even stopping to give me water. It seemed that the farther I traveled from the border, the less concerned the officials became about illegal tourism.

Pockmarked pavement quickly deteriorated into an abrasive white sand as fine as powder—almost like pumice. I learned long ago to refrain from oiling my chain in those conditions, since sand clung to the oil and wore away the chain links. A dry, sandy chain could be brushed off; an oily chain inundated with sand needed to be cleaned with solvent. But the sand of the Taklamikan took its toll regardless of my precautions. When the sun was at its apex, my chain snapped. I was forced to stop and make the repair.

The sand continued to wreak havoc on my time-worn and deteriorated chain while I cycled eastward. Two kilometers after the repair, another weak link snapped. Ten kilometers later, another. I was left with no choice but to use the gasoline from my camp stove to clean the chain. The removal of broken links forced me to once again replace my original derailleur with the shorter one from Greece, and once again I was left with half my original gear selection.

A Chinese character on my map, 220 kilometers west of Aksu, marked my next stop. I was hoping to find water in the town, but found only desert when I arrived. Farther on, I came upon a wooden lean-to shading a solitary man near the side of the road. Was this the town shown on my map? A stack of nang sat on top of a wooden barrel filled with water. I discovered the ingenuity of the Chinese free market when the man charged me seven yuan for five liters of water and ten yuan for a few stale nang.

JUNE 10

Santsako Village—210 Km West of Aksu, China

THE DESERT robbed my body of water at night, even while I slept. Having drained my bottles dry the previous evening, I awoke with no water reserves. Driven by thirst, I climbed up to the side of the road, turned my water bottle over, and began waving down trucks. The first driver who stopped carried only a liter of water. He gave it all to me save one sip. I rationed the meager supply hoping I would come upon an unmarked town, but the effort was futile. I needed a minimum of ten liters of water for a single day's ride. The liter was gone in less than an hour.

Again, I stood on the side of the road with upturned bottles. This time two trucks stopped at once. The first gave me a liter of chai; the second pulled over fifty yards down the road. A short Chinese driver climbed down from the cab of the second truck, heaved a ten-liter water canister from behind the seat, and began running. His face reddened while he ran, his left arm waving wildly in the air and his right, straining against the ten-liter water jug, remained straight and rigid. "Su-ma," he pronounced when he reached me, drinking water.

I ate a lunch of stale nang in the tiny desert village of Santsako. The next village where I could hope to find food and water was a minuscule dot on my map labeled Eejianfaan. Before leaving Santsako, I made an attempt to learn the distance to Eejianfaan, but the first six people I asked gave replies varying from forty kilometers to "at least sixty-five." That type of contradiction was not unusual in Asia, although a consensus could usually be gathered. But this time I was left completely baffled. Down the road I asked a seventh villager, "Fifty-two," he stated, a little too exactly.

I left Santsako in a state of fatigue, facing what I accepted to be a sixty-five kilometer stretch of desert road before finding food. I hadn't been able to buy supplies at any of the desert villages, so my food was gone save some emergency rations. Sandy roads and lack of nourishment caused slow progress. I was forced to rest repeatedly alongside the road while hunched over in the searing sun. An intense hunger drove me the sixty-five kilometers toward food. The sun lowered with each turn of the pedals, and with each sandy crank the kilometers slowly moved by. Tired, hungry, physically spent, I cycled into Eejianfaan at dusk.

The village was nothing but a few shacks, with two lonely inhabitants selling gasoline to passing trucks. I asked for food and water but was told there was none, and only after desperate persistence was I given one liter of orange-tinted water from a scummy wooden barrel.

The absence of food at Eejianfaan put me in a dire situation. I set up camp a few kilometers from the truck stop then, hampered by darkness, I broke into my emergency rations. One small bowl of noodles comprised my dinner, leaving me a handful of cooked rice to see me to Aksu. I went to sleep gnawing on my last stale crust of nang like a dog with a bone.

JUNE 11

deserted shack—100 km West of Aksu, China

I STOPPED A TRUCK for water in the morning, then I ate my last portion of rice. In the afternoon I slipped into a state of such weakness that I was forced to stop and eat sugar cubes, the only food item left in my pack.

Achieving the town of Atcha seemed like cycling up an endless mountain. Again, there was no food for sale in Atcha, and begging turned out to be useless. In desperation, I went to the local military post, where I begged so incessantly that they grudgingly gave me two nang. I was refused when I asked for more. On the outskirts of Atcha, I found one package of sugar wafers and some grape juice at a roadside shack catering to truck drivers. It was all the food available for sale in Atcha. I cut the nang into quarters and ate two, plus half the wafers. I was compelled to save the rest as rations.

With sunken belly, I left Atcha behind. The wadis that had been providing me with nightly campsites two kilometers north of the road disappeared. A flat expanse replaced them, stretching into mounds of dark sand that met a blue sky on the horizon. At times the white-capped Tian Shan could be seen, barely distinguishable from the pillar of clouds stacked up above the mountain range.

With the disappearance of the wadis, camping became more difficult. My tent, torn, tattered, was useful only as a ground mat or pillow, forcing me to camp under bridges, in abandoned shacks, or in the open desert. A two-sided shack provided shelter west of Aksu, one of many in abandoned mud villages I passed at least once daily, as if the desert had engulfed an entire population in one wind-driven sandstorm. Darkness fell, and I unrolled my sleeping bag, ate my ration of a quarter crust of bread, and crawled under my covers in a familiar state of hunger.

JUNE 12

Aksu, China

I FINISHED MY SUPPLIES before reaching Sanchinze, a disheartening town with no truck stop to cater to passing travelers. Once again, I was reduced to begging for food from citizens who did not have enough to feed themselves.

Eighty kilometers remained to Aksu. The supplies which were to carry me there consisted of one bowl of rice given to me by the collective population of Sanchinze, and a handful of sugar meant to augment the coffee which was lost on the floor of the Atcha hotel.

I ate sugar. I walked. Ten kilometers of cycling brought ten minutes of rest. I had rarely in the past experienced true delirium, but the memory of the miles to Aksu became lost somewhere. Lost, in the part of the brain that knew to reach for a patch kit; the part of the brain that knew to think "up . . . up . . . rest."

Too spent to cycle, I walked into Aksu at dusk. Dominating the skyline, an upscale hotel where tourist buses stopped overnight en route to Turpan promised modern amenities. The streets were lined with shops, street vendors and bars. Outdoor grills roasted kabobs and chicken and lamb by the kilo. The smell of mixed spices wafted through the streets, through the alleys and into the market square.

It has been said, "If it has four legs and is not a table or chair, the Chinese will eat it." That night, I followed the motto. I ate kabobs and fish heads and chicken feet. I ate abalone and quail eggs and a local dish, which I found out later consisted of cat and snake meat. I ate until my belly was round and tight, then I ate some more. Excess had gripped me in remembrance of past privations.

I walked through the streets occasionally stopping at a kabob stall or food vendor's shack. Outdoor billiard tables lined some streets, with young Chinese men gathered around watching the action. Makeshift Karaoke stands, nothing but a speaker and a microphone, were as prevalent as food stalls or kabob grills or tea houses. I remained in Aksu for two days, reluctant to leave the comfort of civilization. I left only when my bags were filled to capacity: five days of modest rations and ten liters of water.

JUNE 19

Kuqa, China

THE RIDE from Aksu was typical desert cycling. Typical, because I had become accustomed to thirst, starvation, and bizarre occurrences as normal day-to-day expectancies. My days were spent the way all my days were spent in the desert—waving down trucks for water, begging for food at roadside stands, surviving on my Aksu supplies when no truck stops appeared. The temperature, when the sun rose above the horizon, was always over 100 degrees. It was cooler at night, but the lack of a tent forced me to camp in any slight valley the desert provided for protection.

The first night out of Aksu, I slept under a low-arching bridge made of large stones set in the side of one of the many rolling hills which pervaded the landscape of the northern Taklamikan. Around midnight, a prickly ball against my bare leg sent me fleeing from my sleeping bag. A large rat with matted hair scurried away into the desert night. I awoke the following night to find a two-foot lizard tucked against the warmth of my leg. Since the demise of my tent I was subjected to sharing my bag with an array of bizarre bedfellows. Yet a third night, I awoke to find a scorpion under my pillow.

Four days of desert cycling brought me to Kuqa, an oasis surrounded by ancient grottoes and historic caves only recently opened to tourism. Unlike Aksu, where the tourist bus stopped for the night on its way west, no such stop existed in Kuqa, so the tourist hotel was affordable and virtually empty. I exchanged my travelers checks for FEC at the bank, the FEC for Renminbi on the black market, then I checked into a seven-bed dormitory equipped with the luxury of hot water and an attached bath. A Japanese traveler, Taka, occupied the adjoining room, and between the two of us we represented the entire tourist trade in Kuqa.

During the day I ate and recovered from the past weeks of heat and sun and lack of water, sometimes wandering into town to buy supplies for the onward journey. At night, Taka and I searched the town for a place to eat dinner. For the first time in weeks my skin was clean; the clinging touch of desert sand was gone. The familiar grit in my food was a memory, at least for the night. I sat at our dinner table, satiated, basking in the starlight of a cool Xinjiang evening.

JULY 16
Turpan, China

THE HEAT steadily intensified while I cycled eastward toward Turpan, one of the hottest regions in China at 300 meters below sea level. I thanked fate for the truckers, whose regular trips across the Taklamikan gave them an appreciation, and fear, for the kind of heat the desert could generate. They were my protective angels.

My third day out of Kuqa was particularly oppressive. I had taken refuge under a bridge at midday when a truck driver stopped to give me some water and apricots. Farther on, with a T-shirt wrapped around my head as protection from the sun, a van pulled over with a hand thrust out the window brandishing a bottle of mineral water. A short conversation with the driver ensued, then he drove off, leaving me not one, but three bottles of water. It was as if someone had handed me a sack of gold.

Nearing the village of Yakshi, the heat seemed to melt my legs into worthless baggage. A farmer sat, selling melons from the back of his horse-drawn cart. I bought as many as I could carry and retreated to the shade of a nearby tree, where I sucked on melon rinds until the sun retreated below the horizon. Melons in this dry land were cool and wet; they stood as a symbol that not all of the world is flat and gray and hot. The desert did have boundaries.

I checked into the Yakshi Hotel, a procedure which took over an hour. Some Public Security Bureau officials came to my room later and asked me for my travel permit. I showed them my falsified registration form, which they looked upon with suspicion. Fearing reprisals from the tourist officials, I slipped out of Yakshi before sunrise the following morning.

Yakshi marked the beginning of the demise of Papillon. The previous night, before reaching the village, I spent an hour making repairs to the rear wheel and the following morning more repairs. A scant twenty kilometers out of Yakshi, I was forced to make a two-hour repair to the front wheel. My pannier ripped open five kilometers later and needed to be strapped together with an old tire tube. Papillon II, without spare parts, was becoming a bike beyond repair.

I achieved the town of Mushtala near nightfall, where I ate a rare meal of pears, yogurt and lachman. There was only one other town on my map between Mushtala and Turpan, an expanse of 300 kilometers, so I was hoping to rest in Mushtala's hotel before proceeding into the desert. But there was no hotel in the town, and supplies were scarce. I cycled out into the desert and pitched camp under a bridge.

Before dark, I made some repairs to Papillon's rear wheel and, in the morning, even more. The day's journal entry stated: "I have nineteen broken spokes replaced by old bent spoke pieces and wire.

The chain is so thin and rusted not a day goes by without a repair—only to have the same or yet another link break later."

I ate a handful of stale biscuits and nibbled on bread six-days old for breakfast. Ten kilometers from my morning camp, the road turned to a maddening mixture of dirt and rock and powdered white sand, a combination almost impossible for cycling. The white sand created a reflective surface for the sun; at forty-seven degrees Centigrade, it was like being sautéed on a grill.

Slowly, the rock road tilted up toward the summer sky to begin a forty-kilometer ascent. A debilitating wave of weakness overcame me near the top. It was a weakness that had been haunting me in spells for some days, whether I was in the shade, sun, hungry or well fed. I convinced myself it was due to dehydration and long-term exposure to the elements.

Twelve kilometers into the climb, my wheel gave out. Twenty kilometers later my chain snapped. I was expecting a town shown on the map to be halfway up the ascent, but the town never materialized. Tokshi, the next town shown, would be impossible to reach before nightfall. A small truck stop at the top of the ascent saved me from a night of hunger, but the only food they had was a few stale nang.

As the heat became more unbearable, my notes became less intelligible. The sole notation for June 20th read, "90K—low on supplies." And the 21st, "90K—low on supplies." Which meant I had traveled ninety kilometers and was living on the usual bread and water.

The sun assaulted me with ferocity while I cycled eastward toward the Turpan Depression, the second lowest place on earth after the Dead Sea. Throughout my Taklamikan crossing, the midday heat made it impossible to cycle in the afternoon. When I entered the Turpan Basin, accompanied by the stifling heat that prevailed below sea level, the sun took possession of the hours between 11 a.m. and 7 p.m. No animals dared challenge the sun during those reigning hours.

The ride over the next few days proved to be one of the most difficult stages through the desert. The challenge was a grinding day-by-day mental fight against sand, wind, thirst and hunger—most days a repeated attack by the forces of nature on the human body and soul. When a town appeared, I ate lachman, once a day if lucky. The rest of the time I ate nang. Some days brought me near fainting from a weakness I had never known before. Some days brought me starvation—all brought repairs, three to five per day.

I ran out of water. I crawled on my belly under low bridges to escape the midday heat. I ate six-day-old nang, so hard it crunched when chewed.

I continued toward Tokshi. The sun became wide and intense. Fifteen kilometers from the city, where the road undulated and curled like a flagon's handle, I came upon a truck driver waiting out the midday heat in the shadow of his cab. I sat with him in the shade while he cut up a watermelon and handed slices around to the other drivers who had stopped for the afternoon. The drivers each took one slice of melon, handing it around the circle, then insisted I eat the rest. They watched me with empathetic eyes while I devoured half of a watermelon by myself.

Unlike the water I carried, which maintained the constant temperature of a morning cup of coffee, the melon juices stayed wet and cool inside the husk, making them as valuable as gold in the dry Taklamikan. Nevertheless, I never was charged more than two mao for a melon, a few cents, and more often was given free melons off the back of laden carts by farmers on their way to market in Turpan. I was not sure the gestures were acts of kindness, but more acts of sympathy given out by those who understood the consequences of cycling in the midday heat. Just like I had given a thirsty beetle a capfull of water, so those who knew the desert provided me a melon now and then.

I spent two days in the Tokshi Binguan recovering from heat exhaustion and dehydration. After two days of recovery, I still remained weak and dizzy. It was an effort to walk around town. The only thing that raised my spirits was the fact that Turpan was a short sixty kilometers east of Tokshi. There, I could find a proper hotel, Western amenities, and some basic bicycle parts. There, I could rest and recover in comfort for as long as I liked.

The third morning after arriving in Tokshi, I set out for Turpan. Although the distance was slight, I felt weary, and the kilometers went by slowly. I suffered three breakdowns resulting in an extensive repair halfway to my destination. Since there was no shade in sight, I was forced to make the repairs in the midday heat.

When I approached Turpan, the green oasis showed on the

horizon like a cool emerald in a sea of blinding white sand. I had neglected to shelter myself from the sun during the height of the day, and had pushed myself to the verge of heat stroke. My head pounded until each pump of my heart caused me to wince. My entire body tingled with tiny pinpricks, like a chill running through my spine. On the outskirts of Turpan, half-delirious, I dove into an irrigation ditch where I sat mumbling to myself. The usual crowd gathered to push and poke. It didn't matter. In my delirium, they seemed like echoes. All I could think about was to cling to the bicycle so it didn't get taken, and to soak in the muddy water until my body temperature was lowered.

I soaked in the ditch for a long while. A crowd had long since gathered around when my senses began to return and a farmer on a donkey-drawn cart stopped to investigate the source of the gathering.

"Turpan Binguan?" he asked, after assuring himself that I was indeed a Western tourist. I was helped into the back of the donkey cart, then deposited at the Turpan Binguan near the center of the oasis.

SAME DATE
Turpan, China

AFTER EXPERIENCING almost nothing but drab, gray desert since Kashgar, Turpan seemed to me like an emerald-green sanctuary. The streets were lined with cool shade trees, and grape trestles arched over the tables at the various local restaurants. John's Café, across the street from the hotel, served everything from fried noodles to french fries. There was local wine, and fruit, and all the water a person could drink to be enjoyed along with Western rock and roll broadcast over the café's loud speakers. Turpan was a place overrun with backpackers and veteran travelers, and the locals were surprisingly friendly, having been spared the presence of demanding tourists.

I spent my first four days in Turpan eating and drinking everything in sight, lounging below the grape trestles at John's Café, and making as lasting repairs to Papillon as local materials permitted. I dismantled my rear wheel and hammered it back into a circle by using a rubber tube wrapped around the rim to prevent further damage. No twenty-six inch spokes existed in Turpan, so I bent the longer ones into shape and re-strung the wheel, which took an entire day. Other miscellaneous repairs filled four days: replacing zippers, sewing bags and straps, chain, front wheel, cables . . .

In time, my repairs were nearing completion, so I turned my attention toward nursing my body back to health. I spent afternoons under the grape arbor at John's Café, watching the sun strive in vain to reach me in my shady haven. Despite the abundance of food and water, the clean hotel and shelter from the sun, my body was slow to recover. The weakness that prevailed in the debilitating extremes of the Taklamikan still overcame me in spells while the days moved by. I became so lazy and apathetic that my routine was simple. Wake up, shuffle over to John's Café, eat and drink the day away then shuffle back to bed.

One afternoon, I sluggishly wandered across the street to find the place empty, except for one table occupied by two hippies with travel-worn clothes and shoulder-length hair. They reminded me of Willie, the German from the Tourist Cottage in Gilgit who had not been home in twenty-five years.

In fact . . .

I went closer. One of the hippies looked at me as if in recognition. "Willie?"

I sat down at the table in disbelief. Willie introduced me to his friend, "Bennie," to whom he explained our last meeting in Gilgit and my trip by bicycle. Like Willie, Bennie was a professional traveler. He had been in Asia almost his entire life and had traveled to every country on the continent: Myanmar, Tibet, Bhutan, Afghanistan, Mongolia, Macao, the list went on. Each was proficient in several Asian languages, and Bennie spoke fluent Uyghur.

"Xinjiang," he said, "is one of my favorite places in Asia. I want to buy a house here, but the Chinese will not allow it. Maybe someday."

We ordered lunch and talked into the afternoon while the café slowly filled. Much to my relief, I wasn't stared at while we talked, for Turpan was a haven for odd-looking misfits and I attracted no more attention than anyone else. Bennie fit easily into the crowd as well. He wore a black, wide-brimmed hat, like an old gangster hat from the thirties, dark sunglasses and a leather vest. Although his accent was German, when I asked where he was from he replied, "I'm a world citizen man, from everywhere and nowhere."

For all their oddities, and the fact that their endless supply of money probably came from running drugs, they were kind and gregarious and held sense of camaraderie among travelers.

SAME DATE

Turpan, China

DURING MY FORAYS across the street to John's Café with Willie and Bennie, and my continuing attempts to pour water into my dehydrated body, I was dismayed to only feel weaker while the days wore on. One thing that especially alarmed me was that no matter how much water I drank, my urine remained a deep orange, sometimes fluctuating into a cola brown. Each passing day required a greater effort to get out of bed, and I knew if the fatigue progressed, it would soon be impossible to do so. After four days in Turpan, my symptoms were joined by stomach cramps and nausea. It was impossible to eat, nor did I have any desire for food. The very thought of it made me sick. By the fifth day, I was unable to move a muscle.

Since Willie and Bennie hadn't seen me that day at John's Café, they stopped by my room to see what was wrong. Bennie took one look at me then said flatly, "hepatitis. Look, your eyes are already yellow."

"I know what you mean," Bennie said after I whined about my symptoms. "I had hepatitis in Pakistan. It got so bad I weighed only a hundred pounds when I went to the hospital. They called my embassy and I was flown back to Germany. It took me six months to recover."

THE WEEKS WENT BY. Willie and Bennie came to my room at least once a day. They brought me books and food. Bennie gave me his supply of miso soup he had brought from Japan for his own consumption. He carried it for times of illness, and, when I tasted the broth, I knew that I still had some things to learn. Bennie had found the one thing in the world a nauseated stomach could take. I even craved it. Miso soup became my diet and I looked forward to their visits, another bowl of miso, another book. On my bad days they brought me water, told me travel stories, or gave me one of the books they used their bartering skills to obtain from some passing tourist.

I dreaded getting out of bed, which I only did to use the bathroom. It took a supreme effort just to walk down the lane to the outdoor toilets. One day I slowly staggered across town to the hospital, where I wandered around in delirium trying to find a doctor. Overflowing garbage cans cluttered the hallways of the hospital. Dirt was everywhere. I saw a doctor whose uniform included a cigarette dangling from his mouth, a dingy beard, and two packs of cigarettes stuffed into his front pocket next to a pen. Disgusted, I staggered back to bed. My venture was a waste of time anyway, since the only cure for hepatitis is time.

And time went by. The world in my hotel bed consisted of staring at the ceiling, a few books, and watching roommates come and go in my four-man dormitory. Some of the occupants, at the height of my delirium, seemed like a vague dream. There were two Japanese travelers, Taka and Taka-Shi, on vacation from America where their companies had sent them for the sake of an education. "We cannot go back to Japan for two years," Taka-Shi told me. "We must learn the American way of thinking." They worked for Citicorp Bank, had law degrees from Japan, and were attending Harvard Law School in preparation for the American Bar Exam.

"The Japanese Bar is very difficult," Taka explained." Only two percent of those examined pass, compared to sixty percent in the USA." Not surprisingly, they were specializing in banking law.

Those two roommates were replaced by three more Japanese students on their way to an American fishing vacation. Since most foreign tourists I met had traveled to New York, Washington D.C., and Los Angeles, then flew home with an understandably distasteful opinion of the United States, I was encouraged to learn my new roommates planned to fish in Colorado, Wyoming, and Northern Michigan.

After those two came an Israeli couple. We talked about the Middle East and I tried to describe the places I had seen that were forbidden to Israelis. "We really want to go to Jordan," they confessed, "but we are not allowed."

Next came an English expatriate named Tom, who lived in Hong Kong, and two English professors teaching in Beijing. Tom was by far the oddest individual to join the flow of travelers that came through the dorm during my illness. One afternoon his arm disappeared into his backpack and emerged grasping a three-foot-long, double-speaker, Sony jambox.

"What's that?" I asked, shocked anyone would haul such a large item around China.

"A Sony stereo," Tom said, matter-of-factly.

"Do you ever use it?"

"Naw, I haven't had batteries for six months."

It struck me that his stereo must have occupied over half of his pack.

That was what unnerved me about all my transient roommates: the nature of their gear. I made a list one day of the items sitting out on the next bunk, property of a Dane named Peter. Strewn across the bed rested Nivea skin milk, twenty-two rolls of film, Mata-Sol skin lotion, duct tape, a bamboo fan, Shower to Shower antiperspirant, Skinice Shampoo, two hair brushes, one comb, a large metal chain, Strepsels throat lozenges (with honey and lemon), fifteen cassette tapes, Bostick Rolla Stik glue, tropical strength Aerogard personal lotion, insect repellent (medicated, extra long lasting). Those were only half the items scattered about the bed, along with a stack of clothes two-feet high. All that, and his backpack was still three-quarters full.

The Japanese travelers seemed to have taken the most care in packing. Their gear was always pristine, and everything was carefully sealed in plastic containers. One reached into his bag and began pulling out food: honey corn syrup, cream corn, miso, dried seaweed, candy bars . . .

"Do you want some coffee?" he asked me, and produced what looked like a can of mousse labeled "Coffee In A Bottle."

Some of the items represented luxuries beyond anything I had seen in more than a year. My equipment was all Asian, my clothes matching the poorest residents of the Third World. Constantly surrounded by poverty, my sensibilities and expectations had been slowly transformed. Seeing all the passing travelers with new gear was as if I had been transported from the time of the Great Depression to an era of boom economy. It shocked me, but my Depression-era habits never would change.

TWO WEEKS WENT BY, or so I estimated in my time-frozen

state. Bennie assured me my suffering was almost at an end. "Don't worry," he said, "when your skin turns completely yellow, you know you're almost through it." His words were little comfort, although it was the first time in my life I looked forward to turning completely yellow.

Meanwhile, my boredom in bed during the day caused me to dwell on the frustrations of my illness. Pain is a relative thing. There's the sharp, quick pain that comes and goes with an end in sight. Then there's long, dull pain which requires a long-term mental effort, a pain one must learn to accept. These are the pains people live with— the trials that separate perseverance from failure. Such a trial is hepatitis, a mind-numbing, ceiling-watching, supreme-effort-to-move pain.

JULY ?

Tupan, China

JUST THE WAY Bennie had assured me, my strength slowly returned. I still remained bedridden for most of the day, but began to make small trips into Turpan to satisfy my burgeoning appetite. I managed three walks a day to John's Café where I gorged myself on french toast, scrambled eggs, and yogurt for breakfast; half a dozen mantou (a doughy muffin stuffed with mutton and vegetables) for lunch, and lachman for dinner. While I ate, I felt as if I were grasping some long-sought reward.

My third day of rejuvenation found me at the café with two Americans who taught English near Beijing, and I discovered that comfort is a subjective concept. They were disgusted with the food at the café. Out of curiosity, I asked them if they ate well in Beijing.

"Hell no," one of them replied, "we gotta travel thirty miles just to get to McDonalds or Pizza Hut!"

"Times," as my friends in Detroit used to say, "is hard."

JULY ?

Turpan, China

MY STRENGTH continued to wax, although I still spent much of the day in bed. An American traveler who stayed in the dorm for two days was shocked at my yellow appearance.

"You should fly home immediately!" she told me in hysterics.

"Hepatitis attacks the liver; it's nothing to fool with!"

Despite the warnings, I found the strength to obtain a one-month extension on my visa, the last official extension allowed by Chinese law. That restriction put me in a dilemma. It was not possible to cycle the remainder of China in a month in my condition. I would have to recommence my journey soon. Perhaps in a day or two.

JULY ?

Turpan, China

I SPENT LESS TIME in my room and lingered longer at the café across the street. My strength increased with the passing days. Filled with a newfound energy, I spent a late night at John's Café then wandered back to my dormitory bed to resume my rejuvenation with a long sleep.

Drowsiness overcame me, and I thought of the lands beyond Turpan. A restlessness brought on by a stagnant month in bed took hold. Sleep came, and my night was taken by a dream. I was flying through the clouds. There was a feeling of sheer freedom. Suddenly a trapeze appeared in the middle of the sky, motionless, suspended by nothing. I stopped and I sat on the trapeze.

I sat. I sat for days, weeks, maybe months, I did not know how long. I wanted to fly on but could not. Instead, I looked up toward the azure sky and uncharted territory. But still I sat, unable to move.

In the morning, I awoke in a sweat. It was time to leave.

12

Lost Time

I LEFT TURPAN when August arrived. The Turpan depression slipped by and the remainder of the Taklamikan revealed itself. A blue strip of pock-marked and wrinkled road stretched flat over the horizon into a shimmering nothingness. The sun was made white and round from dust swept up by the desert's currents. The sky, always hazy from sand leached like sweat from the Taklamikan, loomed violet in the morning. During the day it remained light blue, streaked with stark, white clouds stretching through the air in bending waves. My world was flat, and hot. Brown, baked earth arched over the edge of the world in all directions. It seemed as if I were forever cycling atop a huge bubble, with scorched sand descending away as far as I could see. This corner of the earth, 100 kilometers east of Kashgar, was as lonely as a vast, empty void could be. This corner of the earth was slowly burning.

The last of the Taklamikan was in front of me, followed by the grandfather of all deserts, the Gobi. In my weakened condition, it would have been the height of folly to continue east across the Gobi Desert. I decided to veer southeast—across the Gansu desert—which made my first goal Hami, a major town about 300 kilometers away. Since my fourth and last visa extension left me little time to see the remainder of China solely by bicycle, I decided to mix in some hitchhiking until my full strength returned.

Not far out of Turpan, a familiar lethargy overcame me. Stomach pains followed. I was suddenly reminded of the words of the tourist in Turpan, "You should fly home immediately; hepatitis attacks the liver . . ."

I put the bicycle in plain view by the side of the road and began waving down trucks. The first truck that came along stopped, which presented my next problem. My Mandarin vocabulary stood at about fifty words. How then, to ask for a ride to Tsukia, the next town on my map? I patted my chest and pointed down the road, then into the truck.

"Ahh," replied the driver.

That, I guessed, meant "yes, you can have a ride."

To ask about his destination, I patted the side of the truck, pointed down the road, and said, "Tsukia?"

"Ahh, Tsukia."

Off we went . . . although, not to Tsukia. Instead, we bounced along over dirt paths and desert scrub. Thirty kilometers and two hours later, the driver dropped me off.

"Tsukia," he said, pointing down a muddy rivulet, which once must have been a path.

I cycled ten kilometers back to the road and again used the intrigue of the bicycle to hitch a ride. Two trucks passed me. The third truck stopped. It was driven by a shirtless incarnation of Buddha, his belly inhabiting three-fourths of the front seat. This time I asked to go to Hami, 400 kilometers east, with the theory that another detour of 30 kilometers would hardly be worthwhile.

"Ahh, Hami," came the answer . . . which turned out to mean another detour of thirty kilometers. The Buddha dropped me well off the main road, in a small town that existed solely to service the nearby rail line. I began asking around town where the elusive road to Hami might actually lie, but the inevitable response was always a pointed finger down a woebegone piece of dirt track, once road. The path was so blown over with sand that I returned after cycling only a few kilometers, thinking I had been led astray. I was repeatedly shown the same path, and eventually became convinced that the track linked up with the main road farther on.

The track followed the rail line farther into the desert. Dunes covered the way, forcing me carry the bike. My map showed the main road bending away to the north, rejoining the train tracks 100 kilometers to the east. Certainly, if my route paralleled the rail line, then I was not on the main road. I could only hope water would be available somewhere along the 100-kilometer expanse.

Ten kilometers onward I came upon two huts. An idle cargo train sat on the tracks where one building served as a switching station. At first, I thought only of water, then I was struck with an idea. Why not ask for a ride? I propped the bicycle against a mud wall and walked up to the engine of the train. Two engineers lifted their heads when I approached.

"Lanzhou?" I asked, as I tapped my chest then pointed into the train. They looked at each other, then at me.

"Lanzhou, no," one said.

I motioned toward the bike, which was lying unnoticed in the distance, then I showed them my empty water bottles and pointed at the sun.

"Hami?" one of them asked.

The locomotive was divided into two cabs, front and back, each with controls for operating the train. The two engineers occupied the front cab, while I was shown to the rear where I watched the trailing box cars snake along the track. A rotating fan adorned the cab, along with myriad controls, including one remarkably similar to an automobile's steering wheel.

My cushioned chair absorbed rocking and rolling from the uneven track while the train moved eastward. I began to doze, and thought of all the train stories I had heard from travelers—the difficulty in buying tickets, lack of comfort, standing in fourth-class cars for thirty hours. From my comfortable private cab, the stories seemed like fairy tales.

The train was idle when I awoke. One of the engineers came back and led me to a box car because of some checkpoints ahead. If I were seen in the locomotive, he claimed, it would be "not good."

A Chinese youth sitting on a cargo bag already occupied the box car. His only possessions in the oven-like heat of the car were the clothes on his back. He carried no food or water, and there was no way to know how long he had gone without those necessities. I offered him some biscuits and water which he declined with a wave of his hand. He accepted a cigarette, which I carried for bribes, then he sat on the floor and never smoked.

The dunes of the desert rushed by the wide-open cargo doors while the train rattled toward Hami. I stood at the opened car door and watched the desert pass, overcome with a feeling of freedom and contentment. The stoic Chinese boy watched me in silence. Most of the time he sat in meditation, free of possessions other than the knowledge of how to travel through China in a form pure and gratifying. A first-class cabin was not a part of his world.

Still, there were certain aspects of train travel that I had not thought about in some time. On a train, one is doomed to go only where travelers go. After all, trains arrive at destinations— destinations which are the entire goal of travel by train. On a bicycle, the goal of travel lies between destinations.

What represented one glimpse of a passing yurt for a train traveler, might be my home for the night. What for the train traveler was a curious native on horseback, was for me a villager who might provide food, and whose language I had to speak to acquire that food. For the cyclist, language meant the difference between eating and not eating, shelter or no shelter. Ultimately, what for the train passenger was the blink of an eye, for me was an intimate friendship with a mile of countryside—sharing water with a beetle, hearing the roar of a tiger, cresting the top of the Karakoram Mountains.

When the train came to a halt at the next switching station, our engineers were relieved by two new men who indicated that I should once again move to the front. The Chinese youth remained behind, unacknowledged and anonymous. I filled my bottles with water and set one next to the boy before returning to the engine. I would have preferred to remain in the box car as well, but it seemed to me the new crew was paying me a courtesy, so I agreed and returned to the locomotive.

This time I rode with the engineers in the fore compartment. They did me another favor by periodically radioing ahead to Hami in an attempt to find an ongoing train willing to carry me east, but their attempts failed, perhaps due to the illegality of the whole affair.

The train pulled into Hami at midnight, after I had spent several hours in friendly conversation, in mime, with the train crew. We said our good-byes. I thanked them, then I unrolled my sleeping bag under a tree in a nearby wood and went to sleep.

DUE TO THE CONSTANT, lingering fatigue caused by the hepatitis, I didn't awaken until 8:30. I cycled back to the train station in hopes of finding another train traveling east, but I found the station to be a mass of humanity and endless lines.

After searching through the station for several hours, I opted to cycle a few kilometers out of town, then I began waving down trucks bound for Dunhuang. Rides were few, and short when I got them. By midday, I found myself stranded in the desert with no traffic in sight. I was left with no other option but to cycle again. The heat reminded me of the Sahara, with the landscape wavering through a dusty blur. The desert supported nothing but sand and heat and a scorching haze.

Several days of desert cycling brought me to Dunhuang, a city set amidst a trove of archeological sites scattered throughout the Gansu dessert. Three kilometers to the south rose Manshera Mountain, a huge mountain of sand which reminded me of the Himalayan foothills. Twenty-five kilometers north stood the Magau grottoes, a series of 492 caves carved by Buddhists centuries ago. But Dunhuang was a tourist site, and those destinations produced a culture shock for me. I spent only one day in the city, then cycled southeast across the Gansu Desert.

Lanzhou marked the beginning of the expansive central grasslands where nomads wandered and horses ran free unbounded by roads. I felt at home on the grasslands, pedaling along the dirt tracks that crisscrossed the tent-dotted fields of green. I was a free-roaming rider, self-contained and not bound by the itineraries of a mechanized world. Being independent was not only a luxury, but a necessity in the grasslands, where Tibetan nomads traveled by horseback over the pristine and undeveloped countryside.

I cycled into the monastery town of Xiahe, nestled in the foothills outside of Tibet. The single mud road was flanked by a dozen wooden buildings. I entered a bar similar to those in the American Old West, made of adobe-style brick with a dozen horses tied to a post out front.

It was dark inside, and crowded, with shadowy figures showing like a haze through the smoke-filled room. A group of Tibetans, monks, and Chinese were gathered in one corner of the room, shouting and waving as if bartering for stock options. I pushed my way through the throng to discover, seated at a formerly-hidden table, two stark-white tourists at the focus of the activity. A third Westerner was standing between the mob and the table acting as a translator.

"What's going on?" I asked a Tibetan in the crowd.

"Two Germans trying to buy a donkey," the man said.

"What do they need a donkey for?"

"They're going across the grasslands with it."

The two Germans were Stephie and Karlos who, after the negotiations had broken down, took me to the Labrang Binguan where they had pitched camp along with the entire backpacking population of Xiahe. An Australian woman named Sharon, on vacation from her teaching job in Japan, occupied the camp, along with two Canadians who taught English in Wuhon, and Karen, a cyclist from England who had ridden alone across Asia. The six of them were the most carefree travelers ever to don a backpack.

The next three days were relaxing days at the Binguan. We cooked community meals on our combined camp stoves, traded travel tales and explored Xiahe monastery. At night, we all went to the bar to watch the continuing donkey negotiations. It took three days of bartering but, on the third day, the seven of us walked out of the bar and back to the Binguan with a donkey clomping along with us. It was probably the puniest donkey in all of China, but for twenty bucks no one complained. Besides, how much gear would two people need for a few weeks on the grasslands? I had crossed with no supplies at all, relying on the charitable nomads for food and water.

Over the next week, the two Germans began buying supplies. First on the list was authentic Tibetan clothes "so we don't look conspicuous to the authorities out on the grasslands," they claimed. The fact that "authorities" did not exist on the grasslands did not seem to deter them in the slightest. They bought enough supplies to fill three gargantuan flower sacks, each twice the size of a large backpack. When they piled the sacks on top of the shrimpy donkey, all that could be seen was the poor beast's legs.

"Are you sure you guys need that much gear?" I asked them one day, thinking they could mount an Arctic expedition at a moment's notice.

"Oh yes, we'll be out there two weeks, maybe more!"

The next day Stephie arrived at the binguan with a three-liter jug of honey.

"What's that for?" I asked in shock.

"We'll need it on the grasslands."

I hesitated to point out that honey was the one commodity that abounded on the grasslands, even to the point of being a major industry.

The day they set out, Sharon decided to join them. I cycled along for a while, but their progress was so abysmally slow that I decided to strike out on my own across the grasslands then back to the binguan. The last glimpse I caught of the little caravan was Karlos struggling with one of the huge white bags that had fallen off the donkey, while Sharon, clad in her long brown Tibetan coat and John Lennon glasses, was trying to shoo away a promiscuous male donkey that had taken interest in their beast of burden. They were surrounded by a group of curious locals, the Tibetan dress having failed for the purpose of disguise.

AFTER THE DEPARTURE of the Germans, Tibetan clothes became a craze at the Labrang Binguan. An Englishman named Luka spent 600 quai for a coat. Others paid two hundred and up. Out of curiosity, I went shopping with two Canadian English teachers from Wuhon, who had received a hot tip on dead men's clothes. We were led to a musty vault containing a huge pile of articles in various stages of decomposition and bearing the smell of long dead Tibetan ancestors.

Two hundred quai was the asking rate for one of the rancid, lice ridden garments. I didn't claim to be the greatest barterer in the world, but that seemed a bit excessive. Especially since, while in Turpan, I had met a Frenchman who had paid twenty-five quai for a new Tibetan jacket, which meant the Canadians were paying eight to twenty-five times that price for used clothing.

When I mentioned that minor fact, all I heard was, "I hate to be a doubting Thomas, but I doubt it."

The following day an Israeli woman arrived at the binguan with a new Tibetan jacket, tailor-made to her size and build. Everybody was beside themselves to find out the price. "Why, twenty-five quai of course," she said.

I hated to say "I told you so" but . . .

AFTER A TWO-WEEK STAY, I left Xiahe and cycled south through central China. Traveling became easier when I grew nearer to the population of southeast China. The deserts of the north and west became more distant, food was more abundant, and water was no longer an overriding concern. The ever-increasing presence of the burgeoning Chinese population made the privations of the desert seem a distant dream. Just as I'd been doing throughout my trip, I found myself knocking on doors for food, never to be refused.

I cycled consistently southeastward. Chengdu came closer and the mountains of central China leveled off. An unexpected descent brought me into the city, where, with my finances down to a frightening $100, I checked into the only hotel I could afford. My roommate, a traveler from England even more destitute than I was, took great delight in enhancing my discouragement by showing me what his travel guide said about our lodgings:

"The Black Coffee Hotel is a bomb shelter which has been converted into an underground hotel. Unless you like living in a rat hole, this place won't appeal. In the dark maze of rooms, all sorts of things go on: disco dancing, furtive fumbling and even prostitution."

None of that would have bothered me if not for the overpowering smell of chemicals that permeated the dungeon air. When my roommate noted that all the tenants had developed respiratory infections, I decided to occupy the bulk of my time outside the bomb shelter. I went to my room late and left early to avoid exposure, but I became exhausted from lack of sleep after two days of the ritual. It was time to move on. I decided to spend my last day in Chengdu relaxing at the tourist cafés along the river. I would leave sometime in the afternoon.

I checked out of the Black Coffee and took Papillon with me to the riverside cafés. I fantasized about spending another week in Chengdu simply watching the water go by, but my meager remaining money supply would be gone in days if I remained in this expensive city.

I savored my last morning in Chengdu and pushed my lingering plans to leave out of my thoughts. The afternoon moved by as slowly as the river's current, and time went unnoticed while I sipped tea and watched the tourists walk past. There was a girl wearing a sari who wanted everyone to know she'd been to India. A few casually dressed tourists flipped by in sandals. There was a man in a tattered hat dressed like Indiana Jones. A hippie passed wearing a big black hat, dark sunglasses and a leather vest.

"Bennie?" The black hat turned in my direction. Bennie looked at me quizzically, then at the bicycle with sudden recognition.

"Well, it's the yellow man," Bennie said as he sat down. "Where ya' stayin?" Bennie seemed to take our coincidental meeting in stride, but it seemed almost miraculous to me. I had met Willie in Gilgit, then again in Turpan where he introduced me to his friend, Bennie. Now, I was meeting Bennie for the second time, a thousand miles east of our first encounter.

"I was at the Black Coffee," I said after my initial shock, "but I just checked out."

"Good, that place is a dive, man—gives people lung disease. Come stay at the Jinjiang Guest House where I'm at. Best place around, man."

"Can't," I confessed." No bucks. I'm like, out of cash, man." Somehow around Bennie it was easy to adopt hippie speak, but he didn't hear me. He was distracted by the tourist dressed like Indiana Jones.

"Look at that guy," he whispered to me out of the side of his mouth. "You see more and more of those morons every day. Think they're in a goddamn movie." I found the statement odd considering how Bennie was dressed.

"Hey!" he shouted." You can stay in my room. I've got two double beds and I don't even use the other one."

"Thanks Bennie, but I don't want to impose."

But I wasn't imposing. Bennie preferred the company of a fellow traveler over solitude, and I hadn't carried on a substantive conversation in English for weeks. It didn't take me long to accept.

I moved into Bennie's deluxe suite: two double beds, balcony with a view, air conditioning, and a fridge stocked daily with dark German beer. I stayed a week. By day, I explored Chengdu and thought about ways to make some money. At night, I returned to the hotel to exchange travel tales with Bennie and empty the fridge of German beer.

My fifth night in Chengdu, I returned to the hotel early, sat on the balcony under the stars, and listened to Bennie's stories. Bennie had thousands. He didn't even know he was telling them sometimes. To Bennie, simple conversation was one long travel tale.

"You know those grasshoppers they sell in those little wooden cages?" He said while I gazed at the stars.

"Cicadas you mean?" Chinese vendors sold cicadas in one-inch-square bamboo cages. The Chinese enjoyed listening to their high-pitched whine.

"I bought one once. Fed it little celery sticks. The Chinese just buy 'em and let 'em die, but I fed mine. I got so attached to him I named him Charlie and I'd put him on the balcony every night for fresh air. He sang every night 'cause he liked me I think."

Bennie was serious, although he let out a quick laugh to betray an underlying sense of normalcy.

"One day," he said, "I decided it was too cruel to keep Charlie in such a small cage so I broke it open and let him go."

Bennie paused at my laughter.

"But he wouldn't go. He just sat there on the balcony looking at me, waiting for a celery stick. So I shooed him away, but Charlie just flew off a little then came back and looked at me with a sad face, waiting for a piece of celery. I shooed him away again and again but every time he came back and sat next to me on the balcony. Finally, I shooed Charlie away so hard I squashed him! There he was, a dead carcass on my balcony. Poor Charlie."

When Bennie saw me laughing, he turned to me and said, "Hey man, this was serious!"

I LEFT CHENGDU the next day after saying good-bye to Bennie for the second time in three months. Here was a man who saw me through hepatitis, selflessly gave me his supply of miso soup, and shared a deluxe hotel room free of charge. I was sad to leave.

I cycled southeast out of Chengdu into the bulk of China's 1.3 billion individuals. The little Uyghur I had learned in Xinjian long since had turned to Mandarin, only to change to Cantonese east of Chengdu. The fare I had survived on throughout the northwest, lachman, became lamian, while various other types of food became available.

By the time I reached Guangzhou, I thought I had tried everything, from chicken feet to fish heads, dog meat to the unidentifiable. But in Guangzhou, a port city of trade and commerce bordering the South China Sea, I knew I could find some variety.

Since I was tired of lamian, I asked at a local restaurant for the only other thing I knew how to say in Cantonese, nu-ro: beef. When my order arrived, it turned out to be a mounded platter of intestines, topped by a cooked, gray, phallus. After some work with my poor Cantonese, I learned I had, indeed, been served beef: cow intestines accompanied, of course, by the bull's penis. I tasted the thing for the sake of experimentation, but it was beyond me how anyone could eat something so rubbery. I suspected someone was practicing a little local humor at my expense.

After lunch, I wandered through the Cantonese marketplace, a pastime I would not recommend to any sensitive human. Skinned dogs and live cats squashed in crates hung up for sale, like so many ears of corn. There were baby sea turtles in small pools and rare pandas from far away mountains meant for some restaurant's pot. There were insects, snakes—available skinned or alive—caged monkeys watching their relatives be slaughtered, rare animal pelts: tiger, leopard, bear. There were sea creatures of all shapes and colors, from transparent to fluorescent green. In short, more animals were being slaughtered in Canton's market than I had seen in all my travels throughout the world.

But for all the culinary options within my view, I could not afford one of them. I watched a crate of squashed kittens heaved up on two bamboo poles for transport and reflected briefly on my money situation. With less than $100, I had to get somewhere I could earn some money, but how? Where? Surely I could sell my photographs and the story of my trip, or lead a mountain bike tour through flat city streets. One thing was evident, I could not afford to stay in Guangzhou for more than one night.

While wandering the streets of the city in search of an affordable hotel, which probably meant another Black Coffee, I recalled the photographer I had met in Nepal. His magazine was based in Hong Kong. He had given me his card and urged me to look him up if I found myself near his office. I searched for the card in my money belt where it was tucked away along with a year of forgotten names and addresses, all of them crumpled and faded. His card was still there. I could barely make out the name and address while I walked to the wharf, and the ferry to Hong Kong.

13
Journey's End

. . . and mountains stretch away, their towering
peaks an unearthly treasure of distance.

Fragrant chrysanthemums ablaze in woodlands
blooming, green pines lining the clifftops:

isn't this the immaculate heart of beauty,
this frost-deepened austerity? Sipping wine,

I think of recluse masters. A century away,
I nurture your secrets. Your true nature

eludes me here, but taken by quiet, I can
linger this exquisite moon out to the end."

—T'ao Ch'ien

THE OVERNIGHT FERRY to Hong Kong cost me a third of my
money, and that, for a space on deck to roll out my sleeping bag.
Only two other passengers found themselves in such financial straits,
all reduced to sleeping on deck rather than in the one chair allowed
for a fourth-class ticket. Francois, who produced a bottle of rice
alcohol from the folds of his pack, had been hiking through the
remote areas of China for six months. The other deck-class traveler,
Sean, from Ireland, rose to the occasion when he produced a jar of
olives. The rest of the night we drank martinis.

Francois had eaten nothing but noodles and rice during his six-month stay in China, and when the ferry docked in Hong Kong at 9 a.m. we made a frantic dash through the streets in search of Western food. Although our money reserves would have qualified us for food stamps, the up-scale restaurant at the Holiday Inn pulled us in like a giant vortex. I bought a *USA Today* newspaper in the lobby, a luxury reminiscent of another life, then I rushed past Francois in a trance-like surge toward the dining room.

It was the most magical sight I had ever seen. There were petite, round tables with peach-colored table cloths and white linen napkins cradling gleaming silver knives and forks. There was coffee in a steaming pitcher for two, bread and jam, eggs and cheese and bacon. There were warm rolls in a wicker basket, orange juice in clean clear glasses with an optional straw. There were salt and pepper shakers shaped like chess pieces topped with shining silver helmets, hashed brown potatoes cooked golden, served by a waitress who spoke English as if she were from Michigan.

Francois and I sat and stared, too afraid to touch anything, as if doing so would have been to violate something sacred. We shared each other's awe at the silver forks, discussed the white linen napkins and our memories of what an egg tasted like. Then we stared again. We photographed the table as a shrine in our minds. Then we began. I handed Francois a section of the newspaper and we each took a slow sip of coffee, mine black, his au lait with a perfectly measured half-teaspoon of white sugar.

We picked up our forks and felt their weight in our hands. We held them between our fingers as if to confirm they were not some cruel hallucination ready to transform into a pair of wooden chopsticks. I took a small corner of my lightly salted egg, dusted with black speckles from the silver-capped shaker, brought it to my mouth and savored the bite for a full minute. Francois opted for a hash brown corner, with a thumb-sized hunk of cheese in memory of France. We ordered more coffee, more rolls, more cheese . . . and we ate. We ate the bacon, the sausage and ham. We ate the eggs and sopped up our plates with fresh bread. We ate the cheese, the potatoes, the fruit. It took two hours to finish. It was glorious.

On our way out we each grabbed a handful of mints, as if we could clutch the memory of that meal forever in a dozen short-lived cubes of sugar. Francois bought a French comic book, one of those odd pieces of home he never thought he'd miss. When I read it, I could see why. The strip followed the exploits of a secret agent, Tin Tin, who traveled with a talking dog. The excerpt I read depicted the hero doing battle in Pakistan with his arch enemy, the Maharaja Guaiapajama. Subtle humor when one considers the fact that, to the Western eye, Pakistani dress looks like common bedroom pajamas.

Francois and I decided to reduce expenses by sharing a room. We had heard about the Manchurian Mansion through the traveler's grapevine, a hotel that held its place in backpacker lore as a flea-ridden fire trap that was the bane of all those who entered Hong Kong without money. We were not disappointed.

The place was more like high-rise HUD housing than a hotel, designed with the primary concern of cramming as many people into one place as possible. The halls, two-shoulders wide, housed spitting Chinese, cigarette smoke, and terrified backpackers fresh from the West. Our room was large enough to contain two cots, side by side, leaving a two-foot alley for living space. Papillon was left downstairs, locked to a post inside the lobby—a situation that caused me no end of worry.

When we were unpacked, I left the hotel and rode to the offices of *Adventure Asia* magazine. I walked inside wearing my best clothes, a tattered pair of cycling shorts and dingy gray T-shirt. My hope rested in the business card I had been given in Nepal. Although faded and torn, the name could barely be made out: *Harvey Jeffords, Research Director.* The card seemed to carry some importance with the staff, but Harvey Jeffords was on assignment in Pakistan. I was shown to an assistant editor named Jo, who looked at my photos while I told her about the trip.

"These are excellent photos," Jo said.

I was surprised, considering the Praktica camera and single wide-angle lens responsible for every last shot. I was given a business card and told to return the following day, after Jo had consulted with the other editors.

Back at the Mansion, Francois seemed frustrated. He was staring at the walls of our room with his half-read *Tin Tin* laid open to one side. After some prodding on my part, he explained his problem. One of the main goals of his trip was to search out an internationally renowned tattoo artist who was known to reside in Hong Kong. "I've been saving my money and living like a pauper all this time," he complained. "All for a tattoo from this guy. Now, I can't find him."

So Francois began what he coined, "The First Annual Hong Kong Tattoo Artist Hunt." We scoured the streets of Hong Kong armed only with the man's name and the hope that his international reputation would make him easy to find. We explored Hong Kong Island. We searched Kowloon on the mainland.

At length, after following false leads all day, we enlisted the services of a local guide. He led us through a maze of squalid back alleys to a small shop. The interior of the shop was hidden by a dangling blanket that acted as a door. Inside, drawings of tattoo designs hung from the walls of a sparse room. A diminutive man, squat and round, stood in the center of the shop. His hair had turned gray, but his eyes held an intelligent light, and he spoke perfect English.

Here was the man we sought. He traveled all over the world practicing his art and held the confidence of a person who didn't have to prove his competence. Francois described the tattoo he wanted, and where. Some sketches were done, followed by a lengthy refining session, then the price.

"One hundred and seventy-five dollars—American," the man announced.

We were stunned. One hundred seventy-five dollars represented a fortune to someone fresh from the back roads of Asia. Francois had become accustomed to cheap Asian prices, Asian ways. Of course, we knew some bartering was yet to be done.

Francois began bartering, a second-nature task after six months in China. Francois offered a price, but the artist grew indignant, then irate. At first we thought his reaction was a bargaining ploy. The artist set us straight on the point when he ordered us out of the shop with the refrain, "I don't bargain! You want my work, you pay my price!"

We walked back to the hotel, Francois hanging his head in silence.

THE FOLLOWING DAY I called Jo at *Adventure Asia*. She asked me to meet her for lunch at a pub near her office. We discussed my photos and adventures over lunch, but I was not encouraged. The magazine had recently been inundated with mountain bike submissions. The only items with a chance were my photos of trekking in Nepal, which she kept for future discussion with her colleagues.

I left as discouraged as Francois had been the previous day, although the meeting was not a complete loss. Jo had invited me to "The Festival of the Moon" on Llama Island, an annual festival that was to take place the following evening. "Take the Star Ferry," she said, and gave me her home address on the island. "A bunch of us are getting together at my house beforehand."

The invitation gave me little solace. I hardly had enough money left for the ferry. Discouraged, I went to meet Francois at the bar next to the Mansion. He was waiting there to learn the outcome of the meeting. He claimed a vested interest since, unless Francois tapped into his tattoo reserve, neither of us possessed the money to renew our room at the Mansion.

When I arrived, Francois was bearing a smile as wide as Hong Kong harbor. Even the discouraging news about the magazine did not dishearten him. Ultimately, in answer to my questioning expression, he lifted his sleeve. There, on his arm, was the most beautiful tattoo imaginable. A sandy yellow island floated in a sea of white-capped blue, topped by a soaring turquoise sky. A golden orange sun set on the horizon in an all-encompassing globe as it baked the island with shimmering sunbeams. Green palm trees with ochre trunks dotted the sand, while shore birds seemed to fly with motion over the scene. It was a work of art, and it was the first time in my life I considered getting a tattoo.

"I had to grovel some," Francois said, "but he finally agreed to do it for one hundred and seventy-five dollars." I sat in the bar the rest of the day, destitute, hanging out with a Frenchman who had just spent his last dime on a tattoo. My cares vanished for one fleeting afternoon.

I TOOK THE STAR FERRY to Llama Island, a secluded paradise of sandy shores and slow-paced life away from hectic Hong Kong. At the apartment I met Jo and her friends, all energetic women from England who had left their homeland behind in search of adventure. While we drank wine in the living room and talked, I found myself bored and restless. All my communication for the past year had been in pursuit of food, water, or shelter; it seemed odd to babble on about things of seemingly no importance. Eventually, I moved to a corner with my face in a magazine.

Jo's friends tried to alleviate my boredom by explaining the Festival of the Moon. The explanation didn't take long. All they knew was the day provided an excuse once a year to wander around the island with paper lanterns and get drunk. I was amenable to the idea, especially since they had already purchased the supplies.

When evening came, we went. We made our way around the island, one unit in a light-dotted snake that slithered over every beach or hill. From the beach it seemed the mountains were alive with writhing points of light, each connected to the next in undulating lines that wrapped dark, tree-filled hills like a Christmas tree. It was a mystical sight.

At the beach we stretched out in the sand and drank more wine while we watched the full moon turn everything, even the orange lanterns, silver. The night wore on and we played like children, romping and splashing and watching the moon. It seemed to me that it was indeed a special night. Made special by nothing special—only paper lanterns, a full moon, and magic in the silver air.

Slowly, the orange light was defeated by the moon. The lanterns went out one by one and people returned home to sleep, or to take their parties inside. When we ran out of wine our group dwindled to a few who, like myself, wanted to grasp every last minute of the waning night.

A kiosk not far from the beach was still selling wine, so I left to buy some for the remaining few in our group—the last on the beach. When I returned, everyone was gone but Jo, who was lying in the sand with her brown legs crossed and blond hair cocked up to greet me. I sat next to her in the soft sand and could almost feel the moon on my back. In the silver light her face was angelic, framed by her pillowy, reflective hair which caressed her glossy brown skin. We never drank the wine.

THE NEXT DAY I checked out of the Mansion and moved in with Jo. Sue, her roommate, didn't seem to mind. They took interest in the bicycle and shared my journey through the excerpts they read from my journals.

While Jo was at work, I spent my days lounging around the beaches and cafés of the serene island. When she came home, we ate prawns and drank wine at the shore. Some nights we sat up late at the seaside cafés to watch the moon wane and remember the day it was one complete circle. Occasionally, I thought about home, or continuing to Japan in hopes of earning some money—but only occasionally, and then for a fleeting moment. I did call my brother one day who, upon hearing about my monetary status, immediately wired me $300—a fortune to me, which I accepted with some guilt considering my lazy, Gauguin lifestyle.

I took the Star Ferry to Hong Kong island where the American Express office was located. At the counter I picked up the $300 my brother had sent me, along with a mysterious envelope. Inside was a plane ticket home dated for two days later, and a note: "Come home and see us for a while!"

I went back to Llama Island and told Jo. She couldn't understand why I wasn't happy, nor could I. I was gripped by an inexplicable terror. I didn't want to go back. I remembered the American teacher from Cairo I had met in Ajanta who, after fifteen years in Egypt, was terrified to return home. For the first time, I understood her fear.

During the next two days, Llama Island became gradually more beautiful to me. I was overcome with joy at the beaches and reveled in the moon that kept everything slow and soft at night. I savored every prawn and sip of wine on the beach with Jo, where the sea rolled onto the sandy beach. I prolonged our moon-gazing at the seaside cafés well into the night, until the silver moon, which turned everything soft and slow, had been taken by the waiting sea.

The shores of Asia turned into the shores of America in a scant twelve hours, a journey that would have taken half a year by bicycle. My brother picked me up at the airport in his new car, equipped with a cellular phone. I felt I had re-entered the space age.

My Kanha Camp friends in India joked that America would build a statue to me when I returned. But there was no statue, no fanfare, only an emptiness and an overwhelming, inner terror.

My brother had rented me a nearby apartment, but his generosity was lost on me. I didn't know where I was, just knew where I wanted to be—back on Papillon somewhere over a great ocean.

There was a couch in the apartment. I slept on the floor. I set up a small desk in the corner and laid out all my old maps my brother had saved from my research two years ago. The map I hung over my desk was the one that had been there before, of half the world cut off at Turkey. It depicted all of Western Europe and part of Russia.

At its eastern edge the world is cut short as if someone had taken a razor blade just east of Moscow or Istanbul. It's a clean, antiseptic cut with a white border where Ankara should be, and the Black Sea cut in half as if it would pour its waters into India. I owned this map two years ago and, two years ago, I wrote in that white border, "beyond this place there be dragons."

Above my desk where I have written this book, hangs a map with a white border. In the border where Asia should be is written a phrase with one word crossed out and another added in its place. It reads: Beyond this place there be—friends.

Epilogue

Twenty-five years after writing those last words in my journal, I find myself adding an epilogue and answering the questions so often asked by readers of the first edition. Though I fear the answer to the most common question will remain woefully inadequate, even to this day. Regretfully, I do not know what became of most of the people I met along the way, although I've tried to find them over the years through various means. My journey took place before the invention of smartphones—even the internet was not yet in common use—and I returned home years after meeting most of the travelers described in the book. Many of them had moved, some of them were unreachable due to political upheaval, and a lot of them were vagabonds to begin with.

There is one rare exception however. A letter from Bruce, the cyclist mentioned in the foreword who is responsible for the title of this book, reached me when I returned home more than two years later. He was living happily in Thailand with his new wife, the "settle down in England" plan having changed slightly. He had started a scuba diving business, did a little writing about his travels, and remained happily married—at least until I lost touch with him years later.

Another exception is worth noting, even though they are not included in the book. I met a pair of German cyclists in Istanbul, Dieter and Suzie, who cycled along with me for a few days. Years later, the following letter found me.

"We decided to cycle the Karakoram Highway . . . On May 2 we stayed in a hostel in the village of Havelian, where the owners told us of another cyclist with very few baggages named Scott, who had stayed in the hostel on April 27. We immediately checked the hostel list and indeed, it was you! And we were—six months after Istanbul—only five days behind you. But unfortunately we couldn't reach you, you were faster than we. We always looked for your name in the books of the police check points: Scott Zamek, cyclist. And in the "travel book" at the Mountain Refuge Hostel in Sust we read your entry about your trip. And in Shanghai we talked to people who met you in Kashgar in the Hotel Chinibague. Funny isn't it?

"We didn't succeed to cycle in China. We were caught 40km after Tashkurgan at the barrier. Seven military police against two harmless cyclists. They brought us back to Tashkurgan, where we had to take the bus. So we visited China by public transportation."

After the proliferation of the internet, Vice-consul Howard Banks became fairly easy to track down, although I never tried to contact him. Too much time had already passed, and I figured I caused him enough grief for one lifetime. He went on to become a consul in Madrid, then Fiji, Guatemala, London, and is still working today as a government relations coordinator. I changed his name for this book, however, to prevent a possible overflow of emails through his government office.

Because of Vijay Venkatesh's story about Naxalites, I changed the names of everyone who worked at Kanha Camp as well. Even the name of the camp is changed. But I can report that Pradeep, Raj, and Vijay started a new company shortly after I left them. They are still in business and going strong, and they remember the old days around the fire fondly. I follow their progress with interest, for no one deserves success more than they.

As for the remainder of those mentioned in the book, I've had no success in tracking them down. I keep hoping Miguel will read this and contact me, but so far I have encountered only false leads where he's concerned. These days, with all the chaos in Syria, I often think about the judge who argued on my behalf, or the businessman who was excited about the country opening up to exports, and I hope those people are safe. The same applies to other parts of the world and the people who helped me along the way. Perhaps they will read this book someday and their story will appear in the next edition. I hope so.

Many readers have asked me if I would have done anything

differently. Surely, a few things could have been changed: be more wary of thieves, say, in Italy; bypass countries like Syria; start out better prepared in equipment and knowledge. But would I change anything? The answer is, most definitely, no. Those very experiences make travel what it is, and if not for certain difficulties, I would not have come back a changed man. The entire purpose of adventure travel, after all, is to undergo some sort of personal change.

How did the journey effect change? For one, I learned to cherish the basics of life. There's something incredibly secure about reducing one's desires to, what mountaineers call, the essentials of human need—namely: food, fire, water, shelter. Once a person learns to live with those basic necessities, and be grateful for them, the rest of life unfolds in a much more fulfilling manner.

Such realizations make one understand that reducing life down to the bare minimum is the essence to a more enlightened existence. Contentment is not about accumulating more wealth and more material possessions; rather, divesting oneself of such things and focusing on what makes life important to the individual is the key.

I don't worry about material wealth. How can I? When I look back at being stranded in the Sahara Desert without water, without food, without money . . . yet it was the happiest I'd ever been—free to head north, south, east, wherever the wind blew. The trappings of modern American society tell us what we need to own in order to be happy—a house, a car . . . a smartphone. But happiness comes from within, not form a credit card.

I live now in the shadow of Ocala National Forest—in the warm climes of central Florida—my backyard overlooking 600,000 acres of longleaf pine and saw palmetto. Three neighbors occupy the surrounding square mile. It is here for me that the basics become important: the call of a red-tailed hawk; the bald eagle flying toward Lake Ocklawaha; the occasional black bear or white-tailed deer creating a silhouette in the north meadow.

Writing occupies much of my time, and I sometimes wonder if the recounting of my journey conveys any meaning all these years later. In the end, I have learned that the story does still impact readers, but it carries a wide range of messages to a variety of individuals, from simple entertainment to much more. At its core, it is a tale of perseverance—something to add inspiration to one's own life. One emailer wrote me recently, "After reading your book, I decided to go back and get my master's degree." Another person wrote, "As a woman, I was always afraid to cycle across America alone, but now I'm going to try."

What more can anyone ask from such a journey? If it is to inspire, to enlighten, perhaps merely to entertain, all we can ask of ourselves from any inspiration . . . is that we try.

ABOUT THE AUTHOR

Scott Zamek has been writing about distant places and unusual modes of travel for more than thirty-five years. He is the author of many works of fiction and nonfiction, including state park guides, travel articles, and writings concerning wilderness exploration throughout North America, Asia, Europe, and Africa. His latest memoir, *The Hitchhiker's Guide to Life*, takes us rattling through thirty-five states, entailing countless rides from drivers of every conceivable profession, along highways, backroads, and country lanes revealing the true essence of America.

Made in the USA
Middletown, DE
28 November 2018